"A courageous account of what it is like to exist with a life-threatening eating disorder from two quite different standpoints—Lisa, the daughter who stops eating, and her mother, Sheila, a restaurant critic. The irony of this situation is lost on neither, and both are unsentimental and deeply honest about their experience. I especially admire their separate advice for how best to support recovery. This book should comfort anyone confronted with this illness as well as provide much practical help for dealing with it."

—Marion Nestle,
author of *Food Politics*
and *What to Eat*

"Sheila and Lisa Himmel put on paper—with rare vulnerability, wit, and courage—what millions of American mothers and daughters face privately, but fear speaking about in public. Their capacity to mine the depths of Lisa's struggle with eating disorders and Sheila's struggle with Lisa will undoubtedly bring an overwhelming sense of relief and recognition to so many mother-daughter pairs trying to make sense of so much pain. Perhaps most admirable, blame is never a weapon in this extremely personal memoir. Instead, these brave women acknowledge the complex sources of illness and point a way toward real, messy, tentative, hopeful recovery."

—Courtney Martin, author of
Perfect Girls, Starving Daughters

"An engrossing look at the power of food and eating. Mother and daughter have given us a deeply personal story about what happens when that power overwhelms."

—David A. Kessler, MD,
author of *The End of Overeating*
and former commissioner of the FDA

continued . . .

"*Hungry* covers a deadly and serious topic in a poignant story that addresses the irony of our culture's obsession with food. Sheila Himmel brings her talent as a journalist and food critic to show intimately how this disorder took over her family's life for the eight years that her daughter, Lisa, suffered from a spectrum of disordered eating—from anorexia to bulimia to anorexia. As Sheila notes, 'Eating disorders function like addictions, but no, you can't just say no to food . . . America is a twenty-four-hour buffet.' The Himmels bravely share their ups and downs, with honesty and sometimes even humor. Mother and daughter both learned a lot during the recovery process and report on helpful resources they found along the way. I love that the book ends with an optimistic tone and their two lists on Ten Things We Learned About Eating Disorders.

"I highly recommend this firsthand and easy-to-read mother/daughter account of a complex illness that will provide comfort, insight, and support for anyone struggling with or affected by an eating disorder." —Janice Bremis, executive director of the Eating Disorders Resource Center

"Through their honest and compelling story, the Himmels reveal the human impact of eating disorders from multiple perspectives: Sheila as a mother and professional reporter and Lisa as a daughter and eating disorder sufferer and survivor. This book is a gift to anyone who wants a deeper understanding of this often misunderstood disease." —Ellie Krieger, registered dietitian and author of *The Food You Crave*

HUNGRY

A Mother and Daughter Fight Anorexia

SHEILA & LISA HIMMEL

BERKLEY BOOKS, NEW YORK

THE BERKLEY PUBLISHING GROUP
Published by the Penguin Group
Penguin Group (USA) Inc.
375 Hudson Street, New York, New York 10014, USA
Penguin Group (Canada), 90 Eglinton Avenue East, Suite 700, Toronto, Ontario M4P 2Y3, Canada
(a division of Pearson Penguin Canada Inc.)
Penguin Books Ltd., 80 Strand, London WC2R 0RL, England
Penguin Group Ireland, 25 St. Stephen's Green, Dublin 2, Ireland (a division of Penguin Books Ltd.)
Penguin Group (Australia), 250 Camberwell Road, Camberwell, Victoria 3124, Australia
(a division of Pearson Australia Group Pty. Ltd.)
Penguin Books India Pvt. Ltd., 11 Community Centre, Panchsheel Park, New Delhi—110 017, India
Penguin Group (NZ), 67 Apollo Drive, Rosedale, North Shore 0632, New Zealand
(a division of Pearson New Zealand Ltd.)
Penguin Books (South Africa) (Pty.) Ltd., 24 Sturdee Avenue, Rosebank, Johannesburg 2196,
South Africa

Penguin Books Ltd., Registered Offices: 80 Strand, London WC2R 0RL, England

This book is an original publication of The Berkley Publishing Group.

While the author has made every effort to provide accurate telephone numbers and Internet addresses at the time of publication, neither the publisher nor the author assumes any responsibility for errors, or for changes that occur after publication. Further, the publisher does not have any control over and does not assume any responsibility for author or third-party websites or their content.

First edition: August 2009

Library of Congress Cataloging-in-Publication Data

Himmel, Sheila.
  Hungry : a mother and daughter fight anorexia / Sheila and Lisa Himmel.
    p. cm.
  Includes bibliographical references.
  ISBN 978-0-425-22790-9
  1. Himmel, Lisa—Mental health. 2. Anorexia nervosa—Patients—United States—
Biography. 3. Mothers and daughters. I. Himmel, Lisa. II. Title.
  RC552.A5H56 2009
  362.196'852620092—dc22   2009015587
  [B]

PRINTED IN THE UNITED STATES OF AMERICA

10 9 8 7 6 5 4 3 2 1

This book describes the real experiences of real people. The authors have changed the names and disguised the identities of some, but none of these changes has affected the truthfulness and accuracy of their story. Penguin is committed to publishing works of quality and integrity. In that spirit, we are proud to offer this book to our readers; however, the story, the experiences, and the words are the authors' alone.

Most Berkley books are available at special quantity discounts for bulk purchases for sales promotions, premiums, fund-raising, or educational use. Special books, or book excerpts, can also be created to fit specific needs. For details, write: Special Markets, Penguin Group (USA) Inc., 375 Hudson Street, New York, New York 10014.

To our grandmothers:
Elaine Highiet
Tilda Himmel
Hertha Highiet (Nana George)
Edna Phillips (Nana Bill)
Sophie Himmel (Grandma Pancake)
Annie Esenoff (Grandma Soup)

The main thing in life was staying power. That was it: stand around long enough you'd get to sit down.

—ANNIE PROULX,
"The Bunchgrass Edge of the World"

contents

Contents

introduction

LISA'S BLOOD GLUCOSE DIARY: BINGED. One-half choco-late banana. One-third vegan apple nut pastry. Pita chips (about 10–12).

SHEILA'S WORKDAY: Taste-testing french fries at seven restaurants.

On a postcard-perfect June afternoon, green hills going gold, I am driving around Silicon Valley to sample french fries. It is my job. In another universe, my daughter, Lisa, records each bite she takes in her Blood Glucose Diary, a booklet from her nutritionist. She is frantic about veering from anorexia to binge eating. We don't understand each other at all.

As the restaurant critic of the *San Jose Mercury News*, I had noticed french fries popping up on high-end menus, many more than the three instances needed to call it a trend. Was it merely another cheap thrill that posh restaurants could overcharge for, or were these *frites* really that much better than at McDonald's? After all, no less an authority than James Beard, the dear leader of food-ies everywhere, had approved of McDonald's fries.

Food reporting's serious aspects concern safety, fraud, and consumer protection, but this story was just fun. It was also an escape. While I was out judging America's favorite vegetable for flavor, texture, and price, my daughter was home, starving herself. Lisa spent much of her nineteenth year in her room, like a child being punished. Her struggles with anorexia and bulimia had become apparent two years earlier, in 2001, starting with an interest in diet, nutrition, and exercise that was healthful before going very wrong.

Lisa grew up with a lusty appreciation of food. My husband, Ned, is an excellent cook. When we get together with friends, it's in a kitchen or a restaurant. Our vacations are food pilgrimages. Food to us is home, health, family, fantasy, entertainment, education, and employment. Heart disease in the family, yes. Anorexia, never. And bulimia? What was that?

We had experienced none of the common triggers often associated with eating disorders: divorce, death, job loss, sexual abuse. As for the anorexic family stereotype—domineering mother, distant father, perfectionist daughter—um, no. We come closer to the opposite—quietly supportive mother, loving father who cries easily, creatively disorganized daughter. We forced the kids to visit distant relatives and to write thank-you notes, but when they tired of piano lessons and soccer we didn't argue about jeopardizing Ivy League prospects.

After a very bad senior year in high school, Lisa got well enough to go to college in the fall of 2003. There she soon relapsed, but came out of it and had three pretty good years before crashing in an even worse way, just shy of graduation. As we write this book, Lisa is twenty-four, coming back to life, and again we all have hope. But the past seven years brought police cars and emergency rooms into our life, and phrases like "seventy-two-hour hold" and "danger to yourself or others" into our everyday conversation.

As a newspaper writer and editor, I used to love irony. It made for the best stories, especially when they involved an apple falling far from the tree, or at least a little oddly. For example, "Liberal, Matriarchal Family Spawns Pro-Life Leader" and "Anti-Gay Vice

President's Lesbian Daughter Says . . ." What fun when it's someone else! How to explain the intergenerational drama? Too often, the shortcut answer was to blame the mother. "She's so controlling." "She's too lax." "She's distant." "She works too much." "She's always home, interfering in everyone's life." When we need someone to pin to the wall, Domineering Mom is so convenient. I have to admit I did it, too, although I was just as quick to blame the Distant Dad in those deliciously ironic situations. As in "Publishing Heiress Patty Hearst Robs Bank." Extrapolating, I wasn't the only one picturing a love-deprived child of privilege, rattling around the mansion, hungry for the family feeling she was to find, briefly, as a soldier in the Symbionese Liberation Army.

I didn't love irony when it happened to me: Food writer, in the public eye, has an anorexic daughter. Our life was like a movie in which the audience understands what's going on but the main characters are clueless. And I certainly didn't appreciate the armchair psychologists, real and imagined, pointing the finger at me as the cause of my daughter's ED (the catchall term for eating disorders). Our family went into triage mode, trying to help Lisa.

The upside of irony, when it happens to you, is that you have to learn something. Perhaps there's a loosening of attitude. I'm doing a lot less tut-tutting these days, and more tapping into a well of compassion, even for myself and my missteps in our family drama.

Hungry traces our fall from grace as a healthy middle-class family and follows our tightrope walk back to a tenuous perch. In many chapters, Lisa and I write alternating sections, so that families can see eating disorders from both the child's and the parent's point of view. In some chapters, we stop and look at the larger picture of craziness around food.

At first, Ned and I kept Lisa's illness to ourselves and very few friends. All we knew about eating disorders was that if they didn't strike in early adolescence you didn't have to worry, and that turned out to be wrong. Our daughter was older, preparing to leave home for college, when her symptoms first became severe. When she started acting strangely around food Ned and I thought, "This must be stress, it couldn't be anorexia. That would've shown up already." Many denials and common misconceptions later, my editors at the *San Jose Mercury News* asked me to consider writing a story about our experience with ED.

A few months went by, and Lisa seemed to be getting better. We agreed to share what we'd learned. The story would bring a shameful subject out into the open and, who knew, maybe putting Lisa's improvement in print would make it stick. It happened to be Pearl Harbor Remembrance Day, the Sunday in 2003 that the *Mercury News* published our dueling first-person account as the front-page centerpiece, with photographs of Lisa as a smiling six-year-old holding a soccer ball, a pudgy fourteen-year-old, a stick figure at nineteen.

Reader response was overwhelming and heartbreaking. Desperate families appreciated knowing they weren't alone. Like them, we had discovered that eating disorders are moving targets. Just when we thought we'd learned the rules and found the right strategy, the whole game would pack up and move to a new field. We'd been studying anorexia and the test was on binge eating. We had to learn to say, "Okay, that didn't help. Now we have to try something else."

"Something else" was at times a new medication, a therapist specializing in eating disorders, a nutritionist, another medication, a different therapist—all of which helped for a while and then didn't—and an eating disorders treatment center, which was a disaster.

"Looks like you've thrown everything at this," said one hospital doctor. I think he was trying to sympathize with our desperation, but all Ned and I heard was, "Look what you've done to this child." And when we went the route he recommended, it was a different kind of disaster. The lessons of the past several years never presented themselves in an obvious way.

When Lisa was diagnosed with anorexia, I picked up book after book, but none of them gave me what I needed: a sympathetic, articulate expert or parent who not only had been through this hell but also was insightful about food in our culture. This book is our effort to be that resource. Yes, eating disorders function like addictions, but no, you can't just say no to food. At work, at home, on the street, America is a twenty-four-hour buffet. We're never more than steps away from an endless stream of gastronomic options screaming: "Eat me!" Even gas stations have mini-marts serving groceries and hot food. (Pay no attention to the noxious fumes around the pumps.) No wonder we all flail around, from the eating disordered to the healthiest among us. Food overload makes me almost long for the rigid olden days of my youth, when families sat down for three meals a day, or at least dinner on weeknights, at specified times and places. In my parents' house, it looked like this:

3:30 p.m. After-school snack

4 p.m. Kitchen closed

6:30 p.m. Dinner

7 p.m. Do dishes; kitchen closed

When certain guests came over, we brought food into the living room, but never our bedrooms. Grocery stores sold the raw materials to make a meal at home, not hot meals to go. Restaurants were for special occasions. There wasn't a lot of room for individual expression, but the day had structure and families had control.

Now, over forty percent of American adults eat out on a typical day and nearly fifty percent of the family food budget goes to food eaten out or pre-prepared, as cooking is considered a time-consuming craft. Economic necessity may give a boost to home cooking, but it will be a whole new world if we get reacquainted with the dinner table and regularly sit down to meals together, without iPhones, laptops, or TVs.

Revered cookbook author and teacher Marion Cunningham lamented the loss of the family meal in 1998, when only thirty percent of the population cooked at home, even with skyrocketing interest in kitchen appliances. (Perhaps those were for the caterer.) "Home cooking in America has always been considered menial drudgery," Cunningham told the *Los Angeles Times*. This despite all the food shows on TV and sales of celebrity cookbooks. In defense of the family meal, Cunningham wrote cookbooks for children and for adults who didn't know what to do with their saucepans or spatulas.

We like to watch, like Chance the gardener, the Peter Sellers character in the 1979 movie *Being There*, the man who never went anywhere. Everything he knew, he learned from television. On the bright side, a person like Chance could learn to cook from Julia Child, who took to television and books to simplify French home cooking for Americans, knowing "our readers wouldn't have mortars and pestles for pounding lobster shells." (And if the readers didn't, the TV audience certainly didn't.) Now many of us have the mortars and pestles, but they're heavy and inconveniently stuffed way back in a kitchen cabinet because who has time, and who can afford lobster?

Burdened by beatific Norman Rockwell visions of the family meal, we have developed a negativity about eating at home that is shared even by organizations that know better, the ones pushing healthy food habits. Weight Watchers ("Stop Dieting. Start Living.") acknowledges the difficulty of cooking for a family night after night, particularly for the person on a diet, because home is where we know we should comply with whatever diet we've adopted at the time. Restaurants are where we go for a little fun, to treat ourselves, not to control our consumption.

Let's do the math: Food adds so much to our lives that we can lose track of the grand total. We love the feelings food arouses—the sensuality, the comfort of old favorites, the thrill of discovering new treats, the entertainment value of food—just not those pesky calories. We don't want to bother with meal planning and preparation, but we care more than ever about what we eat and how we look. This doesn't compute, except perhaps for those mythical gods with such a "fast metabolism" that they can eat anything and never gain an ounce. They are like students who always ace the exam and claim to "never study." For lesser mortals, passing tests and eating healthfully both take effort. We exist on a continuum of difficulty. Who doesn't have some kind of food addiction? It may be fleeting, like the woman who downs a box of Wheat Thins while sitting in freeway traffic the day before Thanksgiving (me). It may be deadly serious, like the teenager who obsessively counts every calorie as an enemy (Lisa).

Eating disorders fester in an individual's biological and psychological makeup, but we all live in a society that prizes thinness for women above all other qualities. Meanwhile, food gets in your face all the time, the elephant in the room. *Project Runway* and *Top Chef* battle it out for your desires. Want to look like a supermodel (or date one), or do you want to cook and eat like a great chef?

The national panic about obesity provides more grist for obsession. Maybe you didn't feel fat, just a touch overweight, before the U.S. Centers for Disease Control and Prevention revised the height/weight tables, and now your weight is considered morbidly obese. Are you going to exercise more and eat less, or just fuss more about food and appearance? Obsession is what food addiction is all about, and the accompanying compulsion to eat or starve yourself in order to soothe emotional pain, avoid scary feelings, or perhaps narrow your thighs or reach your "ideal body weight." Eating disorders are diagnosable food addictions.

If you're not hungry now, you will be soon, and then you'll have decisions to make. For serious food addicts these decisions take up most of the day. If your addiction is to drugs and alcohol, it is difficult but possible to learn to live without them. But you can't abstain from food. For people with eating disorders, the object of their addiction is in their faces every day, next to media images of impossibly skinny celebrities.

A few stars are finally admitting to eating disorders, but girls still want to look like them—thin hangers for designer dresses. Some centers of the fashion industry have been scared into setting standards. After the deaths of two anorexic models, the fashion shows in Madrid and Milan agreed to ban models whose body mass index falls below what the World Health Organization considers healthy. In the United States, the Council of Fashion Designers of America recognized the problem and formed a committee, which recommended "awareness and education, not policing." Meanwhile, tabloid magazines and websites run galleries of shame, with big yellow arrows noting problem areas in legs and butts, and photo contests like "Guess the Celebrity Cellulite! Can you tell the star by her dimples?"

Models, actors, and athletes set the pace, but at least one in every one hundred female adolescents in the United States is starving herself. Two-thirds of women students could be diagnosed with eating disorders at some point during college. College dormitories have their vomitoriums, where, everyone knows, a resident or two regularly throws up.

ED patients jump all over the demographic landscape, from children as young as six to women in their eighties, to men and boys. Ten million women and one million men have eating disorders, and twenty-five million people struggle with binge eating, the latest wrinkle in the obesity epidemic.

In times of famine, only the rich were fat. Now that anyone can look like Henry VIII—and too many people do—he's gone out of fashion. The most self-accepting among us still despair of our own spare tires.

This scourge hits our children at their most vulnerable. When I was a miserable teenager, my main focus of personal failure was having curly brown hair in a blond surfer-girl culture. But I could look forward to college, where a single standard of beauty wouldn't snuff out all the rest, brains would matter, and the population would be more diverse. We had Barbie, but compared with what came before and after, we lucked out in the sixties and seventies, when there were lots of really bad ways to look. My mother's generation and Lisa's generation have a tougher time with the One-Look-Fits-All dictators.

The Eating Disorder Referral and Information website gets over 3,200 visits a day—and that's only one of dozens of such websites. Anorexia and bulimia are so virulent that even with professional care, forty percent of patients never recover.

Then there are the rest of us, who occasionally diet but are always aware of our weight, and it's always too high. *Psychology Today* found that eighty-nine percent of women want to lose weight. But this statistic is even more stunning: Twenty-four percent of women would sacrifice three years of life to lose weight. Refusing food is a time-honored form of protest, whether you're a child objecting to broccoli or Mahatma Gandhi fighting British colonial rule of India. What's new is the relentless beat that skinny is best (ever more so with big breasts, like the classic Barbie figure) and the common acceptance of that inhuman ideal. We worship deprivation and disdain gluttony as sinful and repellant. Better by far to be hungry. Girls earn bragging rights based on how little they eat, as do women who are old enough to know better. They share tips for reaching the promised land of Size Zero and even better, Size Double Zero.

Pro-anorexia websites are waiting to share ever-more effective techniques of starvation with teenage girls, who love to hang out in digital space. (A recent posting: "I am aiming for 500 cals a day, and I am not exceeding 800. Under any circumstances. FRESH START!")

When Lisa was trawling for "thinspiration," as the pro-anorexia websites call it, I was out reviewing restaurants. People often ask, "How did you keep working?" The real question is, "How *could* you keep working? Your child might be dying!" I asked myself that question many times a day. But being by Lisa's side didn't seem to help, either. She just kept getting worse. Lisa often called my cell phone when I was driving to a restaurant, and sometimes she would say, "I can't do this anymore." By "this" she meant life.

Meanwhile I had the job of my dreams. Besides reviewing restaurants and answering readers' questions, I wrote news and feature stories. It made national news when I found that a prominent local Italian restaurant was substituting pork for veal, a fraud that caused Muslims and Jews to eat forbidden foods. The more I focused on the details of food safety and marketing, the more passionately readers responded. Everybody eats. My predecessor had to quit this job for his health, but lucky me, I have the metabolism for it. I tacked this quote from the great food writer M.F.K. Fisher to my cubicle wall: "First, let's eat," and I followed that commandment.

Also, I had to keep working because we needed my salary. Health insurance covered little of Lisa's care. We finally found a psychologist Lisa connected with, and she's made tremendous progress. Again we have hope, but her treatment has cost $30,000 a year. It comes out of money we had saved for Lisa's education and future.

Faced with a disease of uncertain origin and wildly conflicting experts, I flew into information-gathering like a frantic bird, collecting sticks and leaves to patch the nest. Quick, let's try this treatment or that doctor. When your child is sick, that's all that matters. You feel paralyzed at times, you can't face another day, but you keep going. My job just made the going a little trickier.

People who meet me as a food writer invariably say, "But you're skinny!" It may be my greatest accomplishment ("She ate a ton and never got fat"). But even at my thinnest postcollege depressive self, a knife blade in skinny jeans, I never lost track of the two or three pounds that would have flattened an imaginary bulge in my stomach.

As a food writer and middle-aged woman, I have rounded up a bit. (When I started reviewing restaurants, it was: "But you're *so* skinny!" Mostly I don't hear "so" anymore.) I exercise a lot, and I kick myself for all the mental energy I put into my weight and body parts I'd like to trade in, when I could be caring about something important. How did my body issues and my job as a food writer contribute to my daughter's anorexia? Lisa and I retreat to our own corners on this one. She sees a lot to blame on me, my job, our family's food obsession. And you know, so do I. But I wonder how much can be attributed to my career choice, my personality, or just being Mom. *Hungry* is not about piling on the blame. There's a lot more at work. Like mothers and daughters everywhere, when Lisa and I build up muscles of self-righteous anger and hurt, it's hard to break through. Our book is about the hungers that put us back in the ring.

A Very Bad Day

My daughter stands under five foot three and weighs ninety-three pounds. I can barely see the top of her head in the back of the patrol car as it sweeps by me, standing at the emergency room entrance on this otherwise gorgeous, blue-sky Saturday afternoon in August 2007. An armed policewoman gets out of the car and I can't watch anymore. I retreat into the Soviet-style hospital compound to wait for Lisa, hoping the handcuffs will be off when I get to see her.

Lisa and I had walked out of Stanford Hospital's double-wheelchair-wide doors less than forty-eight hours earlier, after six nightmarish weeks in treatment for anorexia and depression. We hadn't known it was even possible to stay six weeks in a hospital. It was way too long and while she wasn't getting better, she was deemed stable enough. On Thursday we packed Lisa's stuff into paper grocery bags. She hugged the cherubic resident doctor and a couple of the nicer nurses, and got one mile of fresh air as we drove to the new center of our hopes, a cozy, community-based halfway house where she would live for at least the next six weeks. They would have to be better weeks.

Eventually, yes, they would be, but that morning Lisa called 911. She told the dispatcher she had eaten liquid soap and said she felt dead. Two Palo Alto Police Department cruisers, a fire truck, and an ambulance raced to the group home, a place I'll call La Casa, a Tudor-style thirties-era house on a quiet residential street, and took my stunned daughter away in handcuffs. Metal handcuffs. This is police procedure for anyone who's "a danger to him- or herself."

When the officers had appeared at the door, Lisa was stunned. She told them she didn't really mean it. They were calm but stern. Once a suicidal-sounding call is made, there is no going back.

The director of the halfway house called me. He was on his way to the hospital to fill out the necessary forms, and he would talk to me there. He, too, sounded calm. This wasn't all new to him. When he got the call about Lisa's 911, he was buying vegetables at the farmers' market, where normal people went on Saturdays. Ned was out of town or he would have been at the farmers' market, too.

I put down the phone, wishing I hadn't picked it up, that the call had been a prank or I'd dreamed it. Two days free of the hospital, and that was that. What next? But this was no time to explore my feelings. I threw some fruit, bread, and cheese into a sack. All I could think was, We'll have to eat at some point. I wouldn't leave Lisa even for a few minutes to get a sandwich.

lisa: "I need you to just breathe," the policewoman called back to me. But I did not want to breathe, I did not want to see, I did not want to believe I was sitting in the back of a police car, handcuffed and heading back to the Stanford Hospital emergency room.

I had spent two nights at La Casa. I trembled uncontrollably and couldn't think, but mostly it had gone okay. When I checked in, everyone was just getting back from the offsite day program. We had dinner, watched TV, and went to bed. But the second night, a

Friday, most people got to go out after dinner. Being a new resident, I had to stay home to be monitored.

Another resident, Jeff, was in the house as well. The two of us stayed downstairs, he in the dining room while I sat semipetrified on the couch in the living room. The real world scared me and presented itself full of activity, color, lights, and people after being isolated in a lock-down ward for six weeks. I was now in a new place, around new people, and I was still very sick and feared rejection from my new peers. Ron, on duty as the night staff, read a book in the office and waited for residents to come home and take their nighttime medications.

I watched as Jeff got some ice cream and then came into the living room and asked me if I wanted some. It was very sweet ice cream: vanilla with birthday cake flavoring. I ate it at the dining room table, and pretty quickly freaked out about how much I'd eaten, so I went up to the bathroom and tried to calm myself down by washing my face but I couldn't hold back. I stuck two fingers down my throat and made myself throw up, as I had done so many times before. I was used to the taste of vomit, but I also had a soapy taste in my mouth. I realized I must have swallowed some facewash that had remained on my fingers. This freaked me out and I hardly slept at all that night.

In the morning, after breakfast, I felt like my body wasn't mine. Maybe it was all the meds I was taking, but my surroundings became hard to detect. I went upstairs and grabbed my cell phone to call 911. This is what I remember:

"I think I just killed myself."

"Where are you? What happened?"

"I'm at La Casa. I swallowed facewash and OD'd on Prozac." I didn't have access to Prozac or any other medications, and the facewash had been the night before. I just wanted them to come and, as I envisioned, rescue me because I knew something was medically wrong or very off with me and I simply did not feel safe.

Then they were there, and then there were handcuffs. I said, "No, I didn't mean it. I'll be okay. Just let me stay here."

We were supposed to go to the beach on Saturday.

sheila: I was planning to take Lisa to the beach on Saturday. After six weeks of recycled ventilation in a concrete hospital built in 1959, she could use some ocean atmosphere. Psychiatry patients who were stable enough were allowed to sit outside on the deck or shuffle down to the patio for half an hour, but Lisa rarely earned that privilege. She hardly even looked out the window. Most of the time when we arrived, her room's curtain was closed, and she hadn't noticed or cared. She was very depressed, and shaky on an antipsychotic medication, but she was capable of sitting in the car for the one-hour drive to the coast. I calculated the possible restroom stops in case of beach traffic.

We were supposed to have an entirely different spring, summer, and fall. This felt like the *Lifetime* movie version of somebody else's life. Lisa needed two more classes to graduate from the University of California, Santa Cruz, but she was able to walk with her class in June 2007. By now she would have been enjoying the summer; working at O'Neill, an upscale surfer-style clothing shop; and starting to think seriously about her future. She'd still have a couple of classes to finish up in the fall to get her degree in American Studies. She'd considered careers in teaching and in counseling, but needed time away from school before applying to graduate programs. It was a miracle she was even close to graduating with her class. Considering how horrible her freshman year had been—at least one quarter lost to bulimia—Ned and I were thrilled. And we'd been primed not to expect a four-year bachelor's degree at the University of California. Lisa's brother, Jake, spent seven years in and out of UC Berkeley.

I'm trying to make the case that Lisa wasn't under the parental gun when she fell to pieces and lost more than three seasons of her life at age twenty-three. Public school tuition helped us dither. I know parents who carried through on threats of "Four years and you're out!" with regard to college. Was it our permissive parenting that put Lisa on the road to extremely serious eating disorders in the first place? Lisa could have used stricter expectations, for sure. Maybe she felt lost. But I don't know that stricter parents have fewer anorexic kids. Was the attraction to anorexia that it was a way to set limits that we should have been setting? It was also a powerful way to get attention and to manipulate.

During Lisa's last year in college, she was working too many hours at the store, with a full academic load. But she kept saying that she liked to keep busy. She didn't like to have time on her hands. What was that about?

As a young child, Lisa liked to tell us, "I love you to pieces that will never break again!" Now we were even analyzing Lisa's version of Humpty Dumpty. If there had been a fall and something had broken, how could we not have noticed?

Our family had medical history, depression on my side and weight on Ned's. Not just weight. Craziness about weight. Ned's sister started taking diet pills when she was ten and has been on diets ever since. Ned got a little portly and then lost it, but his sister's torture stayed with him. He feared for any child of his, especially a daughter.

Genetics, then, gave Lisa two strikes, but something else must have happened. As with many diseases, the rule you often hear about eating disorders is "Genetics loads the gun, and experience/cultural pressure/trauma pull the trigger." Depression and weight/body image issues are as common as colds in America, yet most of us don't become anorexic. We all navigate relentless media and social pressures to squeeze our imperfect selves into a very narrow band of acceptable appearance and accomplishment. Everyone is exposed, but some are more vulnerable, especially teenagers and young adults struggling to figure out who they are. What comes through clearly, though: Be thin.

And yet, good luck, dear, because you're going to be around food all day, everywhere. Even in a bad economy, Americans have a turbulent relationship with food, more love/hate than appreciative. Rarely are we neutral about eating. Every food and food product is good or bad for our health and spiritual well-being, and the planet's. Give each food an A or an F, rarely a C. While food items shunned one day can be resurrected by new findings or, more likely, suddenly found to be harmful, we feel more comfortable assigning them to one extreme or the other. We aren't the only society to endow food with religious properties, but since the Puritans, it seems, we've never been able to relax about eating. Food is sinful or celestial.

Lisa got caught up in the sin, living in the original hotbed of food worship, the San Francisco Bay Area, with two foodie parents. We obsess. And I'm a food writer. This came as a shock to my family because I used to be the One Who Didn't Eat.

Foodies with Issues
How Sheila Met Ned and Planned
to Eat Happily Ever After

Two frantic grandmothers flutter around one new mom and a child who won't eat. In the 1950s, I am the one in the highchair, batting away all incoming spoons. In the eighties, it is my first child, Jacob. His maternal grandmother has to think, "Just desserts for Sheila" on one hand and "Not this again" on the other.

Maybe the early pickiness helped form me as a food critic, but eating just wasn't that appealing. I stayed small and came late to just about every physical milestone. In photos of birthday parties I am the shrimp among prawns. Would I ever really need a bra? At last, I got my period at fifteen and then grew another two inches in college, to the average American woman's five-foot-four. All that family angst about my eating and growing had been for nothing. I was normal.

Still, when baby Jacob zipped his lips against cereal and bananas and everything most children love, or spit them out, no memory or rational thought could stop me from flying straight into red alert.

Children eat, sleep, and grow. That's their job description. Jacob was a slacker in all departments.

Just like me. In our family, we were the children who didn't eat.

My mother respected the grandmothers, for their child-rearing experience and for their leadership of the family. Mom was not quite twenty-one years old, having dropped out of UCLA after her freshman year to marry a buoyant twenty-four-year-old war veteran who ran the family jewelry business with his brother and uncle. Mom didn't have a lot of confidence that I would survive without my grandmothers' forced feedings. "Very often it was both of them, trying to get you to eat," Mom says. "They were afraid you were going to starve to death."

Medical professionals in the fifties pitched into the kitchen wars by telling Mom to stop nursing and put me on the bottle. I wasn't getting enough milk. "I was not an eater, either," Mom says. "My mother put me through the same thing." We seem to be a line of slow learners.

I was the shortest or next-to-shortest in every class, always in the first row. Each December in our elementary school's unfortunate production of scenes from *The Nutcracker*, Cookie Fukutome and I could not be missed in the "Waltz of the Flowers," despite being the class's clumsiest ballerinas. Being short we were up-front, dancing dangerously close to the edge of the stage.

My sister, nearly three years younger, overtook me early on. She was the one who did eat. In many aspects, Nancy and I divided up the first child/second child duties as if we'd studied Psychology 101. She bounded into rooms, singing and chattering to announce herself. At my most outgoing, it could be said that I was timid rather than shy. I could smile but not speak when introduced to adults. We did a lot of carpooling, and occasionally a father, it was always a father, forgot my stop because I was so quiet. I sank into the enormous backseat, too mortified to tell him I was alive.

Nancy and I exemplified psychologist William Sheldon's classification of basic body types and the temperaments to go with them, a personality lineup taken very seriously for a long time. I was the linear ectomorph, particularly skinny in the arms and legs, as was Jacob. I imagined that I would age into the shape of my dad's father, who in his later years resembled a tangerine on toothpicks. Like Nancy, Lisa was a muscular mesomorph, gaining weight more easily than Jacob. Lisa couldn't help noticing these differences and finding them unfair.

During Nancy's and my youth, being a little more meso than ecto was good for girls. On daily episodes of *The Mickey Mouse Show*, celebrity teenage Mouseketeer Annette Funicello had noticeable breasts under her short-sleeved turtleneck sweater. On Saturday afternoons, we watched the ideal girl handed down from my mother's generation. Impossibly cheerful, apple-cheeked Shirley Temple sang and tap-danced into our hearts in *Curly Top* and *Poor Little Rich Girl*, that like our era's enduring *Pollyanna*, promoted the notion that if you kept your sunny side up things would turn out fine. These were our heroines.

Nancy was the good eater, beloved by grandmothers everywhere, but she had a nonweight health problem that drew concern. Eczema caused her neck, the backs of her knees, and the insides of her elbows to redden, swell, and itch like crazy when she encountered an allergen. For a while, she went to bed with plastic wrap swaddling her elbows and knees, which caused her to crinkle and me to mock. Because of her sensitivity, the nut tree in our backyard had to go. One day she played in the neighbor's tomato patch and broke out so badly that she was sent to the closest grandparents to recover. She endured endless creams. But the biggest effect on her life, on family life, was her restricted diet.

The regimen kept changing. Nancy definitely couldn't eat oranges or eggs, but the other culprits weren't so clear. For several weeks, she ate only applesauce, rice, and lamb. For years she took her breakfast cereal with apricot juice, and later with soymilk. One day Mom gave evaporated milk a shot, but Nancy noticed she was the only one and refused to try it. I offered to pour it on my cereal, too, expecting something that looked like milk to taste somewhere in the same ballpark. It was an early lesson in looks being deceiving, especially for food.

Chocolate and nuts are what Nancy remembers as being more problematic. The best candy bars, the Butterfingers and Snickers bars we got at the Saturday movie matinee, were all about chocolate and nuts. "You got chocolate and I got caramel," Nancy says now, a little edgily. "Luckily I still like caramel." Or not so luckily. Caramel is melted sugar, with none of the antioxidants and endorphins associated with certain kinds of chocolate.

Also less lucky for Nancy, mesomorphs often find weight control a constant struggle. Nancy never got fat, but she never got over the mind-set that food and drink required constant vigilance.

Our grandmothers were German-born Jews, one laser-focused on tidiness and order, the other alert for constant danger. One inspected our drawers for unfolded clothes; the other thought eight was too young to be riding bicycles. They both were short and round, like grandmothers were supposed to be. We called them by their husbands' names. For Nana Bill, a neatnik from Berlin who maybe reached five feet tall, the purpose of dinner was to have the dishes done and put away. While others sat and talked, a redheaded cyclone swept away half-finished plates. The fleshier Nana George had a sweet way of speaking, even when she got mad, using "her" when she meant "she." She must have missed the pronouns lesson in English class. The only scary thing about Nana George was that she kept a bottle of prune juice in the refrigerator and was always ready to use it on the child who admitted to not having a bowel movement that morning.

Nancy pretty much grew out of her allergies, not by puberty as doctors had promised, but by her late teen years. In the college dorm she didn't have to pour apricot juice onto her granola.

As an adult, Nancy stays healthy by walking every morning. She enjoys eating, but not with abandon. Nancy's family attends baseball spring training in Phoenix but has never been to Pizzeria Bianco. Widely regarded as the best pizza place in the United States, Pizzeria Bianco would be my family's first stop, perhaps our whole reason for visiting Phoenix. Nancy keeps kosher and health-conscious. After an anniversary party at her house, I stood by and watched as Nancy *threw out* the remains of an excellent chocolate cake.

When Chez Panisse opened in 1971, I lived a few blocks away and never even looked at the menu posted outside. I was studying journalism and social unrest at the University of California, Berkeley. Soon after, I moved to a cottage in Silicon Valley and, to keep a little Berkeley with me, I became a vegetarian. Sometimes I made my grandmother's blintzes and sometimes an even-richer dish, spinach lasagna, for guests. But mostly I ate vegetables, took up jogging, got very skinny, and dabbled in the New Agey Human Potential Movement. One dalliance involved a three-day fast, an organized event bookended by the group gathering at the start and then breaking the fast together at the end. After the first day's headache went away, I felt light and energetic. I went running. I went to see a new movie, *Rocky*. Bloody fight scenes, screaming, and triumphal music went down easily on an empty stomach, but when Sylvester Stallone swallowed raw eggs to build up his strength, *that* was repulsive. I could have kept fasting much longer. Later, I would compare my experience with Lisa's anorexia, but for me, starvation lacked purpose; It was just something to try.

I was bored. The problem was, my fast occurred over a long holiday weekend. I had made no plans and no one was around. Actually, my plan was to reach some misty point of enlightenment, but it could go the other way and I'd be very grumpy, so I thought it better to keep to myself. Now there was too much time in the day, with no friends and no meal planning, preparing, or cleaning up. I wondered what the other fasters were doing, but I didn't even know their names. I napped a lot. I couldn't wait to get eating back in my life, not so much for the food itself as for the activity.

I never would have met Ned in a fasting group, or even in a restaurant. He loved the hot fudge sundae at Lyon's coffee shop and the chili burger at Original Tommy's in Los Angeles, while indulgence for me was the slightly greasy lentil patty at the Good Earth, an early health-food restaurant. We were introduced by one of my college roommates. When Joyce met Ned, they knew after one date that they were not made for each other, not least because Joyce had so many food allergies. A taste of ice cream made her puff up and break out in hives. Ned could not imagine life without ice cream.

I ate ice cream. On our first date, a scoop of chocolate ice cream was the dessert. We went to Susie's, a fifties-style dinner house featuring chicken-fried steak, not an easy menu item to find in the Bay Area. Still sort of a vegetarian at the time, I ate the iceberg lettuce salad, steamed vegetables, mashed potatoes, and bread, which was unlimited but stale. Somehow at Susie's the bread was always stale, which struck Ned as one of its charms. Did they leave it sitting out to attain the right degree of dryness? I thought he was nuts.

A signature dish from my grim kitchen was soy "meatloaf." Chewy little soy grits formed a loaf that neither mustard, catsup nor any other sauce could moisturize. I liked soy loaf because it made me feel virtuous. Ned thought I was nuts.

But this dark-haired, bearded guy with deep brown eyes liked the fact that I enjoyed learning about places I hadn't been, restaurants as well as concerts and beaches. He made me laugh. We went to see plays and comedians, and waited to see the stars afterward at the stage door. I didn't know you could even do this. After a terrible play, we waited for Katharine Hepburn, and Ned actually spoke to her, asking her to say the famous line from a good play, *Stage Door:* "The calla lilies are in bloom again." She stopped and ripped off her whole opening monologue!

Once we hit the food trail, vegetarianism started dropping like breadcrumbs. Others shun meat for serious reasons: to promote the ethical treatment of animals, to fight factory farming and agribusiness, to conserve resources, to rebel against parents. I just liked saying I was a vegetarian. It gave a person a whiff of superiority, the exhibition of steely control, like a Spartan warrior—in much the same way as anorexics regard themselves. Anyway, fancy restaurants were silly extravagances at a time of social upheaval and there was important community-building work to be done. Not that I did it.

I was willing to be dragged along to all kinds of restaurants by a true enthusiast.

Fish and seafood came back right away. Because, you know, if the restaurant's specialty is roast crab, who are you punishing by not having it? And why live in the San Francisco Bay Area if you aren't going to eat fresh Dungeness crab? It took longer to rekindle a love of red meat, but not all that long. I craved a hamburger every day of my vegetarian years. The occasional lentil burger looked the part, but it didn't drip juices. On our first pilgrimage to Chez Panisse, which had quickly become the West Coast basilica of food worship, wouldn't you know that that night's entrée would be roast pork tenderloin? I could have asked for a vegetarian substitute, but I was starting to understand that my knowledge of food was very limited. If they had selected roast pork as the high point of dinner, who was I to say, No thanks, I'd rather have zucchini?

Our social life expanded to include dinners hosted by Ned's friends and colleagues, where the vegetarian stance felt awkward. None of the options worked very well. I didn't want to tell them ahead of time and have them cook something special for me, or silently push food around and hope no one noticed, or say, "I don't eat the main thing you've cooked here, but don't worry, I'm fine." Dietary restrictions had yet to become common topics of discussion.

At home, Ned melted the rest of my resolve with fettuccine Alfredo and cheese-glazed chicken, which he served together. This was a lot tastier than soy loaf. However, his father had had several heart attacks. My counterpunch was to hector Ned into jogging, which at first he opposed because it was a fad. Ned eventually learned to love daily aerobic exercise. For my part, the fad of vegetarianism was over.

When we got married, the fabulous food gifts included Calphalon pans, Henckels knives, and a gift certificate for dinner at the French Laundry. The little Napa Valley stone building that Thomas Keller would later turn into the country's most difficult reservation was in 1979 just a cool destination restaurant in an actual turn-of-the-century laundry. You got the table for the night, so that between courses you could take a walk in the garden or smoke a cigarette. The framed handwritten menu for September 15, 1979, hangs in our hall:

APPETIZERS
SCALLOPS CHAUD-FROID   3.25

RARE BEEF IN MUSTARD SAUCE   3.00

CURRIED CHICKEN MOUSSE IN CANTALOUPE   2.75

EGGPLANT, BELLS, AND MUSHROOMS   2.25

TONIGHT'S DINNER
COLD TOMATO AND AVOCADO SOUP

DUCKLING IN GREEN PEPPERCORN SAUCE

GREEN SALAD

11.50

DESSERTS

RASPBERRY MERINGUES   3.00

FIGS AND CHOCOLATE IN CREAM   2.75

COFFEE POT DE CRÈME   2.25

We had all three desserts. Then as now, no dollar signs were attached to the menu prices, a graphic style that washes numbers clean of meaning, as if the dish's full name is "Scallops chaud-froid 3.25." The French Laundry was an early adopter of this sneaky fashion in American menu design. Now it's hard to find dollar signs on Chinese takeout menus, let alone the fancy French. Today, a Chef's Tasting Menu at the French Laundry begins with Thomas Keller's trademark humor:

OYSTERS AND PEARLS

"SABAYON" OF PEARL TAPIOCA WITH ISLAND CREEK OYSTERS

AND CALIFORNIA STURGEON CAVIAR

and ends with:

Prix Fixe 240.00 / Service Included

In our family, Ned is the tightwad and I am the spendthrift, and although we each have our irrational moments (Ned: "We need toilet paper *again*?" Sheila: "These shoes are a little expensive, yes, but they will last longer!"), we pretty much agree about spending on food. It's good to eat well. When we argue about restaurants, more likely it's about parking, traffic, or some other difficulty in getting there than about the food. Ned refuses to pay for parking unless all other options are impossible, no matter how upscale the restaurant or how dicey the neighborhood. He is a little bipolar about food, searching for half-off coupons and then buying duck confit for a weeknight dinner.

Before having children, we camped in state parks in order to eat in restaurants up and down the West Coast. We would get dressed in the tent and roll out of camp just as everyone else was huddling around their barbecues and benches. By the time we finished our French Laundry figs and chocolate in cream, coffee pot de crème, and raspberry meringues and drove back into camp, all was peace and quiet. In the morning, we'd find a coffee shop.

Ned's training as a reference librarian gave him extra skills for ferreting out places to eat. In the San Francisco Bay Area, restaurants tended to clump up in Berkeley and San Francisco, but weekend destinations to the north had been newly discovered. When we traveled, Ned made charts and then spreadsheets so that in case we got hungry in Versailles, Brooklyn, or Mendocino, we were less likely to make an unfortunate touristy mistake. Few newspapers ran restaurant reviews, and guidebooks were unreliable.

Sometimes we behaved more like cows than ferrets. We fell back on the herd instinct, and we were reminded that people like restaurants for many reasons, some of which we didn't share. One of the more expensive reminders came during a trip up the California coast, when Mendocino was still an artsy little town. It had yet to become famous in the role of a New England fishing village in the movie *Summer of '42*, but Mendocino had Ledford House, Margaret Fox's irresistible Café Beaujolais, and other restaurants that are still worth the five-hour drive—much of it through beautiful valleys and along spectacular coastline. Those we knew. But one night we found ourselves up near Fort Bragg, and noticed a Hollywood-worthy seafood house on Noyo Harbor, a working port. This place was jammed. It must be great! We waited over an hour in the bustling and quaintly shoddy bar, and then . . . maybe we didn't drink enough. From the relish-and-saltines tray to canned peas to frozen fish, the food droned on. Dining here was like being stuck in a traffic jam, staring at the pattern of holes in freeway divider concrete, thinking, "How bad can it be? Should I get off this road and go another way? Nah, it has to get better soon." But it doesn't. Bad appetizers seldom lead to good entrées, but sometimes dessert is so much better than anything that came before that it feels like you're in a different restaurant. Not this time.

Bad food happens, no matter how extensive the research, but the thrill of the hunt kept us traveling with the sole purpose of trying a new restaurant. Who knew people were allowed to have fun like this? First speaking to Katharine Hepburn, now driving for hours not to visit family or friends, not to see an historic site or a natural wonder, but just to eat.

Ned loved having an appreciative sidekick. He had once taken a thirty-mile detour, on a trip from Los Angeles to the Bay Area, to dine at a French-Asian restaurant famous for its escargots. Despite its being located in Hanford, remote from everything but cattle and cotton, the Imperial Dynasty had served European monarchs and Hollywood movie stars. Ned remembers walking in and thinking, "I really wanted to do this. But it's sad to be here by myself." He doesn't even remember if he had the signature escargots.

At home, the San Francisco Bay Area was leading a white-bread nation into an expanded consciousness of good food, introducing the language we speak today: fresh, local, natural, organic, seasonal. At parties, people talked about restaurants and food rather than jobs and real estate. When our friend Susan's parents were moving to the Bay Area from Los Angeles, friends and colleagues were full of advice: "Oh, the Bay Area. Let me tell you about the best place to get bread." In Los Angeles, restaurant conversation was about real estate, and servers aspired to be movie stars. Up North, in restaurants we talked about other restaurants, and waiters dreamed of opening their own.

In Bay Area home kitchens and restaurants, food allegiances were shifting dramatically. There would be less bowing and scraping to the French on the high end, and much less dependence on canned and processed foods on the low end. We already had high-quality wine, fruit, vegetables, chocolate, Monterey Jack cheese, and sourdough bread. We were about to go artisan, partisan, and often organic in all those areas and more. The West Coast's pioneer spirit and willingness to experiment jibed nicely with a population of adventurous residents who traveled widely and brought back food and recipes. In the seventies, waves of immigrants from Southeast Asia, China, the Middle East, and Latin America opened restaurants and groceries. The mix got even tastier.

How could a person not take part in all of this? It would be like living in Hawaii and never going to the beach. Ned and I searched out Salvadoran *pupusas* and Szechuan peppercorns, hot dogs, and tempura. The night he met my parents, we ate at a French restaurant in San Francisco, La Bourgogne, which I picked because of Ned's research. He was impressed that my dad knew how to talk to waiters. At the first spoonful of lobster bisque, we all looked up and giggled, and by the time we got to the Grand Marnier soufflé, life was so delightful that we all went dancing at the elegant St. Francis Hotel. How could I not marry this man?

Ned and I joined a cheese co-op, which required knife work and attendance at monthly meetings. We saved menus. Ned continued a collection of restaurant matchbooks. Are these foodie obsessions? Did they lead to grief later on?

Maybe as a recent convert to the joy of food, I lost perspective. Where I used to disdain conversations about food—thinking, How can these people keep talking for half an hour about bread? It's just bread!—now I cared deeply. Maybe we put too much effort into procuring, preparing, and consuming food—all the activity, socializing, and sense of purpose that my three-day experiment in starvation had lacked. Of course bread mattered. In France, we took a train trip to Tours just to eat warm brioche at a little place near the train station, famous for selling only brioche. When visiting Los Angeles, we always stopped for corn rye bread at the Beverlywood

Bakery, where I had gone as a child and remembered that no matter how many cakes and onion rolls and loaves of bread you bought, the counterwomen always asked, "And what else?" They still did that. What joy! There was no question that we would pass this joy on to our children.

three

Feed Me, I'm Yours

In 1982, when our first child was born, Ned and I were in our early thirties, not exactly babes in the 'burbs. A librarian and a journalist, we both are trained to track down information, evaluate sources, and talk to experts in subjects that are way out of our realm. We know how to study. But as happens to most parents, in our children's early years much of what we studied turned out not to be on the test.

We read up on pregnancy and took childbirth classes. Child-rearing? Not so much. I found the information hard to store— perhaps a hormonal case of pre-Mommy Brain. But having this unknown future person in our life seemed so hard to grasp. We knew babies are born different and change constantly, and that as soon as you learned what to expect, he or she would push the Restart button. (On our first well-baby visit, when the pediatrician referred to Jacob as "he," after all those months of carrying "the baby," I thought, "Who?") If you think about the impending responsibility, the rational response is overwhelming fear. Ned and I decided we'd read about childcare on a just-in-time schedule. Still, we quizzed every young parent who came near, focusing on things we could control, like what to look for in a good day-care center and what we needed to buy before the baby was born. There was so much unfamiliar equipment to evaluate.

The scariest item looked like an airline-size bottle of dark rum. This was ipecac, used to make your child avoid death by throwing up the snail bait, drain cleaner, or other poison you'd insanely left within reach. Physicians later decided this procedure could do more harm than good. With the advent of eating disorders, bulimics bought ipecac to induce vomiting, so stores stopped stocking it. (Although ipecac lives on. A lightning-fast scan of Google turns up a number of YouTube videos featuring people swallowing ipecac and vomiting, and a record label called Ipecac Recordings whose slogan is "Making People Sick Since 1999.") The American Academy of Pediatrics now recommends that ipecac syrup *not* be stocked at home. Luckily our ipecac never left the kitchen cupboard, but later, Lisa was to remember the creepy little brown bottle and skulk around a drugstore before finally asking if they carried ipecac. They didn't.

For the less ominous items, *Consumer Reports* was a big help. Parents packed up their baby for a walk around the block as if crossing the frontier in a covered wagon. Strollers ranged from handy canvas to handsome buggies suitable for the Prince of Wales. Still, the items then available would have stocked only a mini-mart next to the Costco of products crying out to new parents today.

Besides spending money and interviewing parents, Ned and I practiced childcare on our dear friends' toddlers. Taking care of young children appeared to be a lot like taking care of a dog. I'd always had a dog.

Each outing started pleasantly enough. Sarah played happily with us for a while, and Benjy took one look at us and quickly went to sleep. Then Sarah wanted something unfathomable and Benjy woke up. The dialogue between Ned and me eventually went:

"What should we do now?" (A plea that would bounce back and speak our hopeless anguish during Lisa's anorexia.)

"I thought you knew! Your sister has children!"

"I thought you knew! You used to babysit!"

"Twenty years ago!"

Incompetence didn't keep us from scoffing at others. When our neighbors' adorable two-year-old daughter threw an operatic fit on their front porch, we sat in our childless living room and laughed. When spoiled children dropped food to a restaurant's floor and got up and down, up and down, we clucked disapprovingly. Why couldn't their parents get through the grocery store without a breakdown, holding up the checkout line at rush hour?

There seemed to be a lot of pandering to children's tastes. An actual conversation, overheard in a grocery store, went like this:

"Chelsea, do you want a banana?"

"No!"

"Do you want an apple?"

"No!"

And so on, to everything else on offer that day, until the exasperated mother cried, "What *do* you want?"

"I don't *want* what I want!"

We were to have our own versions of this conversation, but before having children we could float above the fray, like Spock on *Star Trek*, thinking if not saying about other people's child-rearing: "This is highly illogical." Any children of ours, we knew, would eat everything, and they wouldn't have fits in restaurants.

Early on, Ned and I discovered that the best result in splitting household tasks was to focus on areas of competence, and Ned had the cooking competence. He also liked to shop for food. It gave him a sense of budgetary control and ensured we had on hand what he wanted to cook. We loved trying new foods, at home and in restaurants.

In my dreamscapes of maternity leave, I envisioned six months of sitting on a park bench, one hand holding a book, the other on the stroller where "the baby" slept. Our view of taking kids to restaurants was only slightly more realistic. If we trained them right, wouldn't they just sit there and smile?

Baby boomers got the idea that we could control everything that happened to our children, an ego trip foolishly accepted by each successive wave of parents. Perhaps the economy will put a dent in this overconfidence, but we assumed we were the captains of our family ships, much more so than our own clueless parents had been. Certainly we were to be totally in charge of what our children ate. And if they didn't eat well, it was our own fault. Dinner became a show of skill as well as love. Working women brought the discipline we'd honed on the job—control, cause and effect, retraining—to the job of feeding. Books and experts were consulted. During my sister's pregnancy, her bedside table always had a foot-high pile of books on childcare.

Right off the bat, there were skills involved with breast-feeding. Don't let the baby nurse too long on one side. Do consume brewer's yeast, helpful for the letdown of milk. Breast-feed for at least six months—or risk frequent colds, allergies, and low achievement. Bring a breast pump to work, despite there being only a restroom stall to use it in, because the less formula the better.

And then came the complications of solid foods, grown or manufactured by strangers. Solid foods were "introduced" to your child, as if they were new friends. Or enemies. As guardian at the gate of allergies, the wise parent introduces one food at a time. That way, if the child breaks out in hives, you know the culprit. The high performers of parenthood jumped through blenders, grinders, and strainers to make their own baby food.

I focused my anxieties on giving birth to a healthy baby. That is, eating well, sleeping a lot, and taking a Lamaze class, which provided breathing techniques we actually used, but also new things to worry about. One mother-to-be had heard that if you didn't push properly the baby could go back up the birth canal. The rest of us snickered silently at her naivete, but at least one of us was thinking, "I really don't know what's going to happen. My body has never turned inside-out before."

It was the dawn of reality for many of us, that life wasn't practice, with infinite opportunities for do-overs, and that having a baby wasn't just another thing to try, like being a vegetarian. Childbirth classes drive home the awesome responsibility, for the first time since driver's education, with tales of horror and gore. A mother from the previous class gave a stitch-by-stitch account of her emergency episiotomy. We toured the ICU. I hadn't been a hospital patient since having my tonsils out at age four, and that was not a good memory. Even the ice cream at the end didn't soothe the pain.

But when Jacob was born, I would have liked to have lingered in the hospital. He slept, I slept, he was carried in to me, food came to me with no cooking or cleaning, and I had my own room. Except for the crying, it was like a luxury spa.

Which all evaporated when we went home and he became colicky, forgot how to nurse, and slept only when we were awake. I got so groggy that I mistook apple juice for vegetable oil, and served a sweet, rock-hard quiche to guests. Jacob got an ear infection in his second month, and I nearly poured the liquefied antibiotic into his ear instead of his mouth because by the time we got home I couldn't recall what the doctor had said to do with the pink bottle. Luckily the advice nurse was on duty.

Clearly I should have read up on lactation, but it had seemed so obvious. We called the Nursing Mothers Council, a volunteer group that sent over an angel of mercy to help me with technique. From then, feeding went pretty well until it was time for solid foods.

Now came the book buying. The classic *Dr. Spock's Baby and Child Care* for a calm, genial, trust-your-instincts kind of approach and at the other end, books by Penelope Leach and T. Berry Brazelton. These two were steeped in the "attachment theory" that working mothers could not help reading as an attack. If you weren't home all the time, bonding, you were separating, causing anxiety. There were plenty of people around who regarded daycare as bordering on a post-Ceauşescu Romanian orphanage, where starving children were tied to their beds.

I was pretty sure if I stayed home all day, I'd become the Romanian dictator. I wasn't going to worry too much about leaving my children in the hands of recommended professionals. Now that we had a healthy baby, keeping him that way was our purpose in life. *Feed Me, I'm Yours* promised "Baby Food Made Easy! Delicious, Nutritious, and Fun Things You Can Cook Up for Your Kids!" It introduced the "Plop" Method:

1. Take pureed or finely ground foods and "plop" by spoonfuls onto a cookie sheet. The size of each "plop" depends on how much you think the baby will eat at one meal.

2. Freeze "plops" quickly.

3. When frozen, remove from sheet and transfer to plastic bag.

4. Label and date.

The author, Vicki Lansky, also gave the following key advice:

A child needs far less food than many parents expect. A child eats when hungry, and will take just what he or she needs to maintain his/her growth rate. Servings should be small so as not to be discouraging . . . so should the plates or bowls.

I took the plates and bowls part seriously. In our cupboards, small plastic dishes stacked up as if we were Tupperware magnates, but Jacob didn't much care. His eating was erratic at best.

We bought every kind of baby food, even those little hot dogs that look like fingers in water. We'd try anything, if only our fussy firstborn would eat it.

Jacob grew, but very slowly, to sixteen pounds by his first birthday. His arms were so thin that he had to get immunizations in his thigh. He had blood tests, even a test for cystic fibrosis. He was fine. We were nuts. I bought more plates. Another pediatrician had suggested using adult-size plates, so the food looked small.

Restaurants were a breeze at first. But once Jacob reached toddler stage, he dropped plates to the floor and preferred to talk at the table, anything but take in food. Just like at home.

Jacob was a chatty but runty two-year-old when I became pregnant again, and our pediatrician said the presence of a competitor at the table might stimulate his appetite. We'd ruled out all the terrible diseases, and she wanted us to calm down. "Some kids eat just enough," she said. Just like adults, some eat to live and others, like Ned and I, live to eat.

In Jacob's baby book, under the heading Baby's Difficulties, we have this entry at the top:

EATING. Turns his head away, zips up his lips. 10 months.
Throws food to Joby (the dog). 12 months.

Lisa's baby book didn't have a Difficulties page, and if it had, eating would never have been mentioned. She took to nursing right away, went easily to solid foods, and rarely did the dog benefit from hanging around her highchair, like she did with Jacob. Lisa was one of us; she loved to eat.

four

Growing Gourmets

What you worry about is rarely what happens, right? The point of worrying is not to plan or take action, particularly, but just to single out a catastrophe and by naming it ensure that it doesn't happen. Before our wedding, a wise friend suggested I make a list of Catastrophic Expectations, possibly to stop me from talking about them so much. It's a strategy used in business today, as in this advice for jobseekers from GoodPeople, a Baton Rouge–based executive search firm:

> The next time you feel a Catastrophic Expectation about to take hold, confront it. For example, if you're worried that you'll end up sleeping under a bridge if you fail to land a job offer in the next three months, quantify the probability of this happening. You may be amazed and embarrassed by how unlikely it is. Develop some alternatives for what you'd do if you were evicted

from your home. Wouldn't you stay with relatives, rent a room somewhere, or sleep at a homeless shelter first?

In the Himmels' early years of raising a family, our Catastrophic Expectations machine worked perfectly. What we worried about, that Jacob wouldn't grow, didn't happen. In fact, those years were blue skies ahead for us. Jacob was so gentle with his much more aggressive little sister that eventually we told him it was okay to hit her back. Maybe he was too kind. We could worry about that later, if he got pushed around at school. We worried a little about Lisa's mercurial personality, which stood out from the rest of us, who tended to overthink rather than overact. In a family of quiet, shy readers, our incredibly cute daughter quickly became our Sarah Bernhardt, flamboyant star of stage, screen, and opera. Lisa could go from joyful play to pitched combat without any visible means of transport. She regularly woke from naps screaming in sweat, as from a nightmare, and could require half an hour to calm down enough to speak. We named one of her favorite dolls Calm Baby, a squishy toy that lit up when squeezed. Long after Calm Baby's batteries went dead, hugging the doll still sometimes helped. What kicked off the furies? Often it was hard to tell, or it didn't matter. She just had to spin out. Still, she always came back from wherever that was, collected herself, and became charming again. For now, basking in the sunshine of a happy family, we expected that if we kept doing things right, we might get some rain but there'd never be a hurricane. We don't have hurricanes in California.

Much later, I came across the wisdom of the psychotherapist/author Harriet Lerner, whose book *The Mother Dance: How Children Change Your Life* features chapters realistically titled "Are You Fit to Be a Mother?" and "What Kind of Mother Ever Hates Her Children?" Lerner delivers this stunning news: "In the life cycle of a normal family, something will get terribly screwed up with at least one of your kids. If this doesn't happen to you, well, you're just some kind of weird exception to the rule, or very lucky, or in denial, or your time hasn't come yet."

Our time was a long way off.

In Lisa's baby book I wrote on the page titled Special Memories of First Days at Home:

> Lisa is a dream baby. She nurses well (NW as they say in the hospital), is pleasant for a while, then falls back to sleep. In three-hour intervals.
>
> At night she's the same—wakes up to nurse and falls right back asleep.

Now *this* is the way parenting should be.

We started to relax. Jacob had suffered the full first-child treatment, constant vigilance, mirror to his sleeping mouth to make sure it showed a little puff of air and he was still breathing. Jacob's artsy baby book, from New York's Metropolitan Museum of Art, contains a remnant of his belly button cord, long gone to dust. Only two pages of this book are empty: Baby's Christening and Baby Eats at the Table. Elsewhere, Ned wrote that taking Jacob to a restaurant was like eating with Helen Keller (as played unsentimentally by Patty Duke in the 1962 movie *The Miracle Worker*, young Helen was a dinnertime terrorist, grabbing food off her parents' plates).

At birth, our children were the same length and differed by only four ounces in weight. At age nine, when we cut the cord on growth charts, Lisa was half an inch shorter than Jacob had been, but she weighed more than seventeen pounds more.

We neglected to record our second child's statistics for a couple of years. But, sheesh, there was no need. Lisa was doing fine.

How much of Jacob's pickiness did we cause by being so frantic, and how much was just him? Maybe he would have been a connoisseur in any case. When given a tangelo at age three, our serious

	JACOB	LISA
Birth	7 lbs 7 oz; 19½"	7 lbs, 11 oz; 19½"
1 month	7 lbs 11 oz	9 lbs 6 oz
6 months	12 lbs 6 oz	15 lbs 10 oz
1 year	16 lbs; 28½"	19 lbs; 27½"
2 years	19 lbs 8 oz; 32¾"	24 lbs 33"
3 years	23 lbs 8 oz; 36¼"	29 lbs 9 oz; 34¾"
4 years	26 lbs 8 oz; 37½"	36 lbs; 38½"
5 years	30 lbs 8 oz; 41½"	—
7 years	40 lbs; 47"	—
9 years	47 lbs 12 oz; 50"	65 lbs; 49½"

son said, "If you took the seeds out, it would make me much happier." I remember telling his pediatrician that Jacob liked his apples to be peeled, otherwise he wouldn't eat them. The beleaguered doctor looked at me, sighed, and said, "Don't peel apples for him, or you'll always be peeling apples." Still, I peeled.

With Lisa, meals were so much easier. She ate joyfully. Even when she was in a rejectionist phase, the introduction of new foods went like this:

"Want some of this (food)?"

"No. What is it?"

And then, more often than not, she would try it.

Lisa's never-say-never approach to dining became a stream of inputs on her Out of the Mouths of Babes pages of her baby book, such as, at four and a half, when she said, "I feel like I'm going to throw up—after dessert."

Most likely she didn't. Throwing up scared her. Even when Lisa was sick with the flu, she would do anything to avoid vomiting, right up until the time she became bulimic.

However, sleep was a big issue for Lisa. While we rejoiced at how easy she was to feed, she rarely went to bed without a fight and often woke up screaming. As with body type, and the need for orthodontics and optometry, Lisa took after Ned's insomniac side of the family. Later, Lisa's trouble with sleeping would factor into her worst bout of anorexia.

lisa: I have never been a good sleeper, which I can thank Dad's genes for. I was also blessed with bad allergies, flat feet, and extreme motion sickness. My brother got Mom's solid sleeping abilities as well as her lean figure, arched feet, and ability to endure long, bumpy car rides.

Even as a young kid I don't recall sleeping in late or falling asleep easily. I was especially antsy at slumber parties. If I slept at all, I was the last to fall asleep and the first to wake up. I've also never been good at taking naps. My parents claim that as a toddler through about age five, I would rise from naps in a sweat, screaming, crying, and being downright uncomfortable. I suppose that put me off naps.

sheila: Lisa's right, I am a world-class sleeper. If I get less than eight hours, I have to take a nap. For maximum performance, both are nice. At work, some afternoons I go out to my car, put my feet up on the dashboard, and take a twenty-minute snooze. Put me on a train, a ferry boat, or a long drive, and I will sleep. Ned may be talking in the car and notice that I haven't said anything in a while, because I've fallen asleep. On an old comedy album I had as a child, Bill Cosby riffed on the beauties of rest, "I like sleep like a good steak." I'm with him.

It became the family scripture that Jacob took after me and Lisa had more of Ned's genetic gifts. Quiet, thin, serious, judgmental on my side. Fun-loving foodies on Ned's. As a teenager, Lisa wrote to Ned one Father's Day: "You know that I think you're a swell dad; awesome and fun, loving and caring. People tell me that I really am my father's daughter, and I like it that way."

As a first-grader, Lisa wrote to me on Mother's Day: "You are a nice mom but I would like it if you wouldn't yell at me as much. I don't mind if you do it sometimes. On the brite [side], you are so nice and I love you very much."

lisa: I never considered myself a daddy's or mommy's girl, but I did have commonalities with each one. Mom and I could easily talk about our feelings and dissect the reasons behind our particular emotions at a certain time. Mom did all the clothing and toy shopping. She took me to get my hair cut, although that sometimes turned out badly, with Dutch-boy bangs or horrible layers. If I was sick, it was usually Mom who stayed home from work with me. My parents provided equal love, nurturing, and education. I felt equally attached and devoted.

When it came to food, however, Dad was The Man. As contradictory as it may sound for a food critic, Mom failed to display much range in her cooking. Only over the past few years has she come out of her bubble of easy meals into actually reading recipes and producing quite impressive results. Mom taught me to scramble an egg, but when we were growing up, Dad always amazed me with his creativity and skill. I developed a rather mature palate at a young age. Had Dad not been so versatile and skilled in the kitchen I probably would have joined in with most other kids who were stuffing their faces with popular junk food and nutritionally deprived packed lunches. I must have been a little bit of a dream child for Dad, who was so delighted in having a daughter with such a bodacious appetite. My brother actually refused food!

I entered Dad's world as a pleasant surprise and quickly became his kitchen assistant. Dad used to emulate the mannerisms and unique voice of Julia Child as we'd cook together. He'd talk through the steps of the recipe as if filming a cooking show even though his only audience member stood next to him.

Around the age of seven, I felt limited by the children's menu and proclaimed that I wished to order from the adult selections. At eight I tried, and secretly liked, escargots while on vacation in Montreal. While most kids my age considered seafood "icky" and survived mainly on spaghetti, hamburgers, cereal, and sweets, I enthusiastically accompanied my parents out to dinner. They also frequently entertained their eclectic and lively circle of friends—all with a common adoration for food—and I found myself sharing in the dining experience of goat cheese appetizers and Dad's famous caramelized pear tarte Tatin. I even shocked strangers with my mature appetite. On an airplane to visit our family in Seattle, I asked for tomato juice and heard the passenger on Mom's other side whisper, "Your daughter drinks tomato juice?" In fact, I drank a lot of tomato juice and V-8 and took a lot of crap at the lunch table, where sugar-laden Capri Sun was the preferred beverage.

sheila: To get decent tomatoes and stoke the kids' interest in where food comes from, Ned signed up for a plot in the community garden. City officials had started a demonstration garden to show residents how to grow organic crops and quickly turned it over to a hungry populace. Now there are four community gardens sprinkled throughout Palo Alto.

The summer before Lisa was born, Ned and Jacob picked tomatoes, chard, zucchini, and lemon cucumbers—the kind that don't make you burp. On the drizzly morning of October 13, 1984, Ned left me and newborn Lisa in the hospital to pick up Jacob, and before visiting us they swung by the farmers' market. Palo Alto set up a Saturday morning farmers' market in 1981 to offset the disappearance of grocery stores in the downtown area. Whole Foods has long since moved in, but the Saturday downtown market still buzzes and now there's one on Sunday as well.

Lisa took more to the market than to farming. At the garden, Jacob liked to wander around and pick wild berries. Lisa preferred the downtown carnival scene. From the comfort of her stroller, she listened to the banjo players and the shouting about "sweet English cucumbers" and accepted tastes of just-picked peas offered by the professional farmers. She took after Ned in appreciation of free samples. Both also loved Costco, despite its cold concrete vastness, because of the sampling opportunities. The store near us initially made it difficult and foolish to bring young children: There was no riding in the industrial carts, and strollers were not allowed. Costco management soon wised up.

Ned's downtown Saturday rounds included an old-fashioned, frosted cookie–type bakery that made great wheat bread and hamburger buns, and the twenties-era Peninsula Creamery for milk in glass bottles. When we needed staples, we shopped at the Co-Op, a funky nonprofit from the sixties that did not survive the eighties. We joined a produce co-op as well as the cheese co-op.

"That's the store we don't like," Jacob, age two, informed a visitor as we drove by the Safeway supermarket near our house. Apparently we had badmouthed Safeway in his presence. When we did shop there, we read labels to the kids, noted how it was usually crackers and soft drinks piled high at the ends of aisles, and counted the sugary candies and gum while waiting in the checkout line. "Yeah, I see the Kit Kat bars. We don't need them, we didn't come to buy them, but they're placed right here so we'll be tempted. Look at all that packaging. You're paying for that. Does it help the apples to be wrapped in plastic?"

That was one side. The serious Marion Nestle side. Nestle, arguably the most prominent nutritionist in the land, advocates for consumer protection against marketing hype. We taught the kids to make informed food choices, and that new products and packaging are about making a profit, not our well-being. In *What to Eat*, Nestle follows the money: "What industry or group benefits from public confusion about nutrition and health? Here the list is long and includes the food, restaurant, fast-food, diet, health club, drug, and health-care industries, among many others."

On the less serious side, our most-quoted food text when the kids were young was *Yummers!* Writer and illustrator James Marshall is better known for his George and Martha books, about hippopotamus best friends who learn when to tell the absolute truth and when to soften it. *Yummers!* is about being open to new experiences—foods in this case. That's what we thought at the time. A less blessed-out interpretation would be that *Yummers!* is about the hazards of overindulging. It opens with Emily Pig, looking distraught on the bathroom scale: "She was gaining weight and she didn't know why." She resolves to live healthier. Her friend Eugene Turtle suggests getting some exercise by going for a walk, but walking makes Emily hungry. On the way she downs two sandwiches, corn on the cob, a platter of scones, and three Eskimo pies. Then Eugene buys a box of Girl Scout cookies, which need a milk chaser. They stop by a drugstore and Eugene sips skim milk while Emily plows through a vanilla malt, a banana split, and a dish of peach ice cream. When Eugene stops by the supermarket to buy a box of tea, Emily finds free pizza and speaks the line that was our mantra: "It's so important to sample new products."

Is Eugene an enabler? Emily is certainly a binge eater. We didn't see it that way at the time, but rereading *Yummers!* and *Yummers Too: The Second Course* got me worried. *Yummers Too* continues the theme, with the addition of Emily's favorite relative, Uncle Fatty Pig, and Emily eating her way through the inventory of Healthy

Harriet's food store. She has to tell Harriet, "I lost control." Another interpretation: The Yummers books are about what happens when you panic about your weight.

lisa: Emily is a pig! Is she binge eating or just being a pig? I think it would be different if the Emily character was a person, but she's just being a hungry pig. A child wouldn't read that much into it. I loved this book as a kid.

And there is a lesson at the end because Emily gets sick, so there are consequences to her actions. Maybe Eugene, her friend, should have stopped her. But whether or not *Yummers!* carries a positive message, it is charming.

sheila: How do parents find the right books and messages? First, you reconvene the team of advisers from when you were pregnant, and add knowledgeable friends and relatives with slightly older children. As your children grow and their needs shift, you'll naturally recruit new advisers, but the early ones may point the working parent to the right daycare center, which itself will be a great source of expertise and comfort. After my six-month maternity leaves, I went back to work and the kids went to the Learning Center, a highly recommended program with the corny acronym TLC. Nearly three decades later, TLC is going strong, with a long waiting list and an outstanding professional staff who get health benefits. The center closes at 5:30 p.m., early for working parents but powerful incentive to get home. Whenever Ned or I arrived, bedraggled from the office and the rush-hour freeway, TLC teachers were still fresh.

The food was fresh, too, and central to the program. It still is, as the center's website states:

> We do not serve food or snacks with sugar, and we recommend that you feed your child a breakfast low in sugar. Please do not send your child to TLC with any gum, candy, or sweet food. If

you wish to send a treat for snack time or your child's birthday, a holiday, or your child's last day at TLC, please consult the director for a list of healthy possibilities.

We became friends with several of the teachers, went to their weddings, and formed a sort of eating club to explore Asian and South American cuisines in restaurants and in our homes. It was a little like the gourmet group my parents had, dabbling mainly in the foods of Europe, except that then the mothers did all the work. I thought their gourmet group was even dumber than bridge, the card game in which the mothers seemed more often to be the "dummy."

The TLC teachers had a remarkably natural way of talking to young children without patronizing them. It is a place for children with a "whole-child" philosophy, featuring tenets like this:

> We encourage the children to: show kindness, courtesy, and tolerance, be self-directed, develop their potential as loving human beings, to express their thoughts and feelings.

While Lisa and Jacob were developing their potential, we looked for an elementary school to keep up the good work. Palo Alto children have great choices in the public school system: excellent neighborhood schools and three alternative schools, at no extra expense.

We had heard about Ohlone and Hoover, the two alternative schools open when Jacob was ready for kindergarten: one named for the Native Americans of California's Central Coast, the other for Hoover, as in Herbert. Hoover's big contribution to education was to proclaim: "Children are our most valuable resource." More famously, while campaigning for president in 1928, Hoover predicted, "We in America today are nearer to the final triumph over poverty than ever before in the history of any land." That was a few months before the stock market crash.

Hoover Elementary School is about solid academics, fabulous test scores, and "a quiet and orderly environment." Ohlone is about creativity and "open education," which jibed nicely with Jacob and Lisa's training at TLC.

At Ohlone, adults and students go by their first names. Jacob was a popular name, so there might be a Jacob H. and a Jacob R., but by fourth grade Jacob H. had become Jake. In Lisa's kindergarten class, the teacher was called Teacher Lisa to avoid confusion, but never Miss, Mrs., or Ms. At first the name thing struck us as odd. In the olden days, we didn't know our elementary schoolteachers even had first names, and here the principal was just plain Michael. Ohlone gives no grades, only incredibly detailed and helpful written reports from the teachers. Nor is there, remarkably, any homework. Even in an age of test-score anxiety, children work mainly in groups, frequently with students at different grade levels. They learn to work with difficult people. As the manual describes:

> Ohlone provides a "training ground for real life" so that each student becomes a self-directed, thinking, lifetime learner.

Ohlone has a farm with animals as well as vegetables. Students pick corn, feed goats, and collect eggs. They learn that food comes from the earth, not Costco, Safeway, or even the farmers' market. At the annual Harvest Festival, they churn butter, peel apples, and toss pumpkins.

At home, food was central from the get-go. Once Jacob and Lisa were unlikely to stick their fingers in the metal grinder, we unwrapped the Marcato pasta machine we had gotten as a wedding present. We kneaded dough, formed a ball, let it rest, cranked the dough through the machine into our chosen noodle shape. The kids could see how much faster this fresh dough cooked than packaged pasta, and how tender and tasty it was.

We observed the Jewish Sabbath on Friday night with the usual blessings and some innovations like clinking glasses after the wine blessing and then toasting our fortunate life with the pieces of bread we had just broken off. We had healthy children, a community of friends and family, and the resources to buy a house in Palo Alto, where influential residents from Stanford and Silicon Valley ensured highly regarded public schools. We even had jobs we liked, including flexible hours for me, and, for Ned, very little travel and most evenings at home.

Ned was rising into library management, leaving behind the reference work he loved. He put those skills to family use, especially in researching travel and food. He also wrote a restaurant column in the library employees' newsletter, "Out to Lunch with Ned," and started a menu collection. At Christmas, the kids helped him make fudge and cookies for his coworkers. For birthdays, he baked a checkerboard cake, a "How did you do that?" treat in chocolate and vanilla that his grandmother had made for him. He identified his grandmothers with food so much that he and his sister grew up calling them Grandma Soup and Grandma Pancake.

When Jacob was eight and Lisa five, we took a culinary tour of Eastern cities. Along with friends and family, the Liberty Bell, and the Statue of Liberty, each city had food highlights: french fry–topped hot dogs in Pittsburgh, cheesesteaks and the Melrose Diner in Philadelphia ("Everyone who knows goes to the Melrose"), astronaut ice cream in Washington, DC, and just about everything, including the "everything bagel," in New York.

What we didn't know was that Lisa soon would be hiding candy in her room, and feeling very anxious about the deception. It was a small room, and she had posted a sign on the door: "Welcome to Lisa's Very Small Room," but she could have hidden a chocolate factory in there and we may not have found it. Her room was a mess and she was Teflon to any organizational system. She would initially buy into it—this basket for hair things, that plastic tub for puzzles—but within days it was Ned or me or nobody maintaining order. Occasionally we helped her sweep piles from the floor into drawers so our cleaner could vacuum, but basically we admitted defeat and invaded Lisa's space only when something smelled, guests were coming, or I just couldn't stand it anymore. Looking back, I can see that letting this continue, cleaning up myself rather than getting Lisa to take responsibility, was a big mistake, perhaps the initial phase of our happy bubble bursting.

lisa: I wasn't fat as a child. I was average. My parents bought high-quality produce and groceries. This is not to say we never had treats in our house, especially with Dad's cooking skills. I would help him make the holiday fudge just so I could lick the bowl. But my lunch was never one of envy. Too often it was a plain cheese sandwich. The coolest parents packed cookies and other processed foods we loved.

On Saturday morning when Dad would ask, "Who wants to go to the farmers' market?" sometimes Jake chose cartoons on TV and Mom stayed home with him. To me there was no question. I enjoyed the atmosphere, the smell of local flowers mixed with the sweet tang of oranges, and looking back now, I can see that I was being educated in food appreciation. I watched Dad figure out which melon was ripe. If I behaved, we got fresh-made, unpasteurized apple juice.

When I was old enough to start getting an allowance I began to rebel against my healthy upbringing. On the weekends my friends and I would go to 7-Eleven and I'd stock up. Oh, it was wonderful. Snickers, Baby Ruth, Caramello, Laffy Taffy, Pop Tarts. Every bit of junk I could afford, I purchased with joy. When I got home, I stashed the candy in my top desk drawer, so my parents wouldn't find it. I remember sitting in my chair, unwrapping candy bar after candy bar and stuffing them down my throat. It felt so sneaky.

Food would always be there when friends couldn't be found. It wasn't that I hid my emotions. I have always been vocal, often too

vocal. But something was missing. I was never satisfied wi.
I felt ugly and fat, and food solved issues I couldn't even expla..
stopped bringing my parents' lunches. It was better to wait in line
for the mass-produced school lunch and ice cream sandwiches.

I was jealous of my schoolmates' pudding cups, soda cans, and
Fruit Gushers. From fourth grade on, I was just a bit heavier than
most girls my age, but I felt like a complete outcast. I also developed
boobs in fourth grade. At this time girls walked around the room,
grabbing the backs of other girls' shirts to do "bra checks." It was
embarrassing to have a bra but there came a time when I couldn't
wear a shirt, especially a white shirt, without one. Mom and I went
to the Mervyn's kids department and bought two training bras. Really they were just thin cloth made into the shape of a bra. You could
completely see through them, which felt like people were seeing
through me. I was wearing double-digit adult sizes by sixth grade.

At first I thought getting bigger was good because it meant I was
growing up. At age six I got excited when I went from a size 6X to
an 8, and I could fit into my cousin's hand-me-down shoes. At age
eight I knew my exact weight to be sixty pounds. I can recall one
sunny afternoon, lounging on the top of the high monkey bars with
my friends and questioning them on their weight. They were all in
the fifties. By nine years old I started calling myself fat. I was a bit
round but by no means fat. It probably didn't help that my brother
was always a twig.

sheila: We knew it was wrong to push food on Jacob and pull it
away from Lisa, but it happened. When he was a toddler, a pediatrician had us counting bites of banana and whatever else our little
prince would condescend to swallow, and reporting the meager
results. Even as he grew, slowly, we kept an eye on those bites. At
the dinner table, Jacob nibbled on a roasted chicken leg while Lisa
downed a thigh and half a breast. He pushed roasted red potatoes
around the plate, could be nudged to have a couple pieces, and ate

a good amount of steamed broccoli. Lisa went for more of everything. In about fifteen years, we would be counting bites again, this time for Lisa.

In the preschool years, we tried various subterfuges that we thought they might not notice. Usually it was just a chipper comment, like: "Wow, the lasagna is so good! Is this organic chicken-apple sausage in it? We're lucky Dad is such a great cook."

Too often, I imagine, there was an imploring look that said, "Lisa, haven't you had enough? Jacob, won't you have a little more?"

Did we deny Lisa a voice, or stifle her needs, at the family table? That is one of the often-mentioned triggers to eating disorders, especially binge eating.

lisa: Dad has an annual holiday baking extravaganza to make gifts for his staff, and a lasagna-size Tupperware container of "extras" for us always ends up in the freezer. I loved donning the personal assistant hat, proud to be the chosen one. Dad is the executive type of chef, not one to easily share the kitchen, but for me he gave up total control. That's where I got over fearing raw ingredients like the two sticks of butter and pound of semisweet chocolate chips that went into his cookies, which later became my cookies.

Mom was not the most inventive cook although my brother and I most likely did not give her much room to explore. He barely ate anything, while there wasn't much that I would not try. I'm sure my parents found it difficult to cook meals to please the picky versus insatiable appetite. At restaurants I felt limited by the small portions on the children's menu. I knew how I liked my hamburger cooked and rarely did I get one from McDonald's. I preferred the homemade, hand-sculpted thick and juicy patties from the Peninsula Creamery, the one and only diner in downtown Palo Alto. My grandpa also had a knack for making delectable juicy hamburgers, although he often put onions in the meat or served them in an onion roll. I didn't eat onions—one of the only things I wouldn't eat.

I also remained set in my selection of ice cream flavors from the neighborhood parlor, Rick's Rather Rich Ice Cream. I'm not sure if we ever knew the real Rick, but we liked to guess which one he was, the lanky brunet with a mustache or the round, balding elderly man? It didn't matter. Rick's was the place for families. We usually saw someone we knew there. More often than not I ordered a junior scoop of cookies and cream, which had a minty undertone in its creamy vanilla base with generous chunks of Oreos. I still prefer my chunks of cookies nestled within the creamy texture of vanilla, but sometimes I branch out into the land of peppermint, mint chocolate chip, or cookie dough. I'm the same way with frozen yogurt—fairly plain vanilla and chocolate, but always with rainbow sprinkles swirled in.

"Let's have the orange lunch today!" I proclaimed to Mom one sunny Saturday afternoon. My best friend, Feyi, had come over. Like me, like everyone, Feyi loved Kraft Macaroni & Cheese, bright cheese powder sprinkled over bleached white noodles. Mom snuck in some health, by way of carrot sticks and orange slices, on orange plastic plates if they happened to be the clean ones, so that we could have the all-orange lunch or dinner. By age seven, I was making my own. That is, boiling noodles and adding a fat source (butter and milk) with the orange powder.

sheila: In the 1980s, a few grocery stores and supermarkets had little deli departments over by the meat counter, but mostly they were in business to sell the raw ingredients for dinner and other household necessities. Takeout still usually meant metal-handled cardboard boxes from Chinese restaurants. Convenience foods came in frozen packages and boxes that you took home and dropped in boiling water or at least microwaved.

Ned and I are not back-to-the-land lunatics. We allowed processed foods in the house, the occasional soda, and we microwaved leftovers. We had sugar, butter, and chocolate, of course, especially in chocolate chip cookies. As much as we tried to give Jacob and Lisa a love of high-quality food, and in that regard we succeeded, when they were young we weren't serving snails in garlic sauce or only products found in nature. Our children ate a lot of Kraft Macaroni & Cheese, with the scary bright orange powder sprinkled over boiled noodles and butter. (The directions called for margarine, which we did not stock.) Later the noodles came in shapes other than tubes, but that was as far as Jacob and Lisa would bend. They did eat real cheese on bread and crackers, so once I thought what a treat it would be for them to have macaroni and cheese made from scratch. I knew enough to seek out a recipe from Betty Crocker, not Julia Child. On the cover of our well-used 1972 edition of *The Betty Crocker Cookbook*, the fictional Betty looks like a young Lady Bird Johnson, or an old Shirley Temple. Betty's recipe calls for processed sharp American cheese. I used real cheddar cheese and while the dish got positive reviews from the adults, the children never gave it a chance. They had been imprinted by the Kraft brand and weren't open to innovation. But even processed Velveeta wouldn't have saved the mac 'n' cheese. The children of foodies preferred the orange powder.

five

Fat Girls, Husky Boys

When Lisa was born a lusty eater, Ned didn't exactly panic, but it did bring up serious dormant fears. Ned's sister, Elaine, had long suffered for her weight, and Ned wanted to avoid all of that for Lisa. Ned was husky as a teenager, but Elaine has considered herself fat since birth.

We inherited the creaky bathroom scale that used to torture her. I'm not sure the spring-loaded metal antique, black with white speckles, was ever very accurate, but at some point I put it in the garage. Ned and I could find it, but not the kids. Then we couldn't find it either and by the time we did, it was so rusty and cruddy that we threw it away.

I like not having a scale. Considering our middle age and enjoyment of food, Ned and I are resigned to a gradual gain into medium well-rounded senior citizenship. If only our retirement investment charts showed the steady progress of our weight charts.

When Ned's waistbands seize up, he has been known to panic

and eat cabbage soup for three days. He cooks up a five-quart pot that smells like the compost pile to start with and gets worse with reheating. After a few days it goes down the drain, but he feels lighter.

My weight-loss method is to exercise more and drink less. I love wine, but it stokes my appetite, so I rarely drink before a meal. Wine also fogs the short-term memory of what I've just eaten. A few dry days usually restore order. Until recently, I weighed myself maybe four times a year, at the Y and in the office of our internist, who takes a realistic position on weight and keeps a close eye on Ned's constellation of health issues: hereditary heart disease, high cholesterol and blood pressure. However, the gym got a new electronic scale and it gave me five less pounds than the old one, so now I check more frequently.

In an article titled "The Diet Secrets of Slim Women," *Shape* magazine claims that once-a-day weighing provides positive reinforcement. I guess this is true for the rare person who doesn't obsess about weight. But if you've put on a few pounds, the focus on numbers can make you feel so much worse. What's the point? All of your efforts are failing, so you might as well eat. It's an unintended consequence and it doesn't make sense.

That's why constant weighing is counterproductive for most of us. I like the set-point theory, which holds that everyone has a weight we're basically destined for, and within a few pounds of that, who cares? I know this is easy for a happily married, middle-age person to say. But the scale only causes trouble. If I register more than a slight increase, what I've already suspected when putting on my jeans, I get anxious and eat too much. If I weigh less than I thought, it's party time! Again I am likely to overeat.

Ned's sister, Elaine, has the same depraved reactions to weighing herself as I do, yet she climbs the scale at least once a day. Elaine has never been huge. But she's always felt like she was, so reality doesn't matter.

Elaine's lifelong devotion to weight loss intersects far too often with what Judith Moore described in *Fat Girl*, the seminal over-eater's memoir. An extremely unhappy childhood led Moore to believe "that inside every fat person was a hole the size of the world." To compensate, "I built walls of fat, and I lived inside." Elaine's early life was not nearly as crushing, but there are simi-larities, and they had an unintended trickle-down effect on Lisa.

Moore wrote, and Elaine agrees, "I never do not know what I weigh." And Ned has never known a self-confident older sister. He was born when Elaine was three years old, and already her size had been discussed at family gatherings in San Diego. Next to her cousin Ronda, Elaine was a giant. Girls were not supposed to be giants.

My sister, almost three years younger, had only a mild case of body-image issues. Still, I was glad it was Nancy and not me get-ting that kind of attention. In our families, even during Ned's husky phase, he and I were the children who could eat whatever we wanted. For both of us, our sisters' struggles, however imaginary, became cautionary tales. Let's avoid that glare, for ourselves and then for our children.

Ned had bulked up in high school and through college, nipping one hundred and ninety pounds and a portly Jerry Garcia look, before taking up jogging and healthier food. He tried not to think about Lisa's similarities in body type, not to revisit scenes from his childhood when his sister suffered for her size, but it was like trying to push back the ocean. Elaine cuddled baby Lisa and cooed, "She reminds me of me."

As Lisa grew, Ned couldn't help measuring her against Elaine at each age. He had to wonder, would she be as miserable? He tried to focus on buying and eating healthy foods, and getting exercise himself. Ned would be relieved when he noticed differences. Elaine never played sports, Lisa did. Elaine ate with both hands, Lisa usu-ally didn't.

I didn't understand Elaine's low self-esteem. She had great professional success as a teacher, a close family, and a tight, supportive group of friends that anyone would envy. She is very kind and took great care of their mother, who was widowed young and lived five minutes from Elaine's house. Yet she says, "When I think about myself, 'I'm fat' is what always comes to mind first." Until Lisa became bulimic and Elaine saw what that meant, she wished she could purge. She wished that she had the strength to stick her finger down her throat and stand over a toilet.

One weekend when Elaine came for a visit, I asked her to sit down and tell us how weight became the defining issue of her life. It would help us understand what happened with Lisa, how memories Ned pushed away may have crept back in and inadvertently affected how he treated Lisa. Ned and I were surprised and pleased at how ready Elaine was to tell her story. As if she'd been waiting for years. She began, "I don't remember ever feeling hungry. Or full."

Elaine was seven pounds, three ounces at birth. That is, normal. Her parents lived next door to both sets of grandparents until she was two and a half, and she felt surrounded in love. Grandma Sophie had lost her only daughter and was particularly thrilled when Elaine was born. But being next door also meant more than enough attention for one shared grandchild. Two or three grandparents babysat Elaine every Saturday night. With so many arms to hold her, she didn't walk until she was eighteen months old. The family worried that there was something wrong with her legs.

In the seat of power, the kitchen, Grandma Pancake (Sophie) was always baking, always something sweet. The other was Grandma Soup. Whether because of being intimidated or a lack of interest, and later, economic hard times, Elaine and Ned's mother, Tilda, never really learned her way around food. She was a terrible cook. A common dinner for them growing up was Campbell's soup, iceberg lettuce salad, and a can of string beans or creamed corn.

Elaine was always chubby, everyone agrees. Sipping tea in our living room, she remembers, "When people looked at pictures of me as a baby, they would say, 'Oh, look at those pulkies (fat legs)!'" At least that's the part she heard. When people would say, "You have such a nice smile," Elaine took it to mean, "It's just too bad you're so fat."

One day in fourth grade, Elaine's whole class went to the cafeteria to be weighed. There was a scale in front and a teacher calling out each student's name and weight. (Judith Moore recalls a similar torture in *Fat Girl*, but at her school it happened every month. Moore was the only second-grader who needed the metal one-hundred-pound weight to be clanked into place.) The day Elaine, age nine, saw that scale, she started crying and couldn't stop. Her mother had to come pick her up from school. Also in fourth grade, Elaine started menstruating, which was considered very early at the time. By sixth grade, she came close to her full adult height, five-foot-six, and towered over her classmates. There was no place to hide.

Like Lisa, Elaine sneaked food at night. Both ate ice cream out of the carton. And both resented the rest of the family. Everybody in the family loved sweets, but Elaine was the only "fat" one. When the Himmels went to their favorite restaurant in San Diego, Elaine longed for the "Fudge-anna," a hot-fudge sundae with banana, but she knew not to ask for what she wanted. Every time, she ordered sherbet. Unlike Lisa, Elaine has always been compliant and anxious to please, anticipating what others desired of her.

At age ten, Elaine was taken to a mysterious new doctor, with offices all the way downtown. Dr. De La Marquis prescribed the diet pills that Elaine took until she was at least twenty. She didn't take them continuously, and they didn't do much for her weight or self-esteem, but they did help her study. They were speed, after all.

In high school, Elaine didn't date, and in college, she didn't get asked to join a sorority. She felt like a failure. All her social problems, she was sure, were caused by her weight. She told herself, "If only I could lose weight, I'd look better in clothes and have dates." And then get married and have children and life would be beautiful.

At twenty-four, Elaine was doing work she loved. She was born to teach. Still, she felt like a fat, old-maid schoolteacher. Her longtime best friend, Carol, a pretty little thing, had already been married and divorced.

This was 1972, at the peak of the feminist movement. Economic self-sufficiency and equality in romantic relationships were all the rage, with women acting out the slogan "The personal is the political." The landmark Supreme Court abortion decision in *Roe v. Wade* came in 1973. Elaine didn't track any of that. She just wanted to be married and be a mom. When she met her husband, David, he not only made low-calorie foods for her, he thought she was cute. Nobody had ever thought she was cute.

When did she stop taking the amphetamine diet pills? "I only remember starting things that made me thinner," Elaine told us, sadly, "never how they ended."

While Elaine was talking in our living room, Ned had a hard time sitting still. He kept getting up to check the computer, then the refrigerator, then some piece of paperwork. Reliving his sister's struggles in painful detail, Ned felt some responsibility for his role in the family drama. While she got stuck being the good girl in the family, Ned was simply "the boy." He had a lot more latitude. With behavior and food, Ned got green lights while Elaine got Stop signs. And then he wondered how his edginess affected his behavior in raising Lisa. He had tried so hard not to show anxiety, but it had to have broken through.

Brother and sister had a few points of historical disagreement. Ned remembered Elaine wanting to kill herself, even picking up a knife. Elaine had no memory of that.

In their experience of specific foods, especially sweets, it was as if they were raised in different houses.

ELAINE: We were never allowed to have cotton candy. They'd say, "It's all sugar. You can't have it."

NED: I got cotton candy. I don't remember that being an issue.

ELAINE: I had a bite of it somewhere. You must have gotten it.

NED: When we went to a ballgame, we'd have cotton candy.

ELAINE: No. We'd have peanuts when we went to a ballgame.

NED: Cotton candy is one of those things that once you've had it, it's not that good.

ELAINE: Maybe I would encourage somebody else to get it. So I could have a bite.

One weight-related incident was seared in both of their minds. When Elaine was twenty-one and Ned eighteen, they and a friend of Elaine's spent the summer traveling around Europe. Elaine gained twenty-five pounds; Ned lost twenty-five pounds. Elaine couldn't believe the injustice. "We ate the same food!" she said, exasperated. And worse: "When we got off the plane Dad said, 'Oh my god, what happened to you?'" To her, not to Ned.

This is a textbook example of what fathers, particularly, are cautioned not to say to their daughters. Eating disorders are about the hunger for love and acceptance. Girls often yearn for their fathers' affection, approval, and ideas about what's attractive and desirable in women. Their dad was not a cruel man. Les loved his family and liked to joke around. But he had gone bankrupt and had had two heart attacks by then, and though happy to see his children again after their long trip, he probably wasn't feeling great. He made a comment that confirmed Elaine's negative view of herself.

• • •

Elaine's forever best friend, the trim and petite Carol, always got the guys. Elaine resented Carol's good luck in the size department. Now in their sixties, they wear the same size. Still, Elaine is so wrapped up in being the fat girl that she admits, "Now, she's almost irritating me over it. It was okay when I was the one doing all the fussing about weight. Now she's fussing; it's annoying."

Whenever somebody thinner than Elaine complains about her weight, she thinks, "If I looked like that I wouldn't have to always be worried about my weight, so why are they? People have said I look good or I look nice, but nobody has *ever* suggested I should stop losing weight."

Lisa feels the same irritation with friends. Why are they complaining about their weight? Eating disorders are a bad thing, but they're *her* bad thing, not theirs. Skinny friends can be the worst offenders. When they moan that they couldn't possibly have another bite of ice cream, Lisa thinks, "Yeah, right."

Exercise is another of Lisa's things. For Elaine, exercise mainly is painful medicine.

Instead, she diets. She has done Jenny Craig, Weight Watchers, grapefruit, Metrecal, and a dozen diets recommended by the Kaiser Permanente health plan, among others. As a child, one regimen required her mother to make Elaine's sandwiches with lettuce instead of bread. Let's imagine how that went over at school. The Jenny Craig diet plan was successful while Elaine ate Jenny Craig products, but as soon as she was making her own choices, she gained the weight right back.

Elaine has had the best results with Weight Watchers, which she joined in 1974. In those thirty-five years, she has re-upped at least fifteen times. Most recently, Elaine lost thirty pounds, but she still feels she is fifteen pounds too heavy.

"I was once my ideal weight—130," Elaine says, sighing. "It was for one year, between twenty-five and twenty-six. Then I got pregnant. In the past twenty years I've weighed between 160 and 209." Elaine's Weight Watchers range is 135 to 155, but her goal is 150.

How much mental energy this takes! Like people with diagnosed eating disorders, Elaine keeps track of numbers the way baseball fans know batting averages. And she has a system. "I weigh myself at home every day, always at the same time and in the same way: with no clothes on, when I get up in the morning. If I weigh less, I don't have to worry about what I eat that day. If I weigh more, then I worry."

In fact, she worries either way. If not initially about what to eat that day, then remorse later about all she ate. But the system continues:

"I take a diuretic for my blood pressure. I'll take an extra dose if I'm going to the doctor or to Weight Watchers, so I'll weigh a pound or a pound and a half less."

I get this. I take my shoes off when getting weighed in the doctor's office. But Elaine's excessive use of diuretics makes her dizzy and probably contributed to a very scary accident that left her in pain for years. She was touring an aircraft carrier and fell while climbing stairs, requiring a rescue by helicopter that made the evening news in San Diego. Despite a fractured skull, the total loss of hearing in one ear, and excruciating back problems, she still takes the diuretic. As if she'd read some pro–eating disorders guidebook, Elaine puts her health at risk to save a few pounds.

When not on a specific diet, Elaine picks at food all day long, although she claims, "I don't binge, really. I just nibble all the time." Don't we all.

Rather than relaxing entertainment, restaurants are often torture for Elaine. She would never go to a restaurant by herself, even to sit at the counter. She thinks people would notice and judge.

Instead, Elaine would eat in the car. However, she says, "When I go out with friends, I order food they'll think is a good choice for a fat person." This reminds me of a college roommate who was slightly round and similarly self-conscious. In the cavernous dormitory cafeteria, she would ask me to fetch dessert for her. She'd still have to eat it there, but according to her system it was okay to eat ice cream in public, just not to be seen carrying it across the room. People with eating disorders are exquisitely conscious of eating in public, sure that all eyes are disapprovingly on them.

Elaine's friends talk a lot about eating and not eating. She says, "Most of what we talk about is weight and diets. In the teachers' lounge, there are always treats. We say, 'I shouldn't be eating this, but . . .' People check out each other's lunches. I am known for baking, and being the dessert person." When Elaine goes to national conferences, the teachers and administrators who know her say, "Okay, Elaine. Where are we going for dessert?" Of course she keeps a candy dish in her office. Everybody knows it's there and expects it. When it runs out, people ask, "Where's the candy?"

Elaine has been a mentor teacher and Teacher of the Year in the gigantic San Diego Unified School District. When pressed, she'll acknowledge that she had a very rewarding career. She knows she is a good teacher, mother, and friend. But fifteen pounds drown all that out. "Why can't I control my weight? Nothing else I could ever do could ever make up for it. When people say, 'You look good,' I always feel that what they don't say is, 'But you're fat.' I always wished I could have anorexia or bulimia, until Lisa. Then I realized it wasn't something to wish for."

lisa: I'm honestly shocked to come to know that my Aunt Elaine would ever have desired the very disorders that have caused me so much torment. I guess I can see the glory gained by starvation, but bulimia? There's never any glamour in throwing up one's meal. A sickening satisfaction, maybe, even a little high, like, "I have rid myself of something awful," but before I became bulimic I would do anything to avoid vomiting. I thought it was gross and an unrealistic approach to weight loss.

I've always been aware of Aunt Elaine's struggles with weight. I remember as a kid seeing her "I Lost Ten Pounds" ribbon posted on the refrigerator. I loved going to her house because I knew I'd be able to stuff my little face with goodies I never got to eat at home. There were potato chips and cinnamon Pop Tarts in the cupboard. She had American cheese, individually wrapped! As were the Fruit Roll-Ups. There was always soda and Snapple. My parents never let me have soda in the house, only on occasions when we ate out.

My aunt is definitely one of the most loving women one will ever have the pleasure of meeting. I wish for her, as for me, someday to be able to judge our characters based on qualities that matter, like being able to love, rather than what the scale reads.

I remember at my cousin's wedding, under her joy and elation she bemoaned the fact that she hadn't lost an additional five pounds and her one hope was that she didn't look fat in her dress. Of course she didn't look fat, because she's not fat!

I see the way she picks at food, proclaiming to only eat a few bites and that we must stop her if she goes back for more. Food never seems to be pleasurable for her. I wish she could enjoy it more, especially at family events, where we can all sit together and engage in conversation instead of intently focusing on how many calories lie in whatever delicious dish someone prepared.

Food is obviously a major focal point of many gatherings for us. I understand the stress it causes her; I feel it, too. But oftentimes I just have to calm down and realize that eating doesn't have to be such a source of woe. I want for both of us to sit down to a family dinner and enjoy whatever we order or are served, and turn our focus to the joy that is our tight-knit family.

sheila: I'm thrilled that Lisa can be so clear-sighted, now at twenty-four, about someone else. During the worst years of her eating disorders, she barely recognized that other people existed. She didn't have time. Like Elaine, she was spending most of her life thinking about her weight.

When you ask ED patients how much of the day they focus on food, it's always more than ninety percent. This stunning statistic explains a lot. Ned and I learned this at an event we didn't want to attend, a three-hour "Eating Disorders Training" workshop for caregivers. It was midway through Lisa's first year of college, when she'd gone from anorexia to bulimia, and we were scared to death. About half the attendees were parents, the rest nurses, counselors, and teachers. With the first handout, just after coffee and bagels, Ned and I aimed blaming looks at each other, as in, "We are *so* in the wrong place. Whose idea was this?" We already knew the horrifying statistics and many of the concepts, such as, "A caregiver should be nonjudgmental when talking about ED." *Please.* And we really didn't want to hear other peoples' stories. The perky blond trainer's name, Tonja, conveyed ice-skater to me, not a respected authority. We just wanted to grab a to-do list that would specifically help Lisa, and get out of class.

But Tonja Krautter, LCSW, was serious. She kept us on point with useful information and gave us new ways of looking at eating disorders. Even though the statistics were grim, Krautter helped us apply them, so that Ned and I came away feeling a little stronger and more hopeful. We weren't flailing around in the dark. For a few weeks I didn't wake up sweating.

But that one statistic, ninety percent of your time focused on food! No wonder Lisa had such trouble completing schoolwork and maintaining other interests.

I could only relate to the time I starved myself, during a three-day fast with a group. I didn't know what anorexia was at the time, but I was enjoying the lightness and could have continued fasting. Except for one thing: All I could think about was food. What others were eating, how disgusting much of it was, and what admirable foods I'd have when I started eating again. I had nothing but time, but I got nothing done.

In *Hunger Pains*, Mary Pipher addresses this stark irony. She writes, "Most of us worry more about our weight than our wages. We expend more energy on our appearance than on our empowerment."

Oh, the places we could have gone!

"Women are standing on the scales when they could be dancing, measuring their waistlines when they could be writing poetry."

Pipher found that four percent of women (all ages) feel comfortable with their weight. Line up a random one hundred women and girls, and only four of them are okay with their weight!

Many of us have been students of *Seventeen* magazine, like *Fat Girl* author Judith Moore; my sister-in-law, Elaine; and me. A constant theme of this magazine, aimed at girls much younger than seventeen, is weight loss. There are articles on other subjects, as there are articles in *Playboy*, but it seems to me that the reason for reading *Seventeen* is to measure yourself against perfection and come up wanting.

As Moore wrote, "I thumbed through *Seventeen* magazine for hints on how I might make myself more like the girls on the slick pages and the popular, vivacious girls who brightened my high school. I knew, though, deep down in my fat belly, that I would never be a May queen or cheerleader or *Seventeen* girl."

You don't have to be fat to subscribe to *Seventeen* as a monthly announcement of your faults. For me, it was to learn why I didn't have a boyfriend and how the square shape of my face and thickness of my neck (not freakishly thick like a female linebacker, but no Audrey Hepburn) would be lifelong albatrosses, requiring constant attention to makeup and clothing style.

Thirty years later, Lisa pored over *Seventeen*, now one of the more benign of the celebrity-driven teen publications. Still, here's a typical cover from the recent past:

368 WAYS TO LOOK CUTE FOR LESS

FLAT TUMMY TUCKS THAT WORK FOR *EVERYONE*

PRETTY HAIR & GLOWY SKIN
SUPER-FAST!

TAYLOR SWIFT:
HOW SHE GOT OVER JOE JONAS
&
WHY SHE *LOVES* BEING SINGLE!

Except for Taylor Swift, all of these stories could have appeared in the magazines that shaped my generation's views of our bodies and our selves. (For us, the part of Taylor Swift may have been played by Cher.)

Ned has never read *Seventeen*. As a teenager, he didn't subscribe to a magazine that made him feel bad about his hair or thighs. As a teenager he read his parents' *Life*, *Look*, and *Time* magazines. In pediatricians' offices, he liked *Highlights for Children*.

In his *Highlights* years, Ned was a very picky eater, like me. "I like to think of it as being discriminating at an early age," he says, sort of jokingly. But his family catered to him. "The boy" would eat meat only if it came from Bradshaw's, a grocery store that had a butcher. On a visit to a cousin in Los Angeles, the family served a roast and Ned asked if it came from Bradshaw's. His parents had told the cousin to say yes.

When Ned's father had his first heart attack, on the heels of business setbacks, Ned started putting on weight. "The household was very stressful. I don't know if that's why, but my metabolism changed," Ned says. "My best friend, Bill, was skinny as can be, but ate a ton more than I did and he had a fairly large head. We joked that his stomach must be where his brain was supposed to be."

Spontaneous metabolic change is rarely the culprit. More likely, in Ned's case, his body changed shape because he was growing up—and eating too much. He loved his grandmothers' foods, even Brussels sprouts and cooked cabbage. "Grandma Annie made this terrific chicken with onions and we loved to dip challah in the fat and juice. She also made terrific schmaltz (chicken fat). I loved making scrambled eggs in schmaltz and then mixing with Miracle Whip. Hmm, no wonder I have cholesterol problems."

Ned played tennis in high school, which helped keep his weight in check. "I would practice for a couple of hours daily and just eat an apple for lunch and was able to not feel chunky. The word for me was *husky*."

Girls, no wonder so many of us have food issues. Even the disparaging adjectives are harder on us. Who wouldn't rather be husky than fat?

Middle School and the Great Job

Middle school is the worst of times for many kids. It certainly was for Lisa, at least until she developed full-on anorexia toward the end of high school. The ages of eleven through thirteen can make parents yearn for the diaper years. Your sweet child now often despises you, reminds you daily of your shortcomings, and forces you to relive your own painful adolescence. Which was why a big boost at work came at just the right time for me. At the start of Lisa's middle school years, I got to be the restaurant critic for the *Mercury News*—"The Newspaper of Silicon Valley"—at the birth of the dot-com boom. Expense accounts rained cash, celebratory wines were uncorked, and every downtown in the area got rid of its hardware stores and put up wall-to-wall restaurants.

Suddenly I was very popular, holding the keys to many people's dream job. Restaurant critics rarely lack friends. We have to be pretty grumpy or full of ourselves not to attract a flock of suppliants eager to drop everything and dine on the company credit card. Who doesn't like to snoop, criticize, possibly be quoted as "my intelligent companion," and let somebody else pick up the check? Which is great, except when they say something on the order of:

> "Eating in restaurants can't really be a job; it's so fun! I'd love to come with you but if work gets busy [at my significantly more strenuous job] I may have to cancel at the last minute."

> "I've never tried Burmese food, but I'm pretty sure I won't like it."

> "Oh, a restaurant in Gilroy. That's kind of far. Could it possibly be good? I don't want to drive an hour in traffic to spend all evening in aluminum chairs, be ignored by preening servers, and served yesterday's fried shrimp, like that other place you took me."

The last bit they really wouldn't say. More likely, "Oh, Gilroy! I'd love to, but it turns out I have a ton of work. Please, *please* ask me again!"

These people are off the island.

Before I became a critic, Ned and I felt we were the ideal "intelligent companions." We stepped forward when the *Mercury News'* former reviewer needed flexible, adventurous diners who would order whatever we were told, pass plates, and make apt, pithy comments. Only an emergency involving children would have caused us to cancel at the last minute, and it never happened, thank you very much. My predecessor, David L. Beck, returned the favor by thinking of us especially when reviewing a restaurant in our northerly corner of Silicon Valley. When David needed a family to investigate the enduring popularity of an old-line Mexican-American café (combo plates, chalupas, carved chairs), the Himmels gave him experience, enthusiasm, and two children with diverse eating habits. Jacob was polite and picky, while Lisa impressed David with her lusty embrace of enchiladas and the whole experience of eating out.

David, like Lisa, had a good appetite. But after five and a half years of eating his way around the San Francisco Bay Area restaurant boom of the early nineties, expenses paid by a newspaper that couldn't stop making money, David's waistband was tightening. He is a handsome man and a natty dresser. About to turn fifty, he realized that with his family history of heart disease, he might have had enough tiramisu. None too soon. The year David went back to working as an editor, he had to go in for angioplasty.

When the Features editor asked if I wanted the restaurant gig, I said something like Robert DeNiro in *Taxi Driver*: "You talking to *me*?" Except not hostile, just astonished. I loved the entertainment and social sides of restaurants as well as the food, and criticizing them among friends, much the way it's done on Yelp and Chowhound. But to do it in front of 300,000 subscribers people and take the consequences? Bay Area residents are religious about food. Followers of one denomination or the other who disagreed with me surely would call and yell at me and trash me in print. Readers take joy in knowing more than the critic. I know this, I do it myself. ("Famous Critic says these are the best hamburgers west of the Mississippi! Can he be serious? What an idiot!") More important, the responsibility of affecting livelihoods and business dreams weighed on me, especially having come from a small-business family. Restaurants are such a tough way to make a living. Even in a good economy, one in four restaurants closes or changes hands before the first year is up; three out of five fail within three years. People who study organizations often pick restaurants because, like fruit flies, they die so fast. How would I feel if my review put Mom and Pop out of business?

• • •

Reviewing restaurants wasn't on many publications' to-do list in the heady post-Watergate years, when I went looking for a job in journalism. Affirmative action had barely pried open hard-drinking, smoke-filled newsrooms to women and minorities. There were bottles in the drawers and ashtrays on the desks. At the *Mercury News*, female editors and reporters (then dubbed the "Vagino-Americans" by some of the men) lobbied management for parity in merit pay, and for hiring more women in editorial jobs outside of the Living department—home of Miss Manners, gardening, recipes, and heartwarming feature stories. Until recently, it had been called the Women's Section. In 1979, when I came along, no woman had ever worked on the copy desk. A U-shaped bunker in the far corner of the newsroom, the copy desk was where grizzled reporters went when they got too old to chase fire engines and police cars. Two "slot men" sat in the middle and dealt stories to the guys on "the rim." Theirs were the last eyes on every story, the bulwark against bad grammar, pretentious vocabulary and misspelled names. They were just about all smokers, grumpy about being pushed aside, about the newspaper business not being what it used to be, about having a woman in their midst, about the 49ers losing, whatever. When you walked into the newsroom, a dark cloud hung over one corner, not only because of the smoke. That was the copy desk.

I applied for a job, having corrected copy and written headlines at smaller papers, and having friends who could vouch for me at the *Mercury News*. In the interview, the classically crusty managing editor asked if I planned to have children. While I sat there dumbly, trying to remember if he could legally ask me that, he amended: "Oops, can't ask that. Heh, heh." I was twenty-nine and had been married three months. He could guess I would have children, but he needed to hire a woman and at that moment there weren't a lot of seekers for the copy desk. The job was gruelingly sedentary and the hours were unattractive: 2:30 p.m. to 11:00 p.m., Friday through Tuesday. Walking into the building on Friday afternoon, the Monday morning of my week, I passed jolly coworkers heading in the other direction, wishing each other a nice weekend. At dinnertime, we rim guys ate and talked football in an empty cafeteria. The smoke gave me a headache. But my first day on the job, we worked stories ranging from county twelfth-graders' worrisome test scores to Jonestown one year after the mass suicide to the Iran hostage crisis. Two weeks in, Ayatollah Khomeini ordered that the students occupying the U.S. Embassy in Tehran release the women and black hostages. What a rush! Within a year I was promoted to slot man, and two more women had been hired.

All this is sad and quaint now, with newspapers seemingly at death's door. I was supremely fortunate to get in after Watergate and out before the crash, and I worry about sustaining a democracy without the newspapers' vibrant reporting. But there were always people smarter than me in journalism, and there are today. They'll figure it out.

After I'd served two and a half years on the copy desk, Jacob was born. The ideal would have been a part-time job with flexible hours, creativity, and responsibility. It didn't exist in the newspaper industry, which was among the slowest to adopt family-friendly attitudes. I could work part-time as a copy editor, but the desk was a slave to weekends and nights. Also, the copy desk worked every holiday. The most senior people got first shot at the few holiday-off shifts. I could look forward to Thanksgiving at home in twenty years.

When the Sunday Opinion editor job came open, I jumped. It was a one-person, daytime show, with somewhat flexible hours, Tuesday through Saturday. It was a full-time job, though, and Jacob was only six months old. I asked if I could do it part-time and, thinking managers were doing me a favor by even considering my request, I didn't ask about getting an assistant to work the remaining hours. The company was happy to oblige my generosity.

After Lisa was born, though, having two children in daycare and no one to share job responsibilities got difficult. The newspaper's Sunday magazine needed a six-month maternity leave replacement for a managing editor. I stayed for nine years. I got to work with smart people, including the paper's knowledgeable and witty food editor, and I wrote some magazine stories. Most of them had to do with food and family.

A wounding experience at a well-known San Francisco restaurant resulted in "Ten Places to Avoid with Kids." On a Saturday afternoon, usually the quietest meal in a restaurant's week, we four Himmels had a reservation at Wolfgang Puck's Postrio, as part of a family weekend in the city. Postrio had pizza and Pat Kuleto's very cool interior design, with a sweeping staircase by which everyone descends into the dining room, like royalty. (Kuleto is still the über-designer of Bay Area restaurants, now with projects in Chicago, Las Vegas, and Tokyo as well.) As the maître d' took us through the bar on the way to the staircase, a well-dressed matron snipped, "What are *they* doing here?" I think she meant the kids, and wanted to say, "Ruining your meal, ma'am, and with pleasure!" but Lisa wanted to leave immediately.

Another magazine piece, for Mother's Day, explored my disappointment that at the end of the twentieth century people were still surprised that Dad ran the kitchen in our house. By then, Silicon Valley warriors were buying Viking ranges and German knife sets, but apparently only the women or the nannies were using them. In our house, Ned did the food shopping and cooking. This struck people as odd. "Aren't you lucky!" they said, all too often. Nobody was surprised that I was the scheduler, cleaner, launderer, and buyer of essential nonfood items like clothes.

• • •

We went out to restaurants for fun. Did I want to make it my work? David Beck appeared to be relaxed and normal when dining, jotting a nonchalant note every once in while. Two or three weeks later, an entertaining and informative review would appear in the paper, including detailed observations from what had been just an enjoyable evening out for us. Maybe in our enthusiasm for food and restaurants Ned and I were fantasy players like Walter Mitty and Homer Simpson, or like baseball fans who dream of glorious sports-writing careers, being paid to sit in the sun and write about what they loved instead of doing their own dumb jobs.

Not so fast, sports fans. I knew baseball writers. Their hours were brutal; they traveled constantly and churned narrative masterpieces out of grunts from monosyllabic athletes. There must be similar hazards in restaurant reviewing, I worried. But the family didn't share my fears. Suddenly united in culinary self-interest, Ned, Jake, and Lisa chimed, "Are you crazy? At least try it!"

I couldn't argue. Lisa and Jake were on the cusp of their own big changes. Lisa, eleven, was about to enter middle school, and Jake, fourteen, was starting high school. Jake was still picky, but no longer the refusenik, and he liked going out. They were willing food adventurers with highly developed tastes. Pad Thai, chicken teriyaki, dim sum, ho-hum. Those were *so* elementary school. What's new?

Once the kids could be counted on to voice a reasonable choice, they had joined in the tradition Ned and I had adopted from our own parents: The birthday person picks the restaurant. We avoided upscale places with them, but could eat fabulously in Silicon Valley strip malls and the funkier downtown blocks with all the new Vietnamese, Indian, Pakistani, and Mexican regional restaurants. Chinese restaurants diversified even further, from mini-cafés serving only chicken dishes to bejeweled palaces serving fresher seafood than you could get in San Francisco. Jake and Lisa latched onto

Vietnamese hot-rock cooking, with the excitement of having a 500-degree stone set upon your table, and barbecued Afghan kebabs, and soon they were eating the more sophisticated dishes of these cuisines, like *cha gia*, cold Vietnamese spring rolls, and *aushak*, Afghan ravioli spiced with coriander and leeks.

lisa: When Mom got the food critic job, I had a vast and adventurous appetite. I recall our first meals at a hidden treasure of a restaurant called Golden Chopsticks. The incredibly flavorful, authentic Vietnamese cuisine included my favorite hot rock, a sizzling square rock brought to your table with a platter of meats and vegetables to cook yourself. Another favorite that we came drooling back for was the whole crab with roasted garlic. I can still taste the tiny crispy chunks of garlic covering a fresh and succulent crab. We went there five or six times, but after a few years Golden Chopsticks closed. It may have been the bad location. Even the treasures sink in the complicated economy.

Another first-timer for us was the discovery of Afghan food at a restaurant in Sunnyvale. I quickly became a fan of the grilled chicken kabobs served aside a heaping bed of browned rice and a roasted tomato that simply melted in my mouth.

I loved the atmosphere surrounding our delicious meals, all around the Bay Area, in all kinds of restaurants. So many Saturday nights were spent with me, my brother, Mom, Dad, and whomever we invited to accompany us, gathered around a table, talking, laughing, reminiscing, and, above all, eating.

sheila: Where previous birthday dinners had been spaghetti and pizza at Rudolfo's, our neighborhood red-sauce Italian restaurant, now we drove through three cities to get to Afghani House and Golden Chopsticks. The kids' friends often found these restaurants a little weird. And driving half an hour just to eat, what was *that* about? There are plenty of restaurants in Palo Alto. But even as teenagers, Jake and Lisa loved telling people their mom was the restaurant critic at the *Mercury News*, the area's biggest newspaper. The only part Lisa didn't love was the criticism. It didn't matter that *Mercury News'* policy was to skip the review altogether if a Mom and Pop restaurant was bad and that only the big rip-offs earned scorn in print. "How can you say that?" Lisa would ask. "How are they going to feel?" "They" may have been a publicly traded corporation based in Houston, but Lisa hated being party to any deed that could make people unhappy.

Lisa was getting to know unhappiness. Middle school is, at best, a three-year reality spinoff of Judith Viorst's classic *Alexander and the Terrible, Horrible, No Good, Very Bad Day*. At worst, a prelude to *Carrie*. All that sweet talk from parents and teachers about cooperation, inclusiveness, and valuing each individual for her inner beauty goes on the back burner. It will become useful again, but surviving middle school requires other qualities.

A sense of humor, for starters. On the morning of her first day at Jane Lathrop Stanford Middle School, Lisa still had that. As she headed nervously to the garage to get her bike, she smiled and said, with bravado, "I don't feel old enough for middle school, but I guess I have to go!"

Also on Lisa's side was a wonderful sixth-grade teacher, Shauna Rockson. The school made a big effort to ease the transition for eleven-year-olds fresh off the comfy elementary school boat, but there were more than a thousand students.

And there were grades. Jacob and Lisa's elementary school had written evaluations, not grades. Now there were symbolic numbers and letters measuring your performance and worth. Lisa did fine in most academic areas, with mostly fours on a scale of one to five. In Study Skills, she didn't fare so well. Lisa didn't get any I's (Improving) or N's (Needs Improvement), but hardly anybody did. Neatness, attention, effort, and taking responsibility for learning were consistent problem areas.

Mrs. Rockson wrote, "Lisa is an unflaggingly cheerful, bright spot in our classroom! She needs to focus on turning assignments in on time." If this was a signal of things to come, we didn't get it.

Palo Alto's public schools are populated by the children of Stanford professors, Silicon Valley magnates, and run-of-the-mill brainy people. It's a hard place to be average. Lisa had struggled academically a bit in elementary school, but Ohlone was a warm, supportive community. If she had trouble, someone was there to help. Middle school was more like Middle-earth—dangerous and strange. As in the outer world, in middle school you aren't known as a whole person, as you are in elementary school from kindergarten. Appearance becomes the important way to be known.

lisa: In middle school, almost every morning I had a bagel at our 10:00 a.m. brunch, then lunch two and a half hours later. That was healthy enough, but when I got home there was a certain excitement about being out of the scrutiny of my parents and friends. I dove into the ice cream carton with a jar of peanut butter at the side.

When I was twelve I came across a picture my brother had taken of me about two years earlier. I'm lying on my parents' bed, dressed in light-wash Gap overalls and a lime green baby tee. It was a mock photo shoot where I got to be the model and he was the photographer. He had me pose in different rooms of our house with a new outfit each time. I guess this one was my juvenile seduction pose. My mouth is slightly ajar, my eyes gazing into the lens, and I seem to be rather comfortable. I longed to look that way again.

I had discovered anorexia from one of my soccer coaches when I was ten. She had been friends with my best friend's cousin. At our first practice, Feyi whispered in my ear, "That's Melissa, she's anorexic." *Anor-what?* I had never heard the term before. Feyi explained, "Anorexia is when you don't eat. So Melissa doesn't eat." Now with this photo in my hand, I figured that was the most logical solution: to just stop eating. My mistake was announcing to my parents that I had decided to become anorexic. I thought they would say, "Okay, Lisa, you can do that if you want to." But of course my decision was met with much disapproval.

In middle school, food was my comfort and escape. I was never satisfied with myself, I felt ugly and fat, and the only way I knew how to comfort myself was with food. I couldn't face who I was because in reality I had no idea. Food was like my own little support group and in it I could be popular, which was not the story at school. I felt like a complete outcast from all the skinny girls.

Every day I wanted so desperately to lose weight, but soon enough I turned back to food. Perhaps part of my chubby figure in middle school was due to lingering baby fat. I did eat quite a lot, but not enough to gain as much weight as I did. I think puberty caught up with me fast yet mingled with childhood chub that had a hard time saying good-bye.

My weight got noticed by people who knew me, and some who didn't. On several occasions, as I was walking in our neighborhood, groups of juvenile boys would drive by, spot me, and shout out, "Fat!" At a birthday party in seventh grade, we were assigned to two cars and our driver asked who was the biggest girl, so she could sit in the front seat. One of the girls shouted out, mockingly, "Oh, it's Lisa! Lisa is the biggest!" As if I wasn't aware that my body was substantial by twelve-year-old standards. For the rest of the party, at a teddy bear factory, everyone but me was in a group, and when we got our pictures taken at the end, they posed together in happiness. I posed with my bear, my chubby cheeks smiling but inside I was breaking down.

I got my period when I was twelve. I was so ashamed, and prayed it would just go away. Mom reassured me that everything was okay and that this was a good thing, a sign of maturity. I didn't want to be mature, certainly not this soon. My friends were still reacting to the idea of menstruation with a large *eeewww*, even though some of them had gotten their periods, too. Mom didn't get hers until she was fifteen, so what did she know?

sheila: Lisa was dealing with bras and tampons at an age when I still had the body of a little boy. I wanted desperately to "develop," whatever that meant, but it seemed like everybody else had caught the express train and I was stuck at the station. Lisa just wanted the train to stop.

Psychologists point out that girls can't win in their middle school years. Eighth-grade boys hit on sixth-grade girls, ridicule them for having breasts or not having breasts, for being fat or flat. While a girl's body is spinning out of control, she looks at her mother for a hint of the future, and likely is appalled at her bad genes or convinced she will never look as good as Mom. She is dying to look and feel like a teenager, meanwhile holding on to childhood comforts and prerogatives, like having Mom drive her everywhere and Dad cook dinner. It's a push-pull time that repeats in later teen years, when the freedom of adulthood is very appealing, but not the responsibility.

And for Mom, there's a full plate of rejection. Those smiling brown eyes I used to lock with and know would often flash at me with anger and disgust. I couldn't get past the surface. Yeah, yeah, at this age Lisa needed to separate from us and expand beyond the family, and by now she should be secure in our love and values. She was no longer my adorable worshipper, the one who asked, "When you die, can I have your red shoes?" Now she scorned my closet, and most of me. I would have dined out on rejection every day, though, if it would have lessened Lisa's load. Instead, I relived my own mostly unpleasant early adolescence in spite of feeling a dash of jealousy. She was young and I wasn't.

Lisa's room, where we had tried and failed at a series of organizational systems, got more chaotic through the middle school years.

The usual advice to parents is: Just close the door. Except there was an increasingly consumptive aspect to her mess, like she couldn't ever have enough stuff. Amid the mounds of clothes and shoes, hair things, scented candles, stuffed animals, handbags, and jewelry, she often lost her homework. Was that normal girlish sloppiness or a symptom of something deeper? She was furious when I gave away her dollhouse, which had been boxed in the garage for years. It wasn't a handmade treasure, just a large plastic pieced-together dollhouse, sharing limited storage space with all the other outgrown toys, dolls, and artwork that had overflowed Lisa's room.

She wasn't in a party crowd, drinking, or doing drugs. She wasn't cutting herself. She wasn't measuring food or constantly weighing herself . . . yet.

Lisa played soccer, took singing lessons, prepared for her bat mitzvah and did all right in school. But in each arena, accomplishment came with a side dish of trauma. The coach never played her, the math teacher didn't like her, religious school was a minefield of cliques. Minutes before the annual vocal recital, she came down with a sore throat and refused to sing. Maybe she did have a sore throat, and certainly the ramp-up to lavish bar and bat mitzvah parties was intense. Lisa's complaints usually had at least a grain of truth. At an age when old friendships couldn't be counted on and the requirements shifted constantly, she had a short supply of resilience.

Until now, the soccer field had been a haven for girls to run, kick, and yell. I was envious. They learned what in my age group only boys got to learn from sports. They even talked about it: "Somebody wins, somebody loses, nobody dies." "There'll always be someone better than you, and someone worse." "On any given day, anybody can win." All those corny sports lessons do prove useful in the real world, along with the jokey camaraderie. Boys' teams would say, "It's not who wins or loses, it's how good are the treats." The girls' version was, "It's not who wins or loses, it's how good you look." The difference seemed funny at the time. In middle school, boys sometimes came to watch the girls' teams.

Suddenly there were bad teachers. Not mean, usually, just not able to control the class or convey the material, or both. From daycare through elementary school, except for the occasional substitute, Lisa never had a bad teacher. Now, if she fell behind, she was sure it was the teacher's fault. Often she was right. Teaching middle school, where kids are said to go in like lambs and come out lions, requires a special talent. Few have it. But Lisa bad-mouthed some of the good teachers, too.

We signed her up for an after-school tutoring program, and then another. Neither helped, and she hated going.

All the complaining and blaming were getting in Lisa's way. She was tightening up, less able to concentrate and get her schoolwork done. So much for the love of learning. The whole-child foundation of elementary school—giving equal value to emotional, social, physical, and intellectual growth—had slipped away. In middle school, the game was about grades and appearance. We watched Lisa gain weight and lose confidence, and we asked ourselves, "What do we do now?" There was a group at school to help kids organize their time and manage homework, which also taught that not everyone was born with CEO skills and movie-star looks, that others had problems, and that problems could be solved. Lisa agreed to go.

The group helped. Lisa relaxed and did better in school. But still, something was hurting that Lisa was stuffing down with food. She kept asking if she was fat. We kept saying no, and it didn't matter anyway, because she was a wonderful person, compassionate and smart, and she would make a difference in the world. Ned and I weren't popular in school or beautiful ever, yet we had a great life. What was so bad about being like us?

Before Lisa went into full puberty and stopped caring at all about our opinions, we thought about finding a therapist. We investigated and skirted the issue with her. She was horrified. If we insisted, would that make her feel there was something wrong with her? But there *was* something wrong. If we didn't insist, we could miss the opportunity. It could be like the mistake we made with toilet training. Lisa was ready at an early age, too early, according to the books. By the time the world was ready, she'd lost interest and put all her stubborn energy into staying in diapers. Now, though, instead of temper fits our worry was that Lisa could drop into a serious depression, the scourge of my family history.

We told ourselves to relax. Lisa was doing well enough in school; she had friends and interests. This was a developmental stage she'd get through, a "period of disequilibrium" like the ones that hit her at just about every half-year when she was younger. By her birthday, she normally matured and mellowed out. But this time, was Lisa having treatable problems? What should we change about our own behavior? Were we becoming one of those families we used to tsk-tsk about? As if saying, "Of course Jeffrey M. is in a drug treatment program. You could tell in kindergarten. He was always getting sent to the principal's office." Now, in my imagination there had been similar conversations along the soccer field sidelines: "I know, I know. How could the Himmels not see Lisa's eating disorders a mile away? She used to be such a fun kid, but now, you know, she seems kind of depressed. Plus, with all that food in the house, and all they do is cook or go out to eat."

lisa: As if being overweight through my early puberty stages wasn't torture enough, I did not belong to any clique in particular nor did I really have many friends. In middle school, people were judged on appearance and rumors, although I doubt any negative rumors circulated about me, because I wasn't that important. I was mainly gentle and friendly to all, just a bit bigger.

Not that I was a loner. I had close best friends, other friends, and acquaintances, but I think my body structure and all-over proportions caused my peers to steer away. I mean, who wanted to be seen with the fat girl?

Boys became an interest for me, like many young teens, blossoming and discovering their own thoughts on sexuality. Yet, no boy ever advanced my way, nor had I ever been asked to dance. I still went to the school dances, trying to dress cute and hoping I might get lucky one night. I buried my despair with bravery as I often asked boys to dance. I never got turned down, but I'm sure none of those volunteers felt happy about a slow dance with a chubby girl.

I struggled academically, with severe test anxiety and self-loathing, and by seventh grade most of my motivation was gone. Even when teachers offered their support I could never bring myself to seek assistance. I did fine in English and history (social studies then) as well as art and P.E. But math and science were torture. No matter how hard I pushed myself to study I could never grasp the concepts laid out before me. I always excelled in projects, however, giving me some leeway and a boost in my grade. Even with the talents I did possess, such as musical theater, singing in general, and art, I never felt these trades would lead to any success or social acceptance. No matter what, I was a failure. I don't know if anyone really saw me in this negative light, and in a way it didn't matter. I knew myself better than anyone. I knew I belonged on the bottom of the social ladder, and no matter how hard my parents tried to remind me of my positive attributes, nothing could raise my morale. I sucked at life and I especially sucked at middle school.

sheila: When Ned and I look back on Lisa's middle school years, we realize this was a key time and we beat ourselves with an endless lash of sentences starting, "If only." If only Lisa had found a passion to counterbalance her low self-regard. Middle school was when I discovered journalism, which provides armor for many shy people. As in acting, in the news business you get to become somebody else. You are the protector of the public's right to know. You get to call important people, accost strangers, ask all kinds of questions, and keep asking until the story makes sense.

Lisa didn't find anything like that. She was good at sports and singing, but not driven enough to really get better. She played the piano. She got her schoolwork done and got a Student of the Month bumper sticker, but long after all her friends, when to her it wasn't all that important anymore.

I was the one who was thriving. Unlike sports writing, food writing truly can be as good as it seems. Reviewing restaurants turned out to be a natural for me; going places I'd never been, undercover, and criticizing other people's work. What joy! I doubt this had anything to do with the fun of discovering restaurants, but later I tested positive for the supertaster gene. Supertasters have the most fungiform papillae, those dots on your tongue where taste buds live. The French physiologist Jean Anthelme Brillat-Savarin, father of "You are what you eat," said people with more papillae live in different worlds of taste. And in my world, Northern California, your papillae also get to taste lots of wine.

Often during that first year of reviewing restaurants Ned and I would look up from the table and start giggling. Most of my career had been served as an editor in a penny-pinching newsroom. Lunch? If there was time, maybe somebody ran out for burritos. Usually editors and reporters in the newsroom grabbed a plate of something congealing in the cafeteria steam table. Cafeteria workers regularly swept the newsroom for trays people had forgotten to return, after eating at their desks. The food was bad or terrible. One view was that this was to remind us, in the heady years of newspapers, that we were blue-collar workers.

Now I was working nights and weekends again, but I controlled my schedule, and it was fun. The worst that could happen was a bad meal, paid for by my employer. In ten years of reviewing for the *Mercury News*, I never got food poisoning, and the one time I did get sick, it was not the restaurant's fault. I ate too much rich food in a high-toned San Francisco hotspot, and a young woman was spraying her hair in the poorly ventilated restroom, where I stopped before leaving. I just made it to the car in time to puke in the gutter.

My editors sent me to Carmel, the Napa Valley, Mendocino, and Lake Tahoe, the prime weekend getaway destinations for Silicon Valley. Ned and I were forced to spend two or three days in swanky hotels like the Highlands Inn and eat every meal in a different restaurant.

The need to remain anonymous keeps reviewers from getting chummy with chefs and other restaurant people, but it means reporting stories by phone that normally would be done in person. Perfect for a shy yet curious person. On the phone, I developed a banter that would've been hard to sustain in person.

One day I got a voicemail message from a former employee of a prominent downtown San Jose restaurant. The restaurant business is tough in every way, and a lot of people leave mad. Calls from disgruntled ex-employees were almost as common as, "Where should I take my girlfriend for her birthday?" and "Why is restaurant service so terrible these days?" but I called everybody back. This guy had been a waiter at a renowned restaurant, where, he claimed, the executive chef was "cutting corners" in ways that customers should know about.

"Like what?" I asked.

"Like using fake Madeira. And the veal dishes are made with pork." He mentioned something else, something minor like the Madeira, but putting pork in the veal scallopine? Now we're talking fraud with religious implications!

My editor and I went to lunch at the spacious two-story restaurant in a beautifully restored historic downtown San Jose building, crowded as usual with familiar business and government faces. We had veal scallopine and the parmigiana. The meat on both plates was mild and covered in sauce; it almost could have been a very tender chicken breast. I called John Draeger, who oversaw the meat, poultry, and fish department for Draeger's Markets, a third-generation family business with a full-service restaurant and nationally known cooking school. "Pork has a very distinctive flavor, which comes from fat," said Draeger, who had apprenticed as a butcher. "But if the exterior fat is removed, the distinctive flavor wouldn't come through." Also, he said, the texture could be pounded out and disguised by breading and sauces.

I called food-science writer Harold McGee, a Palo Alto resident. He was revising his classic *On Food and Cooking*, which would come out three years later. "Pork has gotten much leaner," McGee said. "It resembles veal more, and would be easier to disguise." He echoed Draeger about cooking diminishing the meats' different flavors: "Browning generates a more generic flavor."

Even the local kosher butcher said he wouldn't bet the store on distinguishing cooked pork from veal.

If nobody could be sure by tasting, maybe science would help. Had the meat been raw, I could have sent it to the USDA or the veterinary genetics lab at University of California, Davis, department for DNA testing. I called Michigan State's department of animal science and Iowa State, too. A private drug company could do it, but they wouldn't. Many of their clients were restaurants.

Marian Burros at the *New York Times* had recently run tests on the freshness and cleanliness of food at salad bars. She generously took my call and gave me the name of a lab in New York City that she'd been using for ten or twelve years. Associated Analytical Laboratories Inc. also did work for the federal government, Burros told me, and, "They don't take just any newspaper case."

They took mine. Finally, I was getting somewhere, although my editor's editor balked at the $200 per sample cost. We would have to send at least three samples to verify the results. We would also send a sample of another restaurant's veal scallopine, to make sure everything wasn't coming up pork.

This restaurant seats four hundred diners, but someone might notice if I showed up repeatedly and ordered the same thing. So I called for takeout, wrapped the meat samples in plastic and foil, and FedExed the boxes to New York. The next day, the boxes came back to my desk. They had started to smell. FedEx workers also had noticed they weren't labeled properly and could have been hazardous. Now the meat was rotten. Back to the restaurant, three more times, eating in and ordering out. I found packing ice and labels, and the *Mercury News* had to spring for next-day delivery to New York. All of this restaurant's veal samples tested positive for pork.

On a rainy President's Day, my editor's editor and I went to talk to the restaurant's owner. In case he got enraged, the big boss said he would be there to protect me, but in fact he had been a police reporter and wanted to make sure the food writer got it right. The owner thought we were there to discuss the case of a dissatisfied customer, and he had a fat file of her complaints and his responses. When I stated the pork issue, he was relieved and so sure it was a mistake that he took us up to his top-floor office to look through the invoices. Rain pounded the rickety skylight, as in a horror movie, as he rustled through his files for an invoice that said *veal*. Still confident, he called his supplier and put him on the speakerphone. The supplier said, "Uh, Bill, we haven't sold you veal in years."

Bill said he would call the chef, who did the buying. Two hours later, the chef called me.

"You guys are right. I thought it (pork) was a superior product. I had received complaints that the veal was tough. Pork had the same flavor, but was more tender."

Pork was also $4.50 a pound cheaper. The restaurant was saving about $15,000 a year.

Had it occurred to the chef, a born-again Christian, that pork is forbidden to Muslims and Jews, or that some people are allergic?

"I never considered religion or health," he said.

I was so stunned that I forgot to ask how long this had been going on. When I called back, the chef was at church. He later said it had been five or six years and, "I don't know where it's going to go. I'm leaving it in God's hands."

This story made news throughout the Bay Area. I agreed to do one TV interview, in silhouette, and sounded like Miss Hathaway on *The Beverly Hillbillies*, mouthing stuffy phrases like "difficult to discern." Despite me, the story got national play, and that weekend was a test question on NPR's *Wait Wait . . . Don't Tell Me*.

Investigative reporting was very satisfying. I had started my career during Watergate, inspired to fight corruption, and now I had a "-gate" of my own. And I'd made some enemies. "Vealgate" began as it ended, with phone messages, such as:

"How does it feel to be someone who makes their living off of other people's misfortunes?"

"You've caused a lot of pain. You're evil. The good Lord is gonna have you pay."

The restaurant owner had to pay $35,000 in restitution (providing "free food to victim customers") and $25,000 in civil penalties ("to address the issue of lack of sensitivity to dietary laws and prohibitions of groups who do not eat pork products"), and the chef faced criminal charges. A group of restaurant supporters took out an expensive advertisement, indirectly recouping some of our FedEx costs.

My next shot on camera was a fluffy feature. My voice was more natural but the rest of me was a mess. I wore a big straw hat, sunglasses, and an overcoat, going for anonymity but achieving bag lady. Still, the genial host of this Bay Area travel show was skilled at loosening up his guests, amid what seemed to me like a very large staff standing around. This same afternoon was Lisa's appointment to take her driving test. I had two hours to shoot the piece and pick up Lisa to bring her for her test. It seemed like plenty of time, but with all the set-up activity and reshoots, I started to sweat under the overcoat and spotlights, mentally mapping out the drive to Lisa's school and then the Department of Motor Vehicles, counting on no traffic tie-ups. Finally, I just had to leave, and let the TV professionals take it from there. Lisa got to her driving test in plenty of time and passed easily.

Bay Area radio notable Ronn Owens did a regular show about restaurants with newspaper reviewers. On the drive to San Francisco I heard the promo, "And this week, we welcome Sheila Himmel of the *San Jose Mercury News* to . . ." I immediately blanked out. What was I to do? Discuss Silicon Valley restaurant history? The booker had assured me that we'd just talk about what we liked and didn't like, but I wasn't great at bantering. The critics arrived early, as instructed, mingled, and ate the croissants one had discovered in her area. Oh no, were we supposed to bring food? Also I was overdressed in a suit. Owens was in shirtsleeves. Michael Bauer, from the *San Francisco Chronicle*, looked cool in jeans and a leather jacket.

Then we went into the studio, put on pilot-size earphones, and sat before massive microphones. I had brought reference material, lists of restaurants in different categories that might possibly come up, but on live radio there is no time to consult notes, and you don't want to make paper-shuffling noises. Except for the time spent staring into the microphone and thinking about how much of the Bay Area was hearing me mumble and the simple question that stumped me, the hour went by quickly. Owens is a dexterous host and he loves to talk about restaurants.

During the call-in portion, someone asked for the best hamburger place in San Jose. Um, hamburgers, San Jose, I couldn't make the connection. Owens quickly changed the subject.

Still, they invited me back. Eventually I got into a groove. As I learned, even a shy person can do radio and television. You just have to do it more than once.

One morning at the neighborhood coffeehouse, I was in line with a companion, talking about restaurants, when the woman in front of us turned around and said, "You're *Sheila Himmel*?" Or she said, "*You're* Sheila Himmel?" I heard it as the latter, my friend as the former. But whether surprised by my size or disappointed in my fashion sense, this citizen was impressed to be waiting for coffee with a marquee player.

lisa: Many people envied Mom's job and talked about it as their dream career. For years I felt privileged to be able to taste gourmet foods from around the world. Not many other middle school kids ate at four-star restaurants or had frequented Boulevard, a San Francisco favorite with great views of the bay. I loved the atmosphere and the food. We ate there as a family, but I loved the time I went just with Dad and we sat at the bar, watching the cooks. I had wonderful scallops and a poached pear dessert before we went to see the musical *Chicago* on stage. We both knew the lyrics by heart. Dad and I did a lot of eating together. If anyone was to accompany Dad on weekend trips to visit family in San Diego or Chicago, it was me, his baby girl. We enjoyed deep-dish pizza in downtown Chicago, fresh fish tacos in San Diego, dim sum on Sundays in San Francisco, and smoky barbecue in Oakland. We'd share molasses chips from See's Candies and nibble at a pound of chocolate truffles. We had our favorite ice cream flavors and burrito fillings and pizza toppings. We bonded over food, over our love for cooking and all the tools and dishes.

But Mom's job fed into my food addiction, this constant supply of oversize portions and richly decadent desserts. My food life took buffet form and my hips took on more fat than they wanted—or my society accepted, more important.

When I was passionate about eating, I loved Mom's job. With food as my very best friend, of course I loved Mom's job. For the first five or so years, I loved Mom's job. After that, I became disinterested and then disconnected and finally disgusted with the whole concept of eating out for a living.

seven

You Are What You Don't Eat

Lisa was too busy to notice, but when she developed serious eating disorders in high school, she wasn't the only one busily crossing foods off the list. Americans increasingly disdain certain foods for religious, ethical, political, and health reasons, imaginary health reasons, and just plain orneriness. We all have our food quirks, but lately in America we are very loud about the feared and frowned-upon, not the favorites. We hear "I don't eat" about everything from red meat to white flour to blue food coloring. Here are a few:

I DON'T EAT	THEREFORE I AM
Traif	Jewish
Haram	Muslim
Red meat	Pescetarian
Red meat and fish	Vegetarian

I DON'T EAT	THEREFORE I AM
Meat, fish, dairy	Vegan
Carbs	Atkins Diet holdout
Food from more than 100 miles away	Locavore (or localvore)
Anything new	Neophobic
Anything blue	Alex H.
Cinnamon	Ellen S.
Honeydew melon	Sheila H.
I Can't Believe It's Not Butter!	Ned H.

I can imagine "Doesn't Eat" as a category on *Jeopardy!*

ALEX TREBEK: "Doesn't Eat for two hundred dollars: This U.S.
   president made about big fuss about broccoli."
ALERT CONTESTANT: "Who is George Herbert Walker Bush?"

The first President Bush set the tone when he reportedly stated at a news conference in March 1990: "I do not like broccoli. And I haven't liked it since I was a little kid and my mother made me eat it. And I'm president of the United States, and I'm not going to eat any more broccoli."

He got a lot of mileage out of this little outburst, refusing to kowtow to the nutrition police who were suggesting that broccoli, among other vegetables and fruits, might have health benefits, like warding off cancer. Bush the elder reminded me of Lisa the toddler, stamping her feet and wailing, "Not gonna!" Our president was letting us know he was a regular guy.

Oh yeah? I have foods I don't like, too. Plenty of them. Since birth I have been a picky eater. Only I'm not president, just a restaurant critic, and part of the job is to push aside personal preferences. Reviewers eat first and criticize later. If a restaurant's specialty is cream of broccoli soup, no aversion to broccoli is going to stand in the way, although the critic may enlist a companion or two to help rate the soup. One of the few downsides of the job is that you can't say, "No, thanks. I don't eat that."

When I started reviewing restaurants a dozen years ago, I didn't eat mussels. Having gotten cinematically ill on mussels, I had maintained a fifteen-year boycott. Oysters, clams, and other shellfish were no problem. The bad guys had come in a package, in the days before sell-by dates. Maybe there was only one offender in the bunch, because Ned ate them too and was fine. My grudge held firm against the sight and especially the scent of mussels. Eventually Ned was allowed to order them in a restaurant, but not to cook them at home. With all the French restaurants on my beat, and mussels commonly harvested on the Pacific Coast, I dreaded the day I would face *moules* in a signature dish.

Alain Rondelli's restaurant was to be my mussel Waterloo. The chef-owner had been executive chef at Ernie's, a San Francisco landmark, and recently opened his own place. Rondelli was a Paul Bocuse protégé and a former chef for the president of France.

I had one dinner at his new restaurant. Other newspapers sent their critics three or four times to each restaurant before writing a review, but mine had decided that once was enough. Our public posture was that reviewers should act like regular customers: You don't like a restaurant, you don't go back. And that the critic's job was to provide a snapshot so that readers could see if the place appealed to them. The expense account was of course the real reason, but after a dozen years of reviewing restaurants, I have to say that this limitation forced me to pay attention and to do my homework.

A reviewer can visit a restaurant nine times and be very confident in what he writes, but the next day the chef has a fight with the owner and disappears, or the produce truck breaks down, or the only well-trained server calls in sick, and it's a whole different experience. Restaurants, unlike movies, are moving targets.

Considering the one-visit rule, Rondelli's eight-course tasting menu was the best way to get a fair sample of his cooking, except that right after the chef's amuse-bouche came mussels and orange soup. I looked at that and thought, "Uh-oh." We had just begun a meal that likely would go three hours. Maybe I'd get sick right away, run to the restroom, and be done with it. I couldn't imagine sitting through seven more courses with waves of nausea.

And yet the orange mussel soup was astonishing. To a base of chicken broth and fresh orange juice Rondelli added squares of fresh fennel and half-dried orange, and plump green lip and Prince Edward Island mussels in a martini glass. Maybe because I was so surprised that the mussels didn't kill me right away they tasted even better, but by any standard those mussels were fabulous, and I've been able to judge them fairly in the line of duty ever since. As a civilian I prefer clams. Avoiding mussels has become part of my identity, just as my friend's son avoids anything blue.

In the twenty-first century, we see so many food products that it is prudent to draw fences around certain of them and say, "I don't go there." We need the "I don't eat" routine so we can pare down the possibilities. In *Mindless Eating*, food scientist Brian Wansink calculated that the average person makes more than two hundred food decisions per day. If even one of those choices didn't have limits, life would be impossible.

Have we all gotten a little carried away? When silly as well as legitimate reasons for avoiding food become central to our identities, my theory is that we're all a little eating disordered. We are what we don't eat.

• • •

In some countries, such as Japan, individuals mainly want to fit in and be like everyone else, and their diets follow suit. America is the opposite. We are all special, and we all have special dietary requirements.

In Silicon Valley, dietary variation is a commonplace cost of business for large companies and meeting and event planners. The giant Cisco Systems has cafeterias that meet Muslims' halal requirements. Google became renowned for its seasonal, local, organic food and its celebrity chef, Charlie Ayers. When he left Google to open a restaurant based on the Google philosophy, it took the company a year and a half to find a replacement who met all of the requirements: five years as a sous chef and three years as an executive chef, plus experience preparing ethnic and vegetarian cuisine using organic ingredients. They would need these skills, the job posting said, to cook an "eclectic menu capable of suiting every Googler palate, from vegan entrées to pad Thai, grilled burgers, and wood-fired pizza."

Of course there are serious health concerns that cause people to reject certain foods, such as lactose-intolerance, high blood pressure, high cholesterol, diabetes, gluten intolerance, and food allergies. People with allergies commonly avoid milk products, wheat gluten, a particular spice, and most notably, peanuts. Parents didn't need salmonella to add to their worries about peanut butter. Once a parent hears about anaphylaxis, a life-threatening reaction to peanuts that requires an emergency injection of adrenaline, she becomes very cautious.

With these and more to keep in mind, home cooks and anyone in the hospitality industry might as well subscribe to *Prevention* magazine. Restaurants receive all manner of special requests and interrogations about ingredients. Menus often encourage this, to avoid poisoning the diner and the expensive lawsuit that would result. Diners with serious food issues may know enough to mention them when they make a reservation. Or to inquire about the ingredients before they order a dish. At Manresa, consistently the top-rated restaurant in Silicon Valley, diners have used a card that says, "Hi, I'm eating at your restaurant, and I'm looking forward to my meal. These food groups will make me severely ill and will be life-threatening." Those foods tend to be onions, mushrooms, garlic, oil, and nuts, says chef-owner David Kinch, who photocopies the card for every station in the kitchen.

Other restaurants have received instructions for "nothing acidic," "no yeast," "nothing fermented," "no seeds," "some kinds of squashes but not others," Lessley Anderson wrote on the foodie website Chow.

And dinner parties, phew, what a headache. Evite should add a box for "Guest Doesn't Eat X." Guests may say, "Oh, don't make anything special for me," and mean, "Just don't make anything that's going to gross me out." Now, do you have to ask every guest if he or she is a vegetarian, and if so what type? The etiquette is evolving.

In an email from Panama, nutritionist Marion Nestle told me about attending a pig roast. "The host told me later that several people complained they don't eat pork," Nestle wrote. "They, of course, had been specifically invited to a pig roast, and there were plenty of other things eat."

In my little circle, Lia is lactose-intolerant, Cathleen can't have wheat gluten, Ellen has a violent reaction to cinnamon. Ellen's husband, Neal, is a pescatarian and eats tomatoes cooked but never raw. If possible, he's fine with picking out the tomatoes. Just having them in the vicinity, even touching the lettuce, doesn't spoil the salad for him. If we served paella, though, most likely we would leave out the pork, just as people who know Ned know to leave the nuts out of cookies and cakes. Ned hates nuts as ingredients but if you put out a bowl of salted Marcona almonds, watch out. What he hates is the textural interference of nuts in food. They disrupt the chewy landscape of brownies, the creaminess of puddings and ice creams.

Food preferences and aversions like Neal's and Ned's often get established in childhood. Ned recalls, "Maybe it was religious. I went to a Jewish preschool and hated it because they often served nuts in lunch foods." Because of the nuts and equally appalling raisins, Ned's whole preschool memory is painful.

Parents are cautioned to respect strong food dislikes, and to keep in mind that while food is prepared and offered with love, children naturally reject some of it. Control and rebellion are powerful motivators. Don't be like the Himmels with their finicky first child, hovering and fretting at every occasion, so that Jacob became the One Who Didn't Eat. Or the older Himmels with their finicky second child, Ned Who Doesn't Eat Nuts, for whom special cakes were baked.

But why do these food quirks stick around, long after they've outlived their youthful usefulness? I had to wonder if biology somehow cemented those feelings into our sense of self. Scientists are finding that more and more human traits and behaviors are based in organic life processes, rather coming strictly from experience or choice. Nearby at Stanford University, preeminent neurobiology professor Robert Sapolsky was the one to ask. Sapolsky studies the biology of every important human behavior, from people who can't stop working eighty hours a week to those who won't eat sushi.

Sapolsky has found that adolescence and early adulthood are the ages when humans and other primates enjoy novelty. And for music and fashion as well as food, that window snaps shut around age thirty-nine. A prolific author and MacArthur "genius" fellow, Sapolsky did a study of fifty sushi restaurants in the Midwest and found that if an adult hadn't voluntarily tried sushi by age thirty-nine, there was a ninety-five percent chance he or she never would. While culture and psychology are the usual suspects, Sapolsky sees biology at work. "It is a rare adult monkey who would try a new food. When you see the same thing in a rat, you're looking at biology," he said. Sapolsky summed up the human quandary in a 1998 piece for the *New Yorker*: "If I'm actually going to die someday, I'm sure not going to waste any of my finite number of meals on some new food that I turn out not to like." Extrapolating on my own, I figure that biological imperative could have something to do with why we hang on to childhood aversions as well. "If I already know I don't like black licorice, why bother? There are lots of other chewy sweets."

As for the current American "I don't eat" phenomenon, biologist Sapolsky suspects culture and psychology. "I don't eat" is not something you hear much in other countries, most of which don't have as many choices. Looking at France, which though more multicultural than it used to be is still a lot more homogeneous than the United States, Sapolsky told me in an email, "I'd say that we are more varied in the what-we-eat department, and maybe even more so, what-we-don't-eat than the French because we are more heterogeneous culturally. Beyond stuff like hamburgers and pizza, it's not that we're great individualists but, rather, lots of us follow an ethnic cuisine that is as defined as is the national cuisine for France." Americans exercise their freedom of food choice in myriad avoidances: pork for Muslims and Jews; meat for people of South Indian heritage; milk for the lactose-intolerant; bread, pasta, and soy products for the gluten-allergic.

Rather than an expression of our uniqueness, Sapolsky sees long-term planning as the reason for refusing certain foods. "If I had to guess what that's about, psychologically, it's because we Americans secretly believe that we can live forever, and somewhere in that irrationality and denial is, among other things, the phrase 'If we only eat right.' So we are battling appetite for, if not our immortal souls, our immortality. Okay, that's a little sarcastic. But something emotionally like that."

Is there something in human biology that's programmed to spend a certain amount of time obsessing about food? Planning, preparing, eating, and dieting take a big bite out of one's day. Are we just hungry hunter-gatherers in new clothes?

Sapolsky eviscerates that little theory, because even the hunter-gatherers had other things on their minds. "From what we know of hunter-gatherers, and given the freedom to extrapolate backward, with ninety-nine percent of human history spent in small hunter-gatherer groups, there was probably not all that much pressure to get yourself fed. Traditional rainforest hunter-gatherers spent only thirty percent of their time or so getting their day's calories. I don't think it has been bred into us as a major obsession."

I was looking forward to blaming everything—food obsession, the way we stick with childhood aversions as adults, the national negativity about food—on biology, but it wasn't going to happen. As Nestle put it, "People do have these things but they usually are socially constructed, not biological. And they can change."

In the sixties, a lot of people did change their eating habits. "You are what you eat" became a mantra, widely accepted to mean that a person's mental, physical, and emotional health depended on putting good substances into his body. As Jean Anthelme Brillat-Savarin wrote in *The Physiology of Taste*, "Tell me what you eat and I will tell you what you are." By that he meant that personality and character were revealed at the dinner table. Later that century, Ludwig Andreas von Feuerbach wrote in his essay "Concerning Spiritualism and Materialism": "A man is what he eats." In 1942, nutritionist Victor Lindlahr adapted the phrase to title his book, *You Are What You Eat: How to Win and Keep Health with Diet*, an explication of the "catabolic diet"—eating foods that, he claimed, take more calories to digest than they contain.

"You are what you eat" hung around to inform America's foodie revolution, long after other sixties sayings fell away. (Such as "Don't trust anyone over thirty.") In the seventies, fresh, seasonal, and organic became the watchwords of foodie faith. Sustainable and local came later.

We speak all these noble words, and their accompanying food philosophies are sound—good for our bodies and for the environment. But when we get specific, often we speak in terms of rejection. Instead of enjoying the bounty of the earth, we push food away, and make a lot of noise about it.

For children, "I don't eat X" is a sure path to family celebrity. Chelsea is the child who doesn't eat eggs, not because of an allergy, just because she's appalled by the idea of eggs. Everyone will remember Mom and Dad buying a special egg substitute product for Chelsea, and that she suffered noisily with cereal when they went elsewhere for breakfast. Not even Chelsea remembers how the egg thing started, but she became the One Who Doesn't Eat Eggs. As with eating disorders, she got attention and power.

Nutritionists tell parents not to fret, that all children refuse food and that many reject foods they've never had (which is everything, but still, don't get alarmed). In the trade, saying no to new is called *food neophobia*, a developmental stage that should end by age five and pick up again in adolescence.

That's a relief. But nutritional advice often changes, conflicts, and gives parents even more to worry about. Consulting *Finicky Eaters: What to Do When Kids Won't Eat!* I learned: "It is not unusual for our daily lives and family mealtime environments to be chaotic and stressful. Environmental stressors can develop from a variety of sources, including chaotic work schedules, cultural beliefs around eating, and the diagnosis of a developmental disability. Family schedules and mealtimes have become increasingly chaotic as children have become involved with more extracurricular activities and parental work schedules are more varied than in the past." I couldn't help noticing the word *chaos* or *chaotic* in every sentence.

The calm, rational adult follows what Susan Baker, MD, and Roberta Henry, RD, write in *Parents' Guide to Nutrition*:

> Parents should be concerned about proper nutrition, but they should not panic or fret if a child fails to eat the recommended number of servings from a food group or a particular iron-rich food. If nourishing meals are offered daily, chances are good that over time children will receive everything their bodies need to grow. Food charts are recommendations that can offer some help in planning meals; however, variety, flexibility, and a relaxed, happy atmosphere are certainly the best ways to keep a child well fed.

We knew this, we just didn't always do it, although we didn't do it in a different way with each child. For a while we counted each spoonful of rice cereal Jacob swallowed, not the ones that ended up on his face and hands. We watched Lisa eat too many cookies and tried not to say anything. We did offer nourishing meals.

Now I can see that what we did do—fret—didn't help and what we didn't do enough was to intervene. We should have picked up on Lisa's comforting herself with food, and tried harder to get her into nourishing activities, or find another adult who could help her, before she became so susceptible to social pressure to be thin.

The trigger to eating disorders often releases very slowly, over years, so you hardly notice: Nine-year-old José won't eat spinach.

Not to worry, many kids don't like spinach, and there are plenty of other leafy green vegetables that provide iron and vitamins A and C, without the mineral taste of spinach. Maybe it's not the flavor, but the slimy mouth-feel of cooked spinach that José finds revolting. So the parent turns to broccoli flowerets, which are crunchy unless overcooked and can be entertaining. They look like little trees! It could end there. He's just One of Many Who Don't Eat Spinach. Or, he gets over his spinach thing and moves to sweet potatoes, another font of nutrition, or he escalates to rejecting all green foods.

And who knows, when José gets a little older he may reverse himself and go green altogether, becoming the One Who Doesn't Eat Meat. Many teenagers do. With increasing interest in health and the environment, the vegetarian diet makes a lot of sense. But teenagers tend to see their choices as full-speed ahead or reverse, and they easily slide off track. Lisa didn't eat meat, then fried foods, then desserts, then carbohydrates after 6:00 p.m., then no carbohydrates at all, until food itself had become the enemy and she had a life-threatening disease.

Vegetarianism has been associated with bulimia, especially for adolescents. Many anorexics started by just saying no to red meat or by developing a repugnance to animal flesh. Eliminating certain foods is a ritual and a way to control your life, the need or hunger that often drives eating disorders. Researchers for the American Dietetic Association found vegetarians "more likely to feel extremely guilty after eating, have a preoccupation with a desire to be thinner, have a tendency to eat diet food, and like the feeling of an empty stomach. In addition, the vegetarians were more likely not to enjoy trying new, rich foods. Also, the vegetarian participants had a greater tendency to feel that food controls their lives, [they] give too much time and thought to food, and [they] have the impulse to vomit after meals compared with nonvegetarians."

When Lisa was in high school, our family internist was the first to diagnose her anorexia. The clinic now makes it easier, with an extensive website that often features eating issues. Recently it linked to a story about Steven Bratman, MD, who coined the term *orthorexia nervosa*, the obsession with quality rather than quantity of food. This focus can be benign or even beneficial when it's about improving health, treating an illness, or losing weight, but people with orthorexia can't stop the train. Bratman provides a list of warning signs:

1. Spending more than three hours a day thinking about healthy food

2. Planning tomorrow's menu today

3. Feeling virtuous about what they eat, but not enjoying it much

4. Continually limiting the number of foods they eat

5. Experiencing a reduced quality of life or social isolation (because their diet makes it difficult for them to eat anywhere but at home)

6. Feeling critical of others who do not eat as well as they do

7. Skipping foods they once enjoyed in order to eat the "right" foods

8. Feeling guilt or self-loathing when they stray from their diet

9. Feeling in "total" control when they eat the correct diet

Orthorexics, like anorexics, become different people, defining themselves by what they don't eat.

• • •

Whenever I teach a food-writing class or give a guest lecture, I like to ask people to name the foods they don't eat. Everybody has something. At a local high school, students quickly named cottage cheese, applesauce, bananas, and lima beans because of their mushiness—a texture they most likely loved when they were younger and possibly associated with immaturity. But how do you acquire an aversion to honey cough drops, olives, or dried fruit? One girl said red licorice made her nose bleed. I wasn't the only one in the room to have a thing against honeydew melon, although to call it an allergy would be a stretch. It gives me a scratchy throat, even if it's just touching the watermelon in a fruit salad. Still, I avoid it.

Anybody know what vegans *do* eat? Beyond beans, vegetables, and fruit, I start to go blank. There must be some kind of emulsifying egg substitute in vegan pastries. But unless you are a vegan or live with one, all you really need to know is what they don't eat: animal products.

Even with religious dietary laws, practitioners as well as spectators tend to be more familiar with what is forbidden than with what is allowed. My father's parents kept a kosher house and didn't eat pork or shellfish ever, but they did eat in non-kosher restaurants. In Stockton, California, there weren't any other kind. My father didn't eat pork or shellfish, but once he left home and tasted a cheeseburger, there went the proscription against mixing a calf with its mother's milk. One of his favorite restaurants, Emil Villa's Hick'ry Pit, specialized in barbecued spare ribs. He never had the ribs, always the chicken. It was okay for me and my sister to have the ribs, however—as long as we weren't dining with anybody who might be offended. Once Nancy forgot this, and ordered the ribs, in the company of Nana George, who opined at the table that pork would make Nancy sick. Mom, whose family didn't go out of their way for pork but didn't shun it, either, put in that really, the cleanliness of pork was as good as any for beef these days. Nancy went home and threw up.

As with Jews and keeping kosher, American Muslims' observance of halal varies widely. "Some Muslims just say a prayer before eating," says Safaa Ibrahim, executive director of the Council on American-Islamic Relations, based in Santa Clara. Another school of thought is that buying meat raised and slaughtered by other "people of the Book" (Christians and Jews) is fine. "I grew up eating kosher meat," says Shahed Amanullah, who founded www.zabihah.com, a nationwide guide to halal restaurants, markets, and stores. "Some say only meat hand-slaughtered by a Muslim. I try not to get too political."

Some halal rules are similar to those for kosher foods. However, halal is certified not by a central authority but by word of mouth. "You just trust the owner of the store," says Tahir Anwar, imam of the South Bay Islamic Association. In restaurants "as long as food we're being served is halal, it's fine to eat somewhere that isn't totally halal. Kosher is also permissible. If we can't find halal meats, we are allowed to have kosher. The method of slaughter is quite similar."

The word *kosher* means proper, and *halal* means permitted or lawful, as in this verse from the Koran: "Eat of that which Allah hath bestowed on you as food lawful and good." But in tune with the food negativity of our times, halal and kosher are commonly known for what they forbid, not what they allow. Both religions have specific words for the opposites of halal and kosher. Pork, alcohol, and products made with non-halal animal content, such as gelatin or a cheese made with rennet, are *haram*. Pork, shellfish, and eating meat with milk are *treif*.

Religious practices, allergies, and vegetarianism are a person's own business. It's when we get all self-righteous about what others are eating, when we disdain each others' choices, when we obsess and fetishize food, that problems arise. The food revolution that rode into town flying the flag "You are what you eat" has taken a forbidding U-turn.

Besides "I don't eat," the other popular foot-stomping about food is "I don't cook." This, too, is said with pride. It is who I am, as in, "I work so hard, my commitments are vast, I'm just so darn important. There's no time to cook." Surely there's a restaurant to grab takeout on the way home, or one that delivers. In an economic downturn, there may be more time to cook, but restaurants have parried with markdowns and cheaper menu items.

Supermarkets used to be all about raw ingredients, which you imported and assembled at home. Now they devote valuable real estate to delis, pizza ovens, sushi, noodle bars, even creperies.

Whole Foods has set a frenzied pace in what the industry calls "meal replacement." As a teenager exclaimed one night at the new Whole Foods store in our area, "I've never seen so much food in my life!" Whoa, a market with the ability to astonish a teenager! Our relatively modest Whole Foods store has a Prepared Foods section with Singaporean barbecued meats on a stick, grilled panini sandwiches, a retro cafeteria line with steam-table all-stars like turkey Tetrazzini and tamale pie, a very good beef brisket near the soup station, and a fabulous salad bar. Across the store from Prepared Foods is another soup station in the seafood department, and all the ready-to-eat fish dishes. Non-cooks of many persuasions feel right at home at Whole Foods.

My own unscientific observation is that fewer shoppers go to the world's largest retailer of organic and natural foods with a shopping list. They browse. They likely spend way too much time browsing, aisle after aisle of exquisite produce and new packaging. It's just so exciting, like a Toys R Us or a casino for foodies.

As at a casino, it's hard to find your way out of Whole Foods without spending money. The high-beam lights and zigzag floor plans can be disorienting. While I was admiring the red army of perfect cherry tomatoes at the salad bar, a man cried into his cell phone: "I'm in the food court area. Where are you?"

But even foodies, who congregate at Whole Foods, farmers' markets, and specialty cheese shops, tie ourselves up in refusing and restricting. We turn up our noses at foods that are out of compliance with our local, seasonal, organic mantra. People who take this to the extreme have been coined *locavores* and *localvores*, proudly by themselves, derisively by others. In San Francisco, a restaurant called Fish & Farm opened in the fall of 2007, featuring a majority of food from less than one hundred miles away (plus an herb garden on the roof, recycled marble countertops, and a bottle crusher for recycling on-site). In December 2007, San Francisco got a self-described "neighborly Cal-Italian eatery" called Local Kitchen & Wine Merchant. Motto: "Drink Global, Eat Local." My town, Palo Alto, offers a series of seven three-hour classes on cooking with California native plants.

As with religion and vegetarianism, there is a continuum of belief and practice among people who consider themselves serious about food, down to the basics of bread and butter. Foodies serve artisan bread, it goes without saying. But, horrors, we come upon restaurants serving salted butter. Worse, our friend Joanne is a fabulous cook, yet puts out a tub of margarine. She doesn't eat it, but her husband, an Australian immigrant, likes its spreadability. Back when cholesterol was found to be evil, my parents converted to margarine and we never saw butter again. In more recent years, my father invested in plastic vats of I Can't Believe It's Not Butter!

Ned and I are Plugra people. Plugra is a modestly priced, European-style unsalted butter from Kansas. We don't splurge on Kerrygold from Ireland and never churn our own. We are butter snobs, but reasonable and correct, just like everyone else who vehemently doesn't eat something. Just like everyone who drives a car, we know that we are reasonable and correct; it's the others who are jerks.

We live in Restriction Nation, where Lisa developed her own brand of "I don't eat." The seeds were planted in middle school, stayed underground through about half of high school, then grew into something awful.

eight

Roots of Anorexia
Lisa's Early Days and a Bit of History

On a warm evening in June 1999, we parents are planted in plastic folding chairs on the blacktop, our backs to the setting sun. Out on the grass, Lisa's fellow middle school graduates squint, the sun in their faces. Maybe this slight discomfort will be the final trial of three turbulent years. The ceremony, unlike the years, is short and sweet, unlike other graduations the parents have attended. Preschool and elementary school promotion ceremonies can be way too much ado, to the point that it scares the graduates out of participating. And once you've had to sit though a high school or college marathon recital of unfamiliar names, you know to bring something to read. But Jane Lathrop Stanford Middle School captures just the right tone: Congratulations, let's move on. Rambunctious kids have practiced the procession from auditorium to soccer field at least three times. Trussed in their serious clothes, with families and teachers assembled, they somehow get the gravity of the occasion.

Palo Alto, population just under 65,000, comes up third in the country in *Forbes* magazine's survey of small towns with the highest percentage of residents holding advanced degrees. At any graduation ceremony in town, at least half of the audience members are doctors, lawyers, researchers, and professors, possibly some Nobel Prize winners.

Lisa's ceremony started with students standing to say, "Welcome to our graduation!" in the several dozen languages spoken at home, from Arabic to Gujarati to Tagalog. Pacific Islander kids wore extraordinary fresh flower leis around their necks. Four students read brief essays about the meaning of middle school, a couple of teachers and administrators got up and sat down, having kept their comments brief, and we went to find our kids on the blacktop. Phew! File the hazardous early adolescent years as Done.

Later that month Lisa was going to Camp Tawonga, a liberal Jewish camp near Yosemite National Park and the one place, she always said, where she felt like she could be her real self. She and Jake had been going there since elementary school. At camp it was possible to feel both special and accepted, to express their creativity and be part of a group, to be somebody else the next year and still feel valued—a combination of needs that for Lisa would later find expression in anorexia. Home, especially when it's the same place since birth, isn't set up like that. Many kids rightly find Palo Alto complacent and materialistic. To parents and real estate agents, comfortable towns like ours, with good public schools and curbside recycling, are the Promised Land. Teens call it "Shallow Alto." Attention and praise are lavished on students for reasons that have nothing to do with the content of their character. Adolescents lacking superior talent, beauty, grades, or test scores are left to resolve their identity conflicts at their own risk, or so it often feels. Think you might want to play the piano or soccer? Be the best, the next Lang Lang or Ronaldinho, or why bother. If you aren't fortifying your résumé, you'll be left in the dust. Maybe homeless. Run the race, touch the bases, jump the hurdles, get into the right college, and then, much later, pause to think about who you really are and what you want in life.

Lisa was approaching high school, gateway to college, with trepidation and hope. Since fifth grade, she had continued to gain weight and beat herself up about it, but she'd gotten through. Toward the end of middle school, academics had gotten easier. She was getting her work done and finding creative outlets in art and theater classes, and she had a leading role in the musical *Damn Yankees*. We hadn't run into any emergency roadblocks. No excessive partying, drug abuse, or cutting, we were pretty certain. Ned and I even crossed eating disorders off the list of Catastrophic Expectations, thinking they would've shown up by now. Lisa was eager to try new things in high school, like choir and water polo.

lisa: As I entered high school, my weight was still slightly above average but had started to even out on its own. The baby fat was going away. In addition, I became three times as active as I had ever been, developing a new interest in the highly vigorous sport of water polo and joining the freshman junior varsity team. With the lengthy practices that challenged my athletic abilities and toned my body, I lost weight fairly quickly. Although I had grown up playing sports year-round, none could compare to the challenge of water polo. I followed each season's sport with a new one: water polo in the fall, soccer in the winter, swim team in the spring.

In middle school, I didn't have the ability to control portions. Two fish tacos, a couple of molasses chips, and then I just kept eating until I knew I'd had too much. I felt terrible, but I'd do it again the next day. Starting high school was scary—the rumor was that seniors got on the roof and threw things at freshmen—but also a fresh start. You could be somebody new.

My sophomore year, the women's water polo team hired two new coaches who decided to make strict cuts. I showed up for tryouts and went through two grueling weeks of all-day practices but did not make the team. At first I cried in disappointment, more from the effort I had put forth than any love of playing water polo. Then I signed up for AYSO league soccer. (The American Youth Soccer Organization focuses on positive coaching, not trophies and scholarships, and everyone gets to play.) I ended up playing soccer through the winter and returned to swimming in the spring.

Playing sports, I kept losing weight and toning my body. Suddenly I wasn't the safety-net friend that made everyone feel good about their own weight (they used to look skinny next to me), as I had been in middle school.

sheila: Middle school is supposed to ease a difficult passage—for anxious near-teenagers. But once they leave the campus shared with five-year-olds and enter the one with kids necking at the Halloween dance, the halls are ruled by teenagers, and they're sexier than ever.

By now kids have had years of experience with the Internet, video games, music, magazines, and movies selling sex, and their parents' attempts to turn back the tide. In an extensive study conducted in 2007, the American Psychological Association concluded that a sexualized society gives girls no good choices: "Teen girls are encouraged to look sexy, yet they know little about what it means to be sexual, to have sexual desires, and to make rational and responsible decisions about pleasure and risk within intimate relationships that acknowledge their own desires." Younger and younger girls are sex objects. Among the injurious consequences are body dissatisfaction and eating disorders.

Highly sexualized lyrics have only gotten grittier since the eighties, when Tipper Gore started complaining, the psychologists found. In magazines, nearly everything girls and women are encouraged to do in the line of self-improvement is geared toward gaining the attention of men. Saddest to me, forty years into feminism, were the new takes on attractiveness, such as revealing clothing designed for four- to eight-year-old girls and thongs in "tween" stores aimed at seven- to twelve-year-olds.

Greater exposure to thin-ideal media correlates with higher levels of dieting, exercising, and eating disorders. Here's a horrifying statistic: From 2002 to 2003, the number of girls eighteen years old and younger who got breast implants nearly tripled, from 3,872 to 11,326. The current ideal, in case you've missed it, is to be skinny with big breasts.

Girls feel pressure to look this way, but then teachers report that girls' "hypersexuality" strikes them as incompatible with academic achievement. So if you're smart and want to be popular, you want to look sexy, leading teachers to think you can't possibly have an intelligent thought in your head. What a setup.

lisa: My parents never shielded me from the reality of sex and sensuality, no beating around the bush stories of the birds and the bees or some other silly analogy other parents use, like, "The man parks his car in the woman's garage." During the news about Magic Johnson's HIV, I heard the word *sex* over and over on the car radio. I was seven and asked, "Mom, what's *sex*?" and, surprisingly, she answered bluntly in plain detail, "Well, sex is usually when a man sticks his penis in a woman's vagina."

"Oh . . ." I still wasn't quite sure what that meant or why people did that, but okay. I had seen some pretty explicit movies. Most of my friends were restricted to PG-13 or less, but I had watched R-rated movies, though my parents would warn that I might not like it, or have nightmares or sometimes Dad would somewhat panic and shout, "Close your eyes, Lisa!" Yet, something about sexual expression fascinated me, on TV and within my own body. Because my parents didn't draw a shield around the subject, I was able to develop my own opinion on sex and sexual expression, and I knew what was too mature for me.

In middle school, I learned terms such as *blow job*, *feeling up* and *feeling down*, *eating out*, and *69* although I had to have a friend explain how *69* stood for a sexual act.

I grew large breasts way before my time, at least before breasts were desirable to boys. And that was the problem; they were all still young boys, barely blossoming as I kicked off the puberty streak for girls.

In high school, I seemed to fade behind the other girls who had caught up with puberty, who had developed breasts and curves that the boys who were finally becoming "guys/men" began to desire. It wasn't until midway through my junior year that I felt at all sexually desirable, when I met my first boyfriend. By that time, the idea of waiting until I was in love for sex seemed unnecessary, and I had grown far too impatient through all the years of self-loathing and body hatred and being passed over by guy after guy. When I had someone to make out with and fool around in bed with I didn't want to wait. My parents had never pressed me to wait or made sex seem like it had to be something hugely important and dramatic. But sex brought on added pressure. With my boyfriend, after the first time, it became expected and I kept denying him, not foreplay, just sex, until he claimed we had moved too fast and dumped me. I started to feel as if sex meant little to most people.

As I got older it became a source of validation when everything else in my life seemed so chaotic. A touch from a guy or a look of desire my way made me feel wanted, and I gave in to what he wanted, but then was always left alone, with no phone calls, no word from him again. Then a new guy came along and this happened over and over. How stupid could I be? Or maybe I was just very lonesome and desperate for attention, even if only for a fleeting moment.

My mind got lost during sex, forgetting why I had gotten myself into that situation again. Somehow, I could never say no and the reality is that I feared if I did, they would physically hurt me. In sex ed and self-defense classes girls are taught to say no when they feel pressured, to resist sexual harassment and unwanted sexual requests. But when I wanted to say no I said nothing. My throat closed up, my mind went numb, and then it was too late.

In high school, I started smoking marijuana on weekends. We'd get high and eat, eat, eat. Everyone in Palo Alto went to this one donut shop, where you'd order one donut and get another for free. And one friend's parents were stoners, keeping all kinds of stoner food at their house. Bingeing was fun. I only smoked on weekends, and I kept exercising, so it didn't add weight, but when I got serious about restricting, the overeating had to stop. Therefore, I quit smoking pot. The allure of food grabbed me so strong that I had to throw my arms out in front of me and just say no to pot and thus no to overeating.

For years, I had no idea what hunger felt like, nor could I really recognize being full. I just felt the same all the time and ate, and ate, because food would never let me down. It was always there for me.

As a baby and young child I loved eating more than Dad, Mom, and Jake did, for sure. They may have loved food, but they understood their hunger and fullness cues, and when to stop.

I fit in perfectly with my family's vast and adventurous appetites, especially on restaurant review nights. But I grew so much bigger than my peers at the very point when it was crucial to fit in, or at least be able to pretend to fit in. I'm not sure what I weighed, but it didn't matter because I felt fat. When you're fat, you can't fake it. I had to choose between bonding with my family and fitting in with my peers, and as I was bad at both; all I felt was shame. And then I ate more.

I decided it was time for me to mold myself into what I saw as the ideal teenage female. I had to limit family meals and control my caloric intake, which meant that eating out could be dangerous. If I didn't know the ingredients and quantities put into each meal, I felt safer avoiding the restaurant altogether. As I became stricter and more motivated in my journey to my ideal body, time with my family significantly diminished.

No one thing happened to get me into anorexia. I got interested in the vegetarian diet and menu options, but not all at once. I exercised a few times at the gym. I started to feel a sense of control over my body, which increased when I cut down on carbohydrates. One of the trainers suggested, "No carbs after six." I added that to my growing list of restrictions.

For dinner I usually had a salad with chicken or tofu, light balsamic vinaigrette dressing, carrots, tomatoes, and some crumbled goat cheese. If my friends had pizza I either forced myself into allowing one slice, or I might scrape the vegetables and some cheese from the top and just eat that. I cut out fried foods, and limited sweets to twice a week. Then none at all. When all this started, I was eating three meals a day and an after-workout snack. Soon what little I was eating would only make up one meal. As my caloric intake decreased drastically, so did the number of statements about my body. People scrutinized me with some worry, dropping a few comments like, "Oh my god, Lisa, you have gotten so skinny!" But their observations and comments only furthered my desire to lose weight. If the public actually *saw* me as skinny then I felt I had to keep up that image. I sat alone during lunch at school, fearful of others' comments toward my limited food choices and fearful they might make me eat more.

I started checking out the pro-anorexia websites (dubbed "proana" online). Many of them had enticing introductions like, "Enter if you dare." I was so lonely. Here were pictures and stories of other girls who understood! That was the "thinspiration" section, and then they'd have diet and exercise tips, like this: Standing is better than sitting, walking is better than standing, running is better than walking, sprinting is better than running. It was stuff you could just incorporate into your day.

I made a point of turning down Mom's invitations to join them when dining out. I wondered if I hurt her feelings, or Dad's. When I did agree to go with Dad to the Afghan restaurant I used to love, I spent more time focused on the calories and quantity of my meal than enjoying the chance to be out with just Dad.

My fixation on achieving the ideal body overpowered my ability to remain an active member of my family.

sheila: In high school, Lisa started swearing off certain foods, then most of the restaurants I needed to review. She never was fat, but she felt that way, so it made no difference. Even if they had something for vegetarians, and a lot of my readers were vegetarians so I looked for those items, Lisa didn't want to come with us anyway. She was revolted by the smell of steak, frying oil, whatever else was off her list on any given day. The tightening self-control was squeezing out any sense of natural balance, that you could just experience food, not as an enemy or ally but just as plain food. We didn't expect a sixteen-year-old to make dining with us her top choice of activities. Still, when an all-vegan café opened in Palo Alto, I insisted that she had no excuse. The Bay Leaf Café was only three miles away and had a menu full of items she could eat.

As was often happening in Silicon Valley, techies with money had opened the Bay Leaf Café—bay for Bay Area, leaf for green environment. Two software engineers had stocked their little restaurant's cheerful blond wood shelves with books like *Eating to Save the Earth* and *The Mediterranean Vegan Kitchen*, and the menu was coded with full circles, half-circles, and three-quarter circles to indicate one hundred, fifty, or seventy-five percent organic for each item. I ordered a grilled portobello mushroom sandwich and an entrée involving brown rice, braised tofu, mushrooms, spinach, red onions, spring onions, and tomatoes in a sesame wine sauce. We missed the Mighty Carrot Roll, which turned out to be one of Bay Leaf's most popular items, but tasted the creamy carrot soup and the unfortunate soy cheesecake, frosted with strawberry jam.

Lisa took a few sullen bites of each dish and was ready to leave. I wasn't. I needed to get a better feel for this restaurant. She snapped at me for trying to make her eat too much, then got up and left me sitting there, like a jilted lover.

Later we learned that teenagers hide eating disorders behind a vegetarian diet. They may initially become vegetarians out of concerns about global warming and cruelty to animals, or disgust with what their parents eat and keep in the house. Maybe the family doesn't eat fried food or red meat; teenagers will find something else to repudiate. They need to find their wings, and the kitchen is a convenient place to practice fluttering. Rejecting Mom and Dad's food puts the growing space between you on the table every day. Plenty of young vegetarians stay on the healthy side, but for teens, there are important, self-defining side benefits of exercising discipline and losing weight, feeling good about the former and getting praised for the latter. What's not to like about shunning meat, a win-win in terms of asserting yourself and saving the planet? Except for some unsettling odds: Vegetarian teens are twice as likely as their peers to diet frequently, four times as likely to diet intensively, and eight times as likely to abuse laxatives. These are all symptoms of eating disorders.

When Lisa started showing anorexic symptoms, Ned and I refused to believe it was more than another ripple of teenage turbulence. A storm we hadn't anticipated, a disease we had barely known even existed; we were certain it would fade away, its place taken by some other problem, and then another, the way they usually do. In my head I was hoping to hear a doctor say, "This is in the range of normal. Lots of kids act and feel this way."

Lisa was overexercising, skipping meals, restricting foods, hating her body overall, and obsessing over how certain body parts (thighs, legs, stomach) looked. We were clueless about the sexual activity, that Lisa's hunger for love and affection made her so vulnerable and exposed to harm. When I read the section she wrote above, I feel sick.

Ned and I finally acknowledged that Lisa's symptoms and behavior were problematic, and that she wasn't going to grow out of them, like a pair of shoes. We went into full librarian and journalist mode. Frantic for a book to help explain Lisa's eating problems, I kept coming back to Carolyn Costin's *Your Dieting Daughter: Is She Starving for Attention?* It still sends one of the few clear signals in a cacophony of advice books. Costin spotlights what she calls "The Real Issues" that draw people to binge, purge, and restrict. They are what everyone wants:

To be heard

To fill up an emptiness

To rebel or escape

To control

To distract from pain

To gain attention

To have fun and entertainment

To have relationships

All that made sense, but was new to us and we had to figure out how these hungers applied in our family. We continued our research. It turns out that people with a family history of eating disorders are twelve times likelier to develop an eating disorder than the general population, but we had no such history.

I had plumped up in high school. Every afternoon I came home from school and arranged a sandwich, chips, and a milkshake on the kitchen table while I read the newspaper. Two and a half hours later, I'd eat dinner. During a fling with candy-making, my sister and I had learned that simply melting butter, brown sugar, and corn syrup in a pan makes chewy butterscotch, swirled around a spoon before it hardens. I'd have that or some ice cream and with my afternoon snack. And what do you know, I gained weight, adding to the usual miseries. An intuitive English teacher had told me not to worry so much, that for many girls high school is torture and real life begins in college. He was right. In college I found a place in the world, like Lisa had at camp. The love handles just went away.

In matters of dress, the sixties were far less constricting than previous and later eras for self-conscious young women. Instead of worshipping one appearance goddess, we could aim for hippie or preppie, or make it up as we went along. Twiggy, the five-feet-seven-inch, ninety-two-pound British supermodel was a blip on the horizon, having only just begun to inspire anorexics like Karen Carpenter worldwide. Miniskirts certainly looked better on thin bodies, but at the same time the women's movement was making inroads into attitudes about body acceptance and self-expression. Lots of women in Berkeley had stopped shaving their legs. Miniskirts were not hanging in their closets.

I had chosen UC Berkeley over UC Santa Cruz because of my hair. All through high school I straightened my hair and shellacked it with hairspray. I knew it would be even frizzier in coastal Santa Cruz, and I'd be miserable. I hadn't counted on the fog in Berkeley, which would have been a disaster had I stuck with the curl-free look. But liberation was at hand, bringing in Afros, ringlets, and every kind of natural and manufactured hairdo. Most different from what kids face now, in my era there was room to experiment with your appearance, and a middle ground.

As when Lisa was born a good eater, I was happy that she wasn't like me—an adolescent nerd. She had a much more active social life. She didn't choose her college based on her hair.

Those are the personal and social roots of Lisa's anorexia. There are historical roots as well.

Eating disorders, especially anorexia, are like what cancer was in my parents' generation, and what tuberculosis was to the generation before that: the shameful, mysterious disease that scares everyone to death. Until somebody discovers the real physical causes, these diseases are invested with all kinds of treacherous powers to invade and destroy. In 1881, one year before bacillus was discovered as the primary cause of tuberculosis, a standard medical text listed these causes of TB: "hereditary disposition, unfavorable climate, sedentary indoor life, defective ventilation, deficiency of light, depressing emotions." That is, getting tuberculosis was mostly your own fault. Patients absorbed the message that they must have done something to bring the disease on themselves. As do ED patients, and parents like me and Ned, today.

"Just have a cracker. A slice of apple. A carrot?" we have pleaded with Lisa. We don't say, but she hears, "How hard is that? Do you want to be sick? Just take a bite. You can start getting better right now!" We are like the people who don't get migraines and don't understand the sufferer lying in bed, wanting to die. We express sympathy but inwardly suspect malingering. Joan Didion describes this brilliantly: "Why not take a couple of aspirin," the unafflicted say from the doorway, or "I'd have a headache, too, spending a beautiful day like this inside with all the shades drawn."

Cancer used to be that way. Even if the patient hadn't done something to make her body turn against her, how could she have been so out of touch with her body not to know? But now, most cancers are not immediate death sentences and even smokers get sympathy when they become ill. The field opened for another disease to be the Next Big Fright. Enter eating disorders.

History has shown us a fair share of starvation as a form of protest, from Mahatma Gandhi to Irish nationalists in the modern era to suffragists and saints before that.

The medieval Saint Catherine pioneered what came to be known as "holy anorexia." She was the champion of the common people, that they should have a more intimate union with God. Fasting was a way open to everyone. For many years, the Divine Sacrament was Catherine's only food, for the eighty days from Lent to the Feast of the Ascension. Born in 1347, Catherine became a saint in 1970, but her story of sainthood is full of earthly parallels for teenage girls today. She chose anorexia as an adolescent, rebelling against the patriarchal medieval Catholic Church and against her family. Her domineering mother sought social status, while her father sat on the sidelines. They fit the anorexic family stereotype.

From Saint Catherine on, anorexics basically hungered for hunger itself, deprivation as fulfillment. At eighteen, Mollie Fancher parlayed a streetcar accident into worldwide fame as the "Brooklyn Enigma." From 1865 until her death fifty years later, she claimed to abstain from food. She did not leave her bedroom, but she did welcome visitors and sell her brand of wax flowers and embroidery, making a little profit on the ordeal. During the Victorian era, other "fasting girls" took to extremes the generally accepted notion that women should keep their appetites in severe lockdown. Living without food became a public spectacle, even inspiring circus sideshow fasts of "hunger artists" who earned their living by starving.

All of this is horrifying to someone who earns her living by eating.

lisa: When Mom first got the food critic job, I thought, "Great! I could be helpful!" As her name became more well-known in the food world, appearing numerous times a week in the paper and often in the news, I never thought, "Oh, my mom is a celebrity." Now, I brag about her work. People are still impressed and envious, and I get to gloat a little.

But I have to wonder how I could *not* have an eating disorder with a food-critiquing mom. She and I grew up in totally different times with different idealized women. For me, a woman's worth, as I learned too often in middle school, was equated to body type and image. Restricting food was a skill in itself, and many of my friends excelled. How could I be like them if food was so highly valued in my family? We were always eating out, trying one new restaurant after the other and always having to order a different meal so that Mom could try everything.

One afternoon during my senior year of high school I agreed to meet Mom for lunch, and it didn't work out well. I had whittled my weight down to 105 pounds, and subsisted mainly on lean protein, veggies, and fruit, in between hours of cardio-aerobic activity. She picked Café Borone, an outdoor, contemporary California cuisine hotspot next to Kepler's, a popular bookstore in Menlo Park. They had plenty of suitable menu items: fresh soups, large salads, and fancy sandwiches. But I freaked out. Nothing appealed to me—or rather nothing fit in the strictures of my rigid diet plan.

I know she just wanted to have a pleasant lunch with her daughter. But I stared at the menu board overhead, while she carefully made suggestions, and I said, "No! That will make me fat, Mom!" She read out one option after the other, and I rejected everything. I wanted to give up, and let my hunger wallow in my tiny stomach, but I could tell I was acting like a child. I settled on a grilled vegetable sandwich on wheat bread, which I broke apart around the edges. The sandwich was fine, but I left most of it on the plate. My love affair with food was over.

I had to break free and find my own image and value. As I got older I began to stray from family dinners and my formerly adventurous appetite. My weight dropped and I seemed to become more noticeable to those who before had never or rarely acknowledged my presence. Words like "fit" and "thin" joined in their compliments of my body. I knew my assistance with Mom's job was done. No longer could I go along for the ride, because each restaurant visit would be a surefire sabotage. Of course I can't deny that avoiding eating out presented me with much less exciting and overall fun meals, but receiving praise about my body was better than a fancy restaurant meal. Even when praise turned into worry as I lost more weight, I only heard "skinny" or "thin" or "she exercises a lot," and I had to keep going.

For her first few years as a food critic, Mom celebrated in the company of an enthusiastic daughter, taking a relieved breath to not have one of those picky kids. But I gave her something far worse. I think that because of her job, shoving unnecessarily large meals in front of my curious young self, I never learned moderation. "Eat more. Try this," is what I heard. Never, "Stop."

nine

High School

While Lisa was restricting, refusing, and turning inward, I was enjoying my spin in the spotlight. Going from copy editor to restaurant critic was like joining a prominent restaurant as a dishwasher and working your way up to chef. At first you do essential work that nobody else wants to do, and then, poof, you're the star. You even have fans.

What great timing, this restaurant gig seemed at first. The kids were old enough that I could ease off Mommy Brain, school committees, and the family GPS, constantly tracking where everyone was or needed to be. Jake and Lisa were moving forward, on their way to college. Our bookcases reflected the transition. We had the usual *Get Out of My Life, But First Could You Drive Me and Cheryl to the Mall?: A Parent's Guide to the New Teenager* and *Reviving Ophelia: Saving the Selves of Adolescent Girls*. But these were sources read once and maybe picked up again, not studied and memorized, like *Your Baby's First Year*. I finally got rid of

Penelope Leach, T. Berry Brazelton, and Dr. Spock. Relying on their popular child-rearing books required swallowing a whiff of disdain, or pity, for mothers who worked outside the home. As if it were a lifestyle choice. Now our shelves were getting populated by life-affirming food writers like Elizabeth David, M.F.K. Fisher, and John Thorne, who planted the idea that you don't have to be a great chef, or even a good one, to enjoy cooking (your own food or someone else's).

We never went nuts about nutrition. White sugar, chocolate chips, Pepperidge Farm fish crackers, and the beloved Kraft Macaroni & Cheese all lived happily in our house. Jake and Lisa usually made better food choices than most of their peers, without being prohibited from enjoying the pizza and burger staples of the teen diet. Often, though, days went by when we didn't eat together as a family. Jake had lots of schoolwork. He and Lisa had been making their own lunches and doing their own laundry since fourth grade. We made sure they had something nourishing for breakfast, but our power over dinner was starting to disintegrate in the face of their activities, my job, and Ned's promotion to library management, upping his travel time and nighttime meetings. Only our two dogs could be sure of eating at the same hour every night.

During Lisa's first year in high school, she started to get interested in nutritional science, possibly as a career. Despite what was seething underneath, she understood what a body needed to grow and stay healthy. She took copious notes in Biology 1A:

Homeostasis and Systems Control
Which four tasks must be performed structurally and physiologically in order for an animal body to survive?

    a. Maintain conditions in the internal environment

    b. Acquire nutrients and raw materials, distribute throughout body

c. Protect against injury, virus, agents of disease

d. Reproduce & help nourish & protect new individuals

Why must homeostasis be maintained in an organism?

Homeostasis is the state of being balanced—stable operating condition. For an organism to survive, cells must be bathed in fluids.

Words about balance and nutrients went into her freshman notebook and, then, out of her life.

lisa: As my sophomore year wound down, I knew I needed to change my lifestyle. I had become all too comfortable gorging on super burritos and making late-night stops at the donut shop. I felt bombarded by diet ads and pictures of thin women, a mold I didn't fit. I was still playing "the chubby girl," overweight and undervalued. I wanted my peers to want to look like *me*, for once, to compliment my figure, and to be told by guys that I was pretty. I grew tired of feeling so average in every way (looks, academics, athletics, talent) and wanted to be better, if not "the best" at something.

As we lived no more than a three-minute walk from the YMCA, I decided to go to that gym after school. I'd never been attracted to the Y before, and at first I dragged myself there and vowed to come back every day. That's when the weight really started to fall off. All I had to do was thirty minutes of cardio daily and alter my diet a bit, and I started to develop a curvaceous yet lean figure. My friends praised my motivation and dedication. And, finally, I was being told I was skinny!

That summer, my friend Feyi introduced me to the Yogurt Stop, and it became my next obsession. There were plenty of frozen yogurt places in Palo Alto, but only the Yogurt Stop would do for me. It was way out of the way in Menlo Park, but had eight flavors to choose from daily, and the option of having two nonfat flavors swirled in harmony. I felt pleased with myself for getting this great deal: half the calories of ice cream for the same price. The Yogurt Stop took the dessert position on the shortlist of places where I would eat out, as the majority of frozen yogurt flavors came as fat free, some even sugar free and therefore low calorie. Even with the Atkins Diet taking off and fat-free/sugar-free labels appearing everywhere, there weren't many restaurants that worked for me. I couldn't eat Mexican anymore as everything seemed to shout out "starch" and "lard" and "massive caloric intake!" Italian was well-known to be an indulgent cuisine. American offered mainly burgers and fries and milkshakes. If I went out at all, it had to be a Japanese restaurant, where still I feared the unknown ingredients and additives and mainly had salad without dressing and a little teriyaki chicken, delicately pulling off any ounce of fat.

sheila: At first, Lisa's restrictions seemed weird but not red-alert worrisome. She was eating more healthily, happier with how her body was taking shape, and still active in soccer and choir. She was not pleased when I volunteered to chaperone the high school choir trip to New York City, which seemed like a great opportunity to hang around her and watch, without being in her face. As outstanding high school choirs bounced "The Battle Hymn of the Republic" off the walls of historic Riverside Church, choir director Bill Liberatore coached, "Altos and sopranos, I don't hear your entrance clearly. Please be aggressive on the attack." Amid the evening dews and damps, the sound was gorgeous. Liberatore also talked about the social responsibility of being in a large choir, and I wondered if Lisa was listening. More often, she seemed to be just mouthing the words. Liberatore had heard the buzz about a Broadway show in previews, so we got to see *The Producers* with Matthew Broderick and Nathan Lane, before the show broke records in box office receipts and Tony Awards. *The Producers* later became a touchstone for me and Lisa, a special moment we shared.

One afternoon while the students were practicing, I had the fun of introducing some fellow chaperones to Original Ray's Pizza and then to Zabar's temple of gastronomy. On a free afternoon, Lisa and I met a *Mercury News* friend in Brooklyn for coal-fired pizza at Grimaldi's. She'd agreed to do what I wanted—eat and visit—and then we'd do a little shopping along Fifth Avenue. Bribery. I bought time with her, and she got a few blouses.

Lisa had way more than enough clothes. She would weed her collection, selecting blouses she may never have worn, when we took boxes to Goodwill, but her room never lost its just-slept-in look. Wasn't this normal? Even the occasional whiff of rotting food wasn't out of the range of reason for teenagers.

I tried chaperoning one more time, when Lisa's soccer team went to a tournament in Las Vegas. Again the more adventurous parents deputized me to pick a restaurant. For something we really didn't have at home, we went to Red Square. The duded-up Russian food was less the attraction than the décor, a post-Communist May Day parade of hammers and sickles, and the vault of two hundred frozen vodkas for drinks with names like the Cuban Missile Crisis. Dinner was fun, but I had the feeling that, more so than the other kids didn't want their parents along, Lisa really didn't want me there.

lisa: I had soccer practice twice a week, which never wore me out. So, after practice I either went back to the gym or ran a few miles. I felt like a failure if I didn't burn at least eight hundred calories. I even left practice early to go to the gym. Occasionally I would cut class if I knew ahead of time that I would not be able to fit the gym in that day. Weight dripped off me like a melting ice cream cone. I had to have been losing three or more pounds a week but I never really weighed myself. I could just tell by how my previously flattering pants hung on my bony hips and sagged, barely nearing my tiny legs. I went from a healthy size 5 to a size 3 but wanted to be a 1, and then that turned into a 0 and even a 0 did not seem quite right. Eventually I got to 00.

My friends really noticed my efforts and complimented me, praised me, and even showed their jealousy. Some wondered how I spent so long at the gym. For a little while, I actually felt very pleased and content in my lean yet fit figure. At the start of my senior year I came back to school with such an obviously flat stomach and toned legs that I got even more praise. At that time I was actually eating well and balanced, exercising daily, and even starting to feel (kind of) pretty. Yet, internally, I still felt insufficient. I continued to dislike what I saw in the mirror. I took my lifestyle restrictions a step further: less food, more exercise, and this continued past my spring break until I had gone too far and couldn't go back. The energetic self I had created a few months prior became replaced by a lethargic and listless little girl.

I was extremely cold at night and tired all the time. I barely went out on the weekends because I had no energy after 10:00 p.m. Even when I did go to a party or somebody's house, my mind was elsewhere, focused on returning to my safety net at home and the audible rumblings coming from my belly. I turned down any invites that included food in the plans, which severely decreased my social life. Every weekend, my friends went to eat and hang out downtown, or to the nearby *taqueria*. If I did go out, I didn't eat. I hated the thought of anyone else seeing me eat as I assumed they were assessing each bite I took, examining my plate thinking how fat I was. I mean these were my friends and I knew in my right mind they *wanted* me to join them—sometimes begging—but my sick mind overpowered everything. I opted instead to remain at home to nurture my stringent meal plans. My friends and schoolmates were starting to notice how much weight I lost and many were concerned. Some would say they were afraid I was going to break if they touched me. Others, more in an effort to comfort me, said I was looking great and really skinny. I felt trapped in a conundrum. Was I really doing right by restricting and overexercising? I felt sick all the time, lethargic, and fatigued and yet I still received compliments. Now I look back and know these people were just trying to be nice and probably felt scared to say what they really thought: that I had become much too thin.

On the rare occasion that I went out to eat with Mom I often became upset, thinking she was going to force me to eat too much food.

sheila: Indeed, I did. But "force" to her was "ask" to me. As in, "Hmm, this looks good. Would you like to try the crispy boneless chicken with mango in a lemongrass-garlic sauce?"

"No! Crispy always means fried."

"Ah, how about . . ." I cast about, pathetically, for some food Lisa would accept. Lisa's restrictions had become set in cement, not quirks that we could wish away. As she moved into red-alert territory, Ned and I felt sick, not knowing where to find help. I have to admit that part of me was also annoyed. Here I had this great job that everyone else in the universe envied, and even Lisa still liked telling people about, but she was spitting on it. Of course I didn't expect her to want to go out with us a lot, but couldn't she enjoy it just a little? Even pretend to?

One of our descents into hell occurred in a stylish Malaysian-Singaporean-Thai restaurant. Lisa hadn't wanted to go, no surprise, but Banyan Garden would have lots of vegetarian dishes, salads, and stir-fries (more sauté than deep-fry), and I couldn't help pointing out, "You used to love this kind of food." Desperate to reignite the connection to happier times, I whined until she finally said okay. But I felt like my daughter was leaving the dock in a rickety little boat, and I was barely hanging on to the sides while she pulled away.

So that she would come with us this time, I didn't mention

where Banyan Garden was—across the bay, a thirty-minute drive if the rush-hour traffic wasn't too bad and there weren't any accidents. The location could have been a deal-breaker.

In the armpit of a gangly shopping center, "Banyan Garden hides its charms under a bushel of Chinese restaurants. Even its exterior looks darkly forbidding," my review would observe. But it often happens in Silicon Valley that good food lurks in ugly strip malls, where new immigrants are able to pay the rent. Banyan Garden's deep red interior gave it a touch of class, and the ambitious, hundred-item menu leaped from Roti Canai to Malaysia Bean Curd, String Beans, Lady Fingers, and Eggplant on to Fish Head Curry Casserole. Ordering was going to take a while.

"We try to satisfy all customers," the manager-owner told me when I called later to set up an appointment for the photographer. Jimmy Cheng had majored in hospitality management in college. Banyan Garden's owners were two Taiwanese Chinese, one Filipino Chinese, one Indonesian, and the Malaysian chef. They wanted to design a menu that appealed to those populations, their base, but also that didn't scare away novices, who in the long run would make or break the restaurant. Thus the very long menu and options like Curry Mix and Match (pick a curry and a meat, seafood, or vegetable). It was like a flowchart or an outline of your meal. Lisa allowed as how the mixed broccoli, green beans, and potatoes were nicely cooked, and bathed in the hot-sweet-sour flavors of Malaysian dry curry. But the Aromatic Chicken and the Siam Jumbo Prawns with Shell both turned out to be deep-fried. Lisa wouldn't touch them or their luscious sauces.

Part of my job was to evaluate the beverages, to determine whether they were appropriate for the menu. Banyan Garden had a brief but helpfully annotated beer and wine list, including two bargain-priced California gewürztraminers friendly to spicy foods and a pinot grigio noted for being especially good with noodle dishes. Ned and I tested a few of their wine suggestions and were studying the desserts when Lisa went to the bathroom for the second time.

She was gone for a long while. We continued talking about mango sticky rice, sweet potato tapioca, and the five flavors of ice cream. Lisa returned to the table, but before ordering, I went to the women's room, and then I had no stomach for dessert. There were two stalls. I considered just picking one, using it like a normal person would, and if I didn't notice anything, oh well, nothing happened. But I had to lift the seat, and yes, someone had vomited.

Lisa wasn't going to own up to it. She was already mad about the long drive, the dithering over what to order, having agreed to come in the first place. I looked around the restaurant and saw plenty of other suspects. It could have been any of the young women or one of the skinny young men, I decided to believe. Compounding my wishful thinking, I mentioned this incident in "A Daughter's Inner Battle," the 2003 story Lisa and I wrote for the *Mercury News*: "Lisa defiantly denied it was her. Today, she tells me the truth, and it is sometimes more than I want to know." That sentence should have read, "Sometimes she tells me the truth, and it is pretty much always more than I want to know."

The women's room at Banyan Garden became my private Gates of Hell. My stubborn innocence died there. It became such a bad memory, I wanted never to see that restaurant again. But three years later a colleague from another paper asked me to meet him for dinner at Banyan Garden, because he needed to review it. The restroom was just a restroom.

lisa: One day at the Y, while getting ready for the first round of my daily elliptical training sessions, I noticed *Shape* magazine. It spoke to me right away. Here were the answers on how to better "shape my life." And so, I got on my machine, plugged in my thirty

minutes, and dove into my new companion. My eyes quickly fixated on an article titled (as best as I can remember, but isn't it always something like this?) "Your Diet and Your Workout." This
article provided a meal plan coordinated to when one worked out.
Since I always exercised in the afternoon, my biggest meal of the
day should be lunch, and the ideal was a burrito with "the works."
By "the works" they meant a whole wheat tortilla, salsa (for all the
great vitamins), some guacamole (watching portion sizes as avocados are high in fat and calories), black beans, and perhaps some
chicken. Definitely skip the cheese. Get complex carbohydrates in
the morning and afternoon, and make sure to wait at least two
hours after completing a meal to exercise. Then, dinner should be
small, no more than 500 calories made up of mainly lean protein
and vegetables (trying to avoid starch!).

Soon I was reading a new magazine every month and trying to
tie in each new workout they gave me to my daily regime. When I
was already fairly deep into my eating disorder, I read an article on
the "butt-blasting diet." I had already starved away my butt, but it
didn't matter. The diet that was laid out on that page said to eat a
small breakfast, an apple for a snack, a lean turkey sandwich on
whole wheat without out any condiments (lettuce was okay), and
then a small dinner. Since I already exercised at least two hours a
day, following a strict plan like this would leave me with no spare
calories and an extreme weight loss.

By the end of junior year in the spring of 2002, my room was
filled with *Fitness* and *Shape* magazines. I still had trouble controlling my dessert intake, so I cut out sweets completely. But for the
most part I was feeling great and my parents were pleased with my
healthy lifestyle. I didn't eat carbs after 6:00 p.m., I stopped eating
altogether after 8:00 p.m., and I rarely went out with friends because usually they ate fast food or pizza.

Then, somehow, I stepped over the line.

sheila: When Lisa started taking her diet in a healthy direction, we were pleased. She read nutrition labels and watched the sizes of her portions. She cut out red meat and fried foods. Even when she reduced her diet mainly to vegetables with maybe a piece of grilled chicken or, more likely, tofu, I cast about for ways to make it work. She could help me seek out vegetarian options in restaurants.

On Mother's Day of Lisa's senior year, we met my parents, my aunt, and my cousin Peggy in San Francisco at the Hayes Street Grill, a well-known restaurant near Civic Center specializing in grilled fish, with lots of low-fat choices and about the best french fries in San Francisco. Lisa only ordered steamed broccoli, and picked at it. The rest of us pretended not to notice. Another day I dragged her to a popular local café that had lots of sandwiches listed on a chalkboard and a long line, so there was plenty of time to decide. We got to the front and still Lisa couldn't pick a sandwich. None of them had the lack of ingredients she was looking for.

Lisa no longer went to new restaurants with us, whether I was working or not. We would take too long and eat too much. As I write this now, I imagine for her it must've been something like being a small child in a restaurant waiting for the adults to finish their coffee. They finish a cup and you think, "Hooray! Finally we can get out of here!" But then the server comes by and refills the cup. It will be another five minutes, which might as well be hours. Especially when you didn't want to be there in the first place, and then, like Lisa, you felt like throwing up.

By this time Lisa could be so unpleasant that when I was working we didn't want her to come. She disapproved of most of what we ate. She barely ate meals with us at home, either, and we stopped begging. It was a rare meal that didn't start in tension and end in tears.

"Come eat with us."

"I won't eat what you're having."

"I know, but just sit down with us."

Strain for safe conversation, as if we are strangers.

"Want to try this?"

"You know I don't eat pork!"

"Aren't you still a little hungry?"

"I knew it! You're going to make me eat so much!"

As Lisa acted even weirder around food—measuring out one cup of steamed vegetables and three ounces of protein and calling that dinner—we grasped for explanations. She was facing college applications, leaving home, life-size decisions. Maybe that anxiety, combined with the crazy-quilt patterns of wealth and the pressures of Silicon Valley, had gotten to her. Or was it the dot-com downturn? She said she feared becoming homeless. Wasn't that just the way adolescents think, fantasizing that a personal catastrophe was about to happen at any moment?

In casting about for explanations of this craziness, we found lists. In source after source, lists of factors leading to anorexia range from emotional states to cultural pressures and genetic history. Parents and patients naturally skip the part that says, "It's not your fault!" and we measure our families against the items on the lists. The following causes, or triggers, turn up on a lot of lists:

1. American society's worship of ultra-thinness

2. An anorexic mother or sister

3. Parents who are highly focused on appearance, frequently go on diets, or make negative comments about their children's bodies

4. Trauma

5. A perfectionistic personality

6. A genetic predisposition to the disorder

And always, the suggestion at the end of these lists is to get help early.

So. We all face the societal pressures to be ultra-thin. I am not anorexic, and Lisa doesn't have a sister, but her brother is not anorexic. If Ned and I are highly focused on appearance, it is to wear jeans and T-shirts as often as possible, although we do clean up when the occasion demands it. Ned grumbles every day when putting on a coat and tie. I have one little black dress, and one blue-green crepe number that I inherited fifteen years ago from a fashion shoot. Henry David Thoreau is our mentor on this matter: "Beware of all enterprises that require new clothes."

What about frequent dieting? Me, never; Ned, maybe once a year when he cooks his cabbage soup. Negative comments about our children's bodies? I don't think so. Negative comments about the revealing clothes Lisa sometimes puts *on* her body? For sure. As for genetic predisposition, how would we know? There was no family history of eating disorders. That left trauma.

Lisa did have a short fuse, but was that because of a trauma? We always thought that was just Lisa. We looked up old school reports for clues.

"She can feel wounded with the slightest confrontation and aggressive exchange, and then will internalize and withdraw into herself," Lisa's wonderful first- and second-grade teacher, Jeannette Wei, wrote at the end of the first year. "It would be very important to help her verbalize and clarify her feelings. She lets go of those negative and depressing feelings when I talk over things with her, point out her erroneous perceptions, and help find some other solutions and options. In time, she will acquire more skills, grow in maturity, and be more able to handle those negative feelings."

At the end of second grade, Jeannette was pleased. "Lisa is a delightful and charming person, full of humor and wit. She is honest and fair, quick to own up to mistakes, and fast to forgive. . . . Now she has learned to present her point of view, use good reasoning power, win people to her side because she now can figure out what is good for all of us as a group. Now, isn't that mature for a child her age?!"

When the kids were young, we belonged to a babysitting co-op. Each family lived within a mile or two and had to be recommended by another family. There were constant phone calls and annual meetings, but the most serious problems ever mentioned were parents who consistently came home later than they'd promised. One night Lisa did run screaming to the car before we left. Did that mean more than "Stay home and play with me"? Lisa always wanted to be in the spotlight. As she had said one day in the kitchen, watching Ned and me kissing, "Stop falling in love, and pay attention to me!"

Now she was in high school and definitely not in the spotlight. Henry M. Gunn High School is known as the city's math-science school, and Lisa was having a lot of trouble in math and science and with taking timed tests. She agreed to an interview with the school psychologist, who wrote, "Lisa self-reports that she worries frequently and has mood swings during school." But a battery of tests was inconclusive. She did consistently well on reasoning tests, written expression, and listening comprehension, although "there is some indication of processing difficulties in the areas of attention and auditory processing especially verbal memory," the psychologist noted. She had a B-plus average. It was recommended that she work with a peer tutor in math and science and check out the adolescent counseling service that coordinated with the school, and that we consider a medical evaluation for auditory processing problems. Practical suggestions, all fulfilled. If there had been an underlying trauma, we were still missing it.

lisa: Early in junior year, we wrote essays for English class about our career aspirations. My eating habits had soured me on nutrition:

> While growing up I often found myself outnumbered three to one. My mom, dad, and brother all played club tennis whereas I never touched a racket, but rather found athletic excitement on the soccer field. My parents both graduated from UC Berkeley and my brother is currently studying architecture there, whereas I will not be joining them. School never came easy for me. My mom would often remind me when I was feeling down that I had a talent that many people struggle to possess. "You have a real understanding for people, Lisa, and you care about what they have to say. Though you might not get a grade for that, find a way to be able to let that talent show in your everyday life." She did not have to actually say the word, but I knew what her advice was adding up to: psychology. Yes, that was it. I wanted to be a psychologist.
>
> Throughout my childhood I yearned to be listened to. Because I struggled to express myself academically, my points of view often went unheard. At home I would try to make up for this by spilling my problems to my parents and not feeling satisfied until I thought that they had truly listened to me. I realized that other people also needed someone to lend an ear to them, and that's where I fit in. Too often people fall into a state of depression from feeling lost and without a mentor. Just knowing that there is a friend who cares can change someone's gloomy mood.
>
> Now that I knew I wanted to be a psychologist I had to practice scenarios of my everyday work life. Friends became patients as I sat in a chair and analyzed their pretend dramas. My friend Feyi became my most frequent patient as she had the most "problems." So

she would lie down on my black leather sofa and I would help her overcome her fears:

"Feyi, tell me what's on your mind."

"I'm crazy. I'm just a crazy person."

"No, Feyi, come on. Be serious. Pretend you have a real problem. I need to practice. I'm going to be a famous psychologist, you know."

"Yeah, yeah, okay, well . . . I think I'm being abducted by aliens."

"Oh, Feyi, you are crazy. I'm sending you to a mental hospital."

I thought about food constantly. It was affecting my schoolwork; it was affecting my life. My friends would say, "Try to focus on something other than food. Just don't think about it."

But there were no safe havens. If I went for a drive, I'd pass countless billboards plastered with food advertisements. Restaurants and coffee shops lined busy streets and the social avenues of every downtown. Everything I did and everywhere I went somehow involved food—or rather the daunting task of trying to avoid food—especially in my own house, which displays more cookbooks and culinary magazines than family pictures. I spent a lot of time in my room, but I wasn't safe there, either.

If I tried to read a book I'd get no further than five pages without getting fidgety in reaction to my stomach growling. I'd say to myself, "It wouldn't be so bad if I had an apple. I kind of want an apple . . . no, you can't have an apple yet, you need to read, just don't think about food!" And I would go back to my reading for a few minutes until my mind wandered back to the apple.

I felt weak for thinking about food and more so for wanting it, even a measly apple. And yet, the more I tried to avoid wanting the apple, the sharper the desire became. Sometimes I would make contracts with myself, like: "You can have this apple if you go for a walk." When I was exercising every day, I'd say, "Because you had this Pria bar, you can't have any more carbohydrates today *and* you have to add ten minutes to your cardio."

Exercise and food restriction had become more than an obsession. I focused all my time and energy on counting calories and burning off whatever I took in times two or even three. If I had allowed what I considered to be an extra serving of carbohydrates or an extra fruit, I burned it off. I purposefully flaked out on friends' invitations, making excuses of illness or too much homework and instead spent hours at the gym. On a soccer trip in Phoenix, I grew frustrated because of my limited playing time and broke down in the car. I felt I was being treated unfairly and was just as good as any of my teammates and that I should be playing more. My friend's mom tried to assure me that I was a vital member of the team and would probably play in the final. In truth, my frustration came from my fear that I wasn't getting as much exercise as everyone else, and I didn't have access to a gym. Even during regular soccer practices I never felt satisfied with two hours of training, because most of the time was spent listening rather than running. I made up for that lost exercise by either running three or four miles or going to the gym after practice.

Each day I took in maybe seven hundred calories at most and burned off about nine hundred. I stopped eating with my parents or with anyone else at all.

I knew I was hurting myself but I couldn't get out of it. I could barely stand, and my stomach was constantly growling. But I got used to the emptiness, and when I didn't hear a grumble I assumed I had gained weight. Finally, I was the thinnest among my friends. What I was doing was working.

sheila: Soon came another unpleasant surprise about eating disorders: Purging can take the form of excessive exercise, not just throwing up or taking laxatives. Inspect the bathroom all you want, but the purge may be going on at the gym. Lisa was spending hours a day at the gym. A sweet trainer at the Y, Rodney Aley, kept track of the exercise addicts. He would tell them, "You've been here for four hours. Go home."

One day he asked me if he could speak to Lisa about her weight. In the past year he had tried to keep her on a sensible workout regimen, but in January of her senior year, the doctor told her to stop exercising for a few months. She was too weak. Later, Rodney met me for herbal tea and told me that when Lisa came back to the Y, "I didn't recognize your daughter."

She didn't want to go to a therapist. Should we have forced her to go? If we forced her, would that tell her something was wrong with her? But something *was* wrong with her.

In March, she was accepted by several very good colleges, but it made no difference.

Spring is the season of thick college acceptance packets, thin rejection envelopes, and their online equivalents. When spring does its job, high school seniors and their parents are put out of their misery. In places like Palo Alto, everybody gets into college somewhere; we have excellent community colleges that take all high school graduates. And nobody dies if the first place is not the right place. This is a truth that teenagers rarely buy. Even the adults don't believe that things work out, at least until their first child makes it happen. I clung to the vision of the perfect launch, like a NASA spacecraft against blue skies in Cape Canaveral. They're off—phew! Over the years there was often more *stop* than *go*, but now our children are in new orbits and, hope against hope, they'll learn something useful and splash down in a safe harbor, with a job and a family and . . . are we getting ahead of ourselves? Of course we are. But high school is when we get way ahead of ourselves, pedaling to the rest area just over the next hill. The next hill is college, and, okay, as soon as they figure out what to major in, then they'll be set. Everyone can relax. Until they change majors or drop out for a while, and so on.

We chose to live in Palo Alto, where houses cost more because the public schools have always been good and test scores are phenomenal. When *Newsweek* and *US News & World Report* publish their annual rankings of high schools, Palo Alto Realtors carry them around like Bibles.

The year-end high school newspapers run maps showing where their graduates are headed. Seniors by then are pretty sick of the whole subject and might rather have one summer not to think about what college means: leaving home and growing up. This issue of the student newspaper is for the parents. We study their graduation maps for our own grades in child-rearing: How have I done raising my child to survive the competition? Our eyes go immediately to the little dots representing college-bound graduates who bunch up on the coasts: Stanford, UCLA, and UC Berkeley on the left, Ivies on the right.

Lisa most likely would have done better by starting at a community college. Living at home would have been torture, but that wasn't the deal-breaker. The deal-breaker was having to tell others and facing the polite condescension of her peers and their parents. ("Where are you going?" "Foothill." "Oh.") Her ego wasn't up for that. Lisa looked wounded when we mentioned the idea. Her brother went to Berkeley, her friends were going to Stanford and Princeton, and we were sending her to Foothill? We might as well have suggested the army.

From preschool through fifth grade, the headline had been: "Learn for the joy of discovery, not for competition. Attention, parents, this means you." But the minute kids hit middle school the clock on college acceptance starts ticking. Were you in the most advanced math class? Spanish was so ordinary (yet so vital in California). Would taking German or Japanese improve your prospects? And on it went, until that fat packet, or some packet, arrived in the mail and parents imagined wiping their hands in bittersweet victory and sighing, "My work here is through!"

Ned and I had a middling case of the college vapors. Products of the University of California, we nurture a populist bent against private schools. However, did we like having our kids attend the University of California? Yes. Did we want to say Lisa was going to the community college? Not so much. It would require explanation. We didn't know that later we would be explaining issues that really were hard to talk about.

Years ago, there was a bright girl in Jacob's kindergarten class. That summer after kindergarten, I ran into her mother, so naturally I asked which teacher her daughter had gotten for the fall. The mother named a kindergarten teacher. I said, "No, I mean next year," and she said, "Right, next year." And then I got it. She was repeating kindergarten. This poor woman must have faced off with lamebrains like me all summer long, and again when school started in the fall.

Recently I saw the mother of a boy who had been in Jacob's class since kindergarten. Her son had gone to the California Maritime Academy, a state college forty miles away but way off the status radar, and he'd become a ship captain. The long stretches away from home were hard, but he loved the work. "Can you imagine?" she said. "A Palo Alto kid is a ship captain!" He's happy, she's happy, except for all the explaining.

lisa: The week before spring break of my senior year of high school, I got my wisdom teeth out, which proved to be a huge mistake. I had already been seriously restricting my caloric intake and exercising for more than two hours a day, but I had not yet reached a weight so low that people gasped in shock. With oral surgery's heavy medications and giant chipmunk cheeks, I couldn't exercise at all. I compensated by barely eating. I picked at bananas and measured out one single cup of low-calorie, low-fat vegetable soup. I asked for sugar-free, nonfat pudding and when Dad returned home with regular (even though it was organic), I wouldn't touch it. I also requested organic one hundred percent juice and products like sugar-free angel-food-cake frozen yogurt, and left most of them untouched, too.

For spring break, my three best girlfriends and I drove to San Diego, where I began my love affair with starvation. More precisely, my day's menu was half a banana, one cup Special K cereal, and half a cup of nonfat milk, always leaving something in the bowl. Sometimes I'd pick at steamed tofu or nonfat yogurt in the evening.

One day as we all lay on our beach towels, letting the sun beam down hoping for a deep tan (I usually just burned), I stared into the sky while desperately attempting to keep a conversation going with my friends and trying to ignore the painful hunger in my stomach. Instead of the sound of waves crashing before us, my stomach crashed with gurgles and swishing of its own fluids and bile, waiting to be joined by food that was highly unlikely to come. After about three hours of fighting off my hunger, my closed eyes began to see sparks dancing before me like fireworks on the Fourth of July. I had to give in and eat *something*. It had been six hours since any of us had eaten, so Olivia and I walked over to the nearest street with stores, where five or six restaurants and delis lined up next to one another. They offered gyros, pizza, tacos and burritos, deli sandwiches made with sourdough rolls, and more pizza—all forbidden foods. Olivia and I kept walking. We looked and debated, and I turned down everything. Olivia remained patient with me; she knew she couldn't force me, but I'm sure she wanted to shout, "It's just food, Lisa, make a fucking choice. I'm hungry, too!" Finally we stumbled on a small ice cream shop that had a sign for smoothies. I gave in because that was probably my best and only option. Olivia suggested with some hopeful excitement, "Look, Lisa, they have mango. You love mango!" I needed no time to decide on this one, I knew the mango with banana and orange juice was my pick. However, hoping to be a good anorexic girl, I made one odd and I'm sure horribly annoying request: I asked the gal working the counter to leave out the frappé mix in order to reduce the sugar content. She looked at me in slight shock but tried politely not to say anything other than that my smoothie would be more ice than anything. I didn't care as long as I had less sugar and saved some calories. It was in fact quite icy and a little unenjoyable, but I pretended to be satisfied.

This scene occurred over and over again during that week of spring break. At a Chinese restaurant, the others enjoyed sharing dishes, while I picked at steamed tofu and broccoli without sauce, and at McDonald's, I just went to the bathroom. After a few days of this, I found it difficult to complete easy tasks. We stayed with my cousin and made him dinner on our last night. Or, the others did. I couldn't even boil water.

sheila: Three years earlier, Lisa had been the first one home to find Jacob's acceptance package from UC Berkeley, and she had been so excited she called me at the newspaper. I had to work that night. The gaming reporter, Mike Antonucci, and I were doing a story about the new Dave & Buster's, the Goliath of arcade restaurants. I was meeting Mike there, plus my panel of experts: a game-designer friend of ours and two of his sons. A long night of fried food, loud music, and shoot-'em-up games stood in my way of getting home to celebrate Jacob's getting into the school he most wanted. Lisa took up the challenge. She may have been a dorky freshman, but she was proud of her brother. She made dinner for the two of them. Ned also had to work that night.

When Lisa's turn came, there was no little sister to be excited for her. She had gotten into a couple of good schools and had been rejected by a couple, but she didn't much care. When the large envelope she was waiting for came on Saturday, March 1, 2003, Lisa was working out at the gym, as usual. I walked to the YMCA, carrying the packet from UC Santa Cruz and waited for Lisa outside. I waved as she walked out. She scrunched her eyes in the sun and flashed a look that said, "Why are you here? Who died?"

Our Big Nights

In a rational world, Lisa's college acceptances and her decision to attend UC Santa Cruz might have relieved some of the anxiety she was feeling, but they didn't seem to make a dent. She continued to overexercise and undereat. At the end of spring, she and I reached a chasm. On each side was an event each of us had been hoping for, envisioning, for years. And they were scheduled for the same weekend.

lisa: I couldn't sleep at night. I was scared to sleep on my back because my stomach would growl, so I rolled onto my side. Unlike other anorexics, I hated the emptiness. I liked having the willpower but I wanted to be able to go hungry without feeling or hearing it. My hips protruded so severely that lying on them for even a few minutes caused me to wake up sore and bruised. I was afraid to fall asleep, and helpless to find any way out.

My heart rate and blood pressure were dropping significantly due to malnutrition. My doctor told me to stop playing soccer and exercising. She referred me to a nutritionist. She noticed how tired and depressed I was, and asked if I wanted to try an antidepressant. I didn't.

My body contour changed frequently. I was bloated, so that it appeared I was gaining weight. I cried to one of my friends that the weight was coming on too fast, that I had to stay below 110, and she tried to reassure me that it was water retention. I started having nightmares in which voices mocked me and forced me to drink salad dressing and eat donuts.

sheila: "What should we do now?" Ned would ask. As a child Lisa had been so close to Ned. From his family, she inherited playfulness and warmth in addition to nearsightedness and body type. When she had something to work out in her mind, she often went to Ned. They shopped for food, planted vegetables, and cooked together. When he took a class in improvisation, she, as opposed to me and Jake, enthusiastically played games like Panel of Experts, in which you carry on as if you have special knowledge of some obscure topic. Now she had no interest in any subject but her weight.

When Ned said, "What should we do now?" I thought I should know. I'm the mother. Lisa called me at work many times a day, with some worry or complaint, often crying. Her eyes bothered her. Yes, her contact lenses had been rechecked two weeks ago, but now they didn't fit right. She needed to go to the optometrist again. Her stomach hurt, she was cold, her hair was falling out. Somebody said something she took as hurtful. She didn't stop ranting unless I interrupted, with a comment meant to be reassuring that often angered her, or said I had to call back later. In the office I tried to stay calm and productive, as around me people talked about the Iraq war, the mayor's shady dealings with a garbage company, our list of restaurants serving Mother's Day brunch. The newsroom looked like an insurance office, although a messy insurance office, just a sea of desks in cubicles. For any kind of privacy, I would bend over and duck under my desk, talking upside-down, very softly. That, too, would annoy Lisa.

Nobody in our house was sleeping. Many nights, Lisa brought a futon mattress into our room and curled up like a fetus, while Ned wandered from bed to the living room couch to the family room couch. The Himmels became regulars at the Safeway pharmacy window. Before this, Prozac had helped lift me out of chronic depression, which made a case that it might be something to consider for Lisa. When Lisa went to the family physician, Deirdre Stegman, she had lost too much weight and hadn't gotten her period in several months. Prozac was mentioned and refused, but Lisa liked Dr. Stegman, and agreed to see the psychologist she recommended. Several nudges later, Lisa went a few rounds with a psychiatrist. She rejected one medication after the other because it made her gain weight or feel "not herself." I hadn't wanted to take an antidepressant, either. Who would? But now that I was a poster child for better brain function through chemistry, I didn't hesitate to seek medications for heart-pounding panic and sleeplessness. Meanwhile, Ned discovered Ambien.

When I could sleep, my dreams were disaster movies, but waking hours at home were worse. Lisa was leaving a trail of garbage, gum wrappers, and water bottles all over the house. Asked to clean it up, she would explode. Who *was* this child?

Once she had loved company and watched old videotapes labeled "Family & Friends" until they fell apart. Now she stayed in her room when family and friends came over. It felt as if we'd lost Lisa to a cult or a coven of witches. We could see her, what was left of her, but not touch her. Ned asked, "What should we do now?" What I really wanted was an expert to move into our house and tell us all what to do.

• • •

Lisa's behavior took me back to my own teen years, not a time anybody revisits willingly. The trouble starts when your body changes from the way you've always known it to be. One day you're playing with Barbies, the next you're wrestling with bras and tampons. You likely put on a little weight with the curves—for me, more weight than curves. And just when your body goes out of control, how you look becomes essential to your being. Some fat is a normal part of adolescent development. But these days, nobody wants that part of being normal.

I went to UC Berkeley in 1968, a tumultuous time when many parents were directing their daughters somewhere safer. But Berkeley came up with so much real life that I needed a lot less comfort from food. By graduation I had grown happier, slimmer, and two inches taller.

Despite my heartening story, as a high school senior Lisa was sure her life was never going to get better, that whatever worked for me meant nothing to her, that she and I had little in common temperamentally or physically. At the time it was true, we were running on different tracks, though food was central to both. Now we were about to collide.

Prom was Saturday, May 3, 2003, in coastal Santa Cruz, the same weekend as the James Beard Foundation Awards, the food world's biggest honor, in New York. It didn't look like a problem, because I had no expectations of getting an award. We were just trying to make it day to day. The whole concept of looking forward, that good things could happen in the future, didn't fit in a house where one of the children was ill. We all had lost the ability to think ahead.

Except for the prom. For that, Lisa had plans.

lisa: I kept studying the pro-anorexia websites. Girls post their pictures and their weights. Many of them are fine and normal, but they call themselves fat and ugly. I felt this way, too. I absorbed their rules, like the Ten Commandments: Thou shalt not eat. Thou shalt remain thin. This is where I learned to use a toothbrush for purging instead of my fingers, and to eat lots of soft foods or to drink milk after a binge, to get more of the food out.

I can recall standing in front of my parents' full-length mirror in a white spaghetti-strap tank top, oversize sweatpants folded over three times at the top, with my twig-like arms drooping at my sides, hip bones sticking out, and staring at myself, saying, "This is good, right? I'm skinny—so skinny, and this is good?!" My head appeared too big on my extremely shrunken frame. Part of me wanted to believe I had reached something amazing with my new emaciated body and the other part of me knew I had landed in dangerous waters.

sheila: The family physician who diagnosed Lisa's anorexia also referred us to the HMO's nutrition department, which unlike psychopharmacology held a lot of interest for Lisa. She pored over food labels and diet plans, websites and magazines, and talked about becoming a nutritionist. Prom was four weeks away when Lisa and I went to her first appointment with Karen Astrachan, a clinical dietician who turned out to be a valuable resource even after Lisa stopped seeing her. Astrachan looks like Lisa wanted to look: trim figure, straight blond hair, attractive. Lisa didn't dismiss her as yet another adult who would never understand. In the dietician's office, Lisa said that her goal was to stay her current weight for the prom, to gain not one pound.

"After the prom, there will be something else," Astrachan warned, explaining that another event or reason to stay thin would always come up. She spoke knowledgably and convincingly, but without lecturing or talking down to a very sick teenager.

Astrachan was very likable and Lisa seemed to absorb some of what she said about nutrition. She piled up plastic models of various foods to demonstrate how much it would take to gain even one pound. As she told Lisa how she worked and that she didn't want Lisa to weigh herself, I thought, "Please, please let this be the person who breaks through."

lisa: I wanted to go to Karen. I thought she would tell me: "This is the way." My first question was how I could maintain my weight, especially with prom around the corner. I wanted an exact eating plan. I thought if I ate even a little bit more than I was currently eating, I'd gain weight. Karen said it takes 3,500 calories to gain a pound. She had a basket of toy food to show me: a slice of pizza, a tortilla, a piece of cheese, a bowl of rice, a piece of tofu, a chicken breast, a bowl of cereal, a banana, a piece of bread, a brownie, a scoop of ice cream. She said that she does not do eating plans, that it was my job to figure out what it was my body needed. She recommended that only she weigh me so I would not obsess. She said we would start slow, with added fats, since obviously they were my biggest fear.

I thought it would be easy enough, just six servings of added fats each day. But I couldn't do it. Adding a tablespoon of peanut butter or a slice of avocado seemed like so much to me.

It felt like all food was bad. I often found myself crying after finishing a sandwich or a small wrap. I was tired all the time and anxious. I was prescribed, with much resistance, Remeron, an antidepressant that would aid in sleep. However, it also increased my appetite. I had to check in with Dr. Stegman again to see if I would have to go on hormones since my estrogen level was getting low.

I knew I needed to gain weight and eat more, and yet I really didn't want to nor did I want it done artificially, with all these pills. In a way I felt cheated out of my chance to be thin, with doctors telling me I did not have the body type to support a low weight. I had spent the majority of my important preteen and high school years overweight and self-conscious and now I had finally seized control, able to be labeled in the "skinny" category. Why did it have to be taken away? I wanted to stay this weight and still be normal. But I didn't feel normal. All my focus on restricting calories and exercising in turn caused my attention span to be swarmed by thoughts of food. The less I ate, the more I thought about it. My mind was in a constant state of negotiation. I would try to study but the rumbling in my stomach grew louder and my mental debate worsened: "Should I have an apple? No. Be strong. Just finish this homework and then you can have an apple." But in the end I didn't do the homework or eat the apple.

I started having anxiety attacks, especially at the end of the day when my blood sugar was at its lowest. I constantly tried on certain clothes to make sure they were either still too big or fit a certain way. I checked my face in the mirror when it seemed bigger. I would complain to my parents that I was ballooning up. They would tell me I was crazy, and that I wasn't seeing things clearly. They would say, "What I see is a very skinny girl."

sheila: Did we really tell Lisa she was crazy? It's possible. We were not in the running for Parents of the Year.

With a year like ours, I hadn't even thought to look when the Beard nominations email went out. But my colleagues did, and there was my name, attached to the long-winded award category: Newspaper Feature Writing About Restaurants and/or Chefs with or without Recipes.

The James Beard awards are the Oscars of the food world. For chefs, cookbook authors, restaurant owners as well as food writers and TV show hosts, the Beards are the big leagues.

I was nominated for my story "Serve You Right: Caring for Diners Is a Learnable Art." I was proud of this story, which had grown out of an experience with good service one night with friends. The server had picked up on Diane's disappointment with her entrée, asked her about it, and taken care of it with absolute efficiency.

What struck me was how rarely this happens, unless you're in a very expensive restaurant, and even there, you can feel uncomfortably full of attention overkill. In good economies and bad, service is always the number one complaint among diners. I had heard so many horrors that I had to wonder how a restaurant ever got it right, so I went about asking owners, servers, and customers why they thought service, though so important, was mostly flubbed and what were the steps to correct that, for diners as well as restaurants. Bad service spoils the best food. The point was that diners want to feel that some hunger—for nourishment, hospitality, community, or entertainment—has been satisfied by the time they've paid for dinner.

The journalism awards were to be given at a banquet in New York City on Friday, May 2—the night before the prom.

lisa: The day Mike asked me to the prom, I happened to have one of my worst breakdowns so far. I hadn't expect to be asked. I had never been asked to any dance ever in my high school career. I had been to many dances, but I had either gone stag or with a group of friends.

Mike was in a band with my friend's boyfriend. I thought he was cute.

My last class of the day was physics, and for months I'd been having extreme difficulty holding it together for that hour. Whether because of six hours of various other draining classes, or low blood sugar, or just because it was physics, it had become my hour of doom. This day, I spent most of the class with my head buried in my arms, folded across the desk. My friend Gaelin did her best to talk me through, and when the class got let out, I felt like running to safety but could barely lift my head. All I could do was shuffle out, like a very old woman. I just wanted to go home, hoping to find some solace in front of the TV.

But Mike was waiting for me. Standing with his hands nervously tucked at his side, he called to me quietly, "Hey, Lisa . . . um, I wanted to ask you to the prom." He extended his hand, which held a single rose.

My eyes fixed on the rose for a second. It seemed so lonely and almost hopeless, like me. And yet, somehow endearing.

My mind was in so many places, it took some time to process his proposition. Finally I lifted my head enough to meet his eyes and slipped out a yes. Then, I don't know why, I fell into an awkward hug with him and whispered, "Thank you."

I drove home to tell Mom the good news.

sheila: How could I go to New York? Fly across the country for an award I had only a one-third chance of getting, dine like a celebrity, and gad about at cocktail parties? A month earlier I'd canceled a trip to Washington, DC, where Ned had a conference, because both of us couldn't be that far from Lisa at the same time. We hadn't even gone to visit nearby friends for a weekend. Canceling had been the right thing to do then, and maybe was the right thing now.

But how could I not go? I'd never been nominated before, and may never be again. Besides the journalism awards banquet, the rest of the weekend, through Monday night, offered chances to meet the luminaries of my field. And there were panel discussions at the renowned Institute of Culinary Education. *New York Times* writer R. W. Apple would be moderating an exchange with cookbook author Marion Cunningham, *Gourmet* editor Ruth Reichl, and Judith Jones, the editor who discovered Julia Child and Anne Frank. These legends of food writing do not pass through my town on their way to San Francisco.

The Monday night gala also has its legendary aspects. Like the Oscars, the Beards always run far too long. For years the food awards were held in a vertical ant colony, the Times Square Marriott Marquis. (In 2007 the fete moved to Lincoln Center.) Two thousand attendees warmed their auditorium seats for four hours, then streamed into another windowless ballroom, set up like the world's tastiest trade show. As a restaurant critic I had been a regional judge for the restaurant awards, which got me a ticket to the gala every year. This time, Ned could go, too.

If you want to go and you're not a member of the James Beard Foundation, no problem. What you get for $450 a head are fine wines matched to dishes made by world-famous chefs who stand there cooking and chatting. The food is fancy, but not necessarily the behavior. Go back for three servings of Hudson Valley Foie Gras with Caramelized Three-Pear Salad. Who's going to know? As at a theme park, strangers swap suggestions about which culinary ride is worth standing in line for, and which to skip. There are very few tables, and if you sit down you might miss something. The 2003 awards marked the centenary of James Beard's birth, with celebrity chefs including Daniel Boulud, Jacques Torres, Suzanne Goin, Jacques Pepin, and Andre Soltner. Wines would be poured by Cakebread, Far Niente, Domaine Drouin Oregon, and a dozen other top-notch wineries.

It would be fun. Are you allowed to have fun when your child is sick? Could there be circumstances that permit enthusiasm? Doubtful, but in thinking about it I remembered maxims of motherhood, such as: Children would always rather have you committing suicide in the next room than enjoying yourself away from them. And who can forget this one: You are only as happy as your most unhappy child. In the twenty-two years since our first child was born, the usual work-family conflicts had come up. Ned had a meeting so couldn't get to the daycare center by 5:30 when they closed, but I had a deadline. Jacob or Lisa was sick—whose work could be done at home or whose boss was more understanding of childcare issues? But now, Lisa was always sick. Ned and I had eliminated most everything in our lives other than work that wasn't about her care, but she wasn't getting any better.

How could I go to New York? Lisa was very fragile and the

prom was so important to her. I felt guilty about her whole life, way beyond the prom, that she had come to this sickness. I was also furious. All those years, focusing on the kids. In the past two years I'd done research, made appointments, stuck by Lisa's bedside, and instead of getting better she had turned our home into a forcefield of fear and dread. She didn't want to be sick. No one would choose to live this way. We know depression runs in the family, so certain genes stacked up against her, but the trigger wasn't obvious. What part of it was my fault? Did I not applaud enough when she needed it, or did I applaud too much and let her feel entitled to endless praise? My job surely didn't help; we talked about food all the time. Still, I felt manipulated and rotten for feeling that way. Children force us to be generous. No question, my kids made me a better person. But not perfect. If I didn't go to New York, I might file it at the top of my Sacrifices Made for Children list and hold it against Lisa forever. Ned was dying to go, too. For him, it was the Superbowl. We decided to change his ticket, so he could fly back Saturday to be there when Lisa got home from the prom. Jake and my cousin Peggy would be there till then.

lisa: During the weeks leading up to the prom, I still couldn't sleep. I kept setting goals for myself, like to be better by this date or try to eat an added fat with dinner, but every date passed and fats were left out. Prom was my new goal. Then Mom got this great news and I felt like shit. Her James Beard–award nomination meant she would have to fly to New York for a few days—and that just happened to be the same weekend as the prom. I didn't think I could do it.

Without her, how was I going to prepare for the biggest night I would have in a long, long time? Dad was going with her. I felt abandoned. Every mother loves to be there when her daughter goes off to her senior prom, and Dad was supposed to pep-talk my date to make sure he would treat me well and get me home safe. They weren't going to be there to take group pictures and hundreds of pictures of me, until I got sick of smiling and yelled, "That's enough! I'm leaving now!"

They weren't even going to be there to embarrass me.

sheila: I didn't even go to my high school prom. In 1968, I wasn't the only one in the country who skipped the prom. What with Vietnam War protests, the continuing Soviet nuclear threat, and the assassination that spring of Martin Luther King Jr., the prom seemed silly. But in my town, debutante balls were big deals and so was the prom. Two boys asked me to go. Two boys even nerdier than me, and I was the frizzy-haired editor of the school newspaper. No way was I going to be stuck for a very long evening in uncomfortable clothes with either of them. I'd rather stay home and watch *Rocky & Bullwinkle*, and would still today.

At some point in the evolution of social etiquette between Lisa's generation and mine, high school kids smartened up about proms. Now they go in groups, and their dates are often friends. During prom season, you see a lot of rented limos seating ten or twelve very dressed-up high school kids. They don't stand around with one person all night. Prom is still a very big deal, maybe even bigger because just about everybody goes. Rituals include pre-prom photo shoots and dinner for the parents, and intricately planned after-parties. Girls pour energy into hair and makeup, but the really big thing is the dress.

lisa: The dress I decided on was the only one that could really work with my body. My butt had been exercised into oblivion, and I had lost any sign of female curves. On one of many scouting trips to the mall, I found a black Jessica McClintock gown, with layers of lace and chiffon, and an empire waist decorated with a maroon rose on the right side. It ended just above my ankles. In the dressing room I discovered the dress had perfect "twirlability." For the short time I spent in that dress in that fitting room, I felt pretty.

But that was a month before the prom. I was supposed to be gaining weight. Would it still fit?

sheila: In the best of times, I am a terrible shopper. But that's only one of the Mom skills I flunked. Hair was another. My method is wash and let dry, while Lisa collected ribbons and barrettes, and wanted her hair twisted into a French braid. She had to show me what she was talking about. My ideas for Lisa's birthday parties lacked the pizzazz she sought, and I was not the soul of patience when other kids came over. Ned baked the cakes.

But by her teenage years, Lisa had either accepted my areas of incompetence or figured out how to maneuver me into position. For the prom, she wisely scoped out the mall on her own, so that I could come back with her, approve the dress, and pay. I even looked forward to it. We could spend a little time together outside the home battlefield, and the mall had a food court we could check out.

lisa: A mall is the worst place for someone with severe anxiety. It was like somebody had slipped me a psychedelic. As sleep-deprived as I was, with all the mall's sounds and colors, I felt detached from reality. I was overwhelmed by the crowds, and by the task at hand. I took Mom to the Jessica McClintock store, where I'd tried on the twirly dress. They didn't have my size anymore. I knew that Macy's carried Jessica McClintock, and they had the dress, but we could only find my size in a petite.

Now here's what I feel is a difference between my anorexia and many others'. I looked emaciated and many people assumed I weighed less than 90 pounds, but I still weighed 110. In most clothing brands I had dropped to a size 0 or a 1, but Jessica McClintock dresses seemed to run small.

We grabbed a size 4P and a 6P, and one other possible dress. I tried on the 4 first, which fit just fine although there would not be much room to grow. Not that I wanted to, but this seemed to be a concern of Mom's. I did a few sit-ups in the dressing room. The 6P allowed some room. I was scared of gaining weight before the prom, Mom was hoping that I would, and my friends tried to convince me that I wouldn't. I wanted the 4P to work, to verify my success at restricting and losing weight. We settled on the dress with room to grow in it.

For shoes, Mom actually picked out pink strappy sandals to match the rose on the dress—shoes with a four-inch heel!

We ate lunch in the food court, which was torture for me. Mom had to pick a place to review and wanted to try a shrimp shack or something along those lines, with a menu of clam chowder and fried fish. Yeah, right.

The only place I let myself agree on served salads and sandwiches, and I was able to find something I thought would be okay: salad with chicken and low-cal raspberry dressing. I thought I ate too much. Mom pushed me to eat more. Either way, the salad wasn't very good and I immediately felt fat and regretful and certain that the waist room on my dress now would be filled in.

sheila: Lisa and I had shopped together at the Valley Fair Center's Jessica McClintock store once before, a time I now remembered as impossibly happy, buying her a dress to wear as flower girl in my sister's wedding. She was four years old and everything about being a flower girl filled her with joy. Fourteen years later I waited in a chair for a sullen, sunken young woman to come out of the dressing room and model the dress she had already chosen. Lisa conferred with the saleswoman and found out her size wasn't in stock. They could get it from another store, but Lisa didn't want to wait. She didn't have a meltdown. Instead, she took me to Macy's, which had the right size and a shoe department where Lisa liked the shoes I picked out—a miracle.

At Victoria's Secret, Lisa tried on strapless bras while I went on an anthropological dig through sections of the store labeled Sexy Little Things and Bustiers & Merry Widows. And then I suggested lunch. The mall had recently expanded to accommodate a nine-hundred-seat food court, on the second floor near the stores most frequented by teenagers. It looks like a stone mountain lodge. I needed to check out some of the new eateries, and Lisa would have been the perfect companion—had she eaten. Instead we argued. Ivar's Seafood, Rubio's Tacos, no way. Finally she agreed to try California Crisp, which offered made-to-order salads and sandwiches. Lisa picked at her chopped salad and piece of grilled chicken breast, drizzling a fine mist of no-fat raspberry vinaigrette from its side dish. Her side of the table was an empty desert with one green oasis. My half was Mount Everest, piled with a bowl of minestrone soup, a turkey sandwich, a vegetarian panino, and a cheddar cheese–stuffed baked potato. Most of it came home for dinner.

lisa: My parents went to New York a few days before the prom, and I was left alone at home. My brother came home from Berkeley to stay with me, but he provided nothing more than a sleeping body on the couch in front of the TV with the History Channel turned on low. I don't know what my parents thought he was going to do. He had problems of his own, and taking care of his anorexic sister was not going to be his call to greatness.

My doctor had finally prescribed a sleeping pill. On Ambien I was awarded a few nights of six or seven hours of sleep, but it was barely enough to feel rested. I had developed astigmatism in one eye, so even on nights when I did get some sleep, I still had blurry vision. Wearing my glasses made me feel disconnected, but my contacts were very uncomfortable. I dreaded the idea of wearing glasses to the prom.

Thursday and Friday before the prom were two of my worst days. The Ambien had either stopped working, or I was too anxious about the prom and couldn't sleep. Sometimes on particularly bad nights Mom had even come into my room to sleep on my floor, like I was a child again, afraid of the dark. In a way I was afraid of the dark, and I had become afraid of my room. It had established itself as a doomed chamber, stripped of slumber. Sometimes having Mom there quieted my mind and I felt safe. But she was gone.

Thursday night I took two Ambien and woke up to a spinning room, falling out of bed as I was trying to get to the bathroom. I was so dizzy, I softly yelped: "Too much Ambien. It didn't work."

Friday was torture. I stayed home sick from school. At that point, my teachers knew I was going through something traumatic. They pardoned most of my absences. I don't remember much from that day except lying on the couch in the family room, staring at the wall and crying. I saw no way I could make it to the prom. And I don't think there could have been a way if Peggy hadn't shown up.

sheila: On the Friday before the journalism awards, I had my nails done, for probably the third time in my life. The technology had improved a lot from the old days of poking pointed sticks into cuticles. Now it was all about comfort, warmth, and massage. I stepped back onto Sixth Avenue with hot pink nails to jazz up my little black Ralph Lauren cocktail dress. We had a fabulous lunch at Le Bernardin, showcasing a James Beard Rising Star Chef nominee from the Bay Area.

Lisa called us in New York so many times that Ned and I still shudder when we hear that particular Nokia cell-phone tone. The pressure of the prom was too much. She hadn't been out late at night in months. She wasn't ready. She talked and talked, and whatever we said was either hideously stupid or just vapor, it didn't really exist. She would calm down and then call again. She behaved like our friend's elderly mother, who phoned thirty times a day.

Guilt doesn't come close to what we felt. We were unfit parents, betraying our child. Still, we told ourselves, she was not going to die. I was sure I would feel that level of danger in my bones, if only because I couldn't live the other way. We would find the key, turn it, and the real Lisa would come back. Like the scary night she got the croup as a baby and wheezed helplessly for breath, but Ned turned on the shower for steam, and soon she slept peacefully again. We just had to find the anorexia key.

That afternoon, I did my hair in the usual way: shower and let dry. I applied the usual traces of eyeliner, mascara, and lipstick. Ned said I looked great, and once again, I was happy to be going to a food event as a size 4, not 14. It is an undeniable source of envy to be a food writer, especially a restaurant reviewer, who doesn't look the part. We stayed with friends in New York, and took the subway to the Grand Hyatt Hotel, atop Grand Central Station, for the journalism awards.

The 2003 awards featured some of James Beard's favorite foods. Before sitting down to specialties of his home state, Oregon, we mingled and tasted what Beard called "doots," little dabs of food like truffle-scented popcorn and Depoe Bay Dungeness Crab Cakes with Red Pepper Coulis. I introduced myself to Ruth Reichl and gushed stupidly about her book, *Tender at the Bone*. Ned and I spoke with a charming gray-haired woman, and soon her daughter joined us. They turned out to be Perri Klass, the pediatrician author, and Sheila Solomon Klass. Three years later, they published a dual memoir, *Every Mother Is a Daughter: The Neverending Quest for Success, Inner Peace, and a Really Clean Kitchen*. It is a model of good humor and surprising aha moments for Lisa and me.

Newspaper Feature Writing About Restaurants and/or Chefs with or without Recipes came during the second course: Oven-Roasted Asparagus on a bed of Willamette Valley Fromage Blanc scented with Herbs and Black Truffle Oil, topped with Crispy Julienne Parsnips, accompanied by Willamette Valley Whole Cluster Pinot Noir 2001.

At the Beards, as at the Oscars, presenters announce the nominees and there's a second or two of paper rustling. Then they said, "And the winner is: 'Serve You Right' by Sheila Himmel!" I kissed Ned, walked to the front without tripping, and said a few words about the servers who do the hard work, just as a platoon of them reentered the ballroom, as if to illustrate my point. Foundation President Len Pickell helped drape the Olympics-type medal around my neck. At the front table, the mistress of ceremonies, an award-winning middle-aged TV and Broadway actress, looked anorexic.

Ned ate my asparagus and started in on the Kobe beef entrée while I headed out of the ballroom to call the West Coast, where it was 5:30 p.m. Lisa was home with Jake. When I told him about my award, he worked up a little enthusiasm, but his mind was on getting out of there, because he wasn't in great shape at that time, having trouble with school and depression. Being with Lisa was making him feel worse. Lisa barely had anything to say, except that my cousin Peggy was coming. She had been great with our kids since they were young. Holidays, birthdays, babysitting—Peggy was there. Maybe Peggy was the one person Lisa would allow to help her.

To share the moment with someone who cared, I called my editor.

lisa: Mom's cousin Peggy lived in San Francisco, and my family had always been close to her. Peggy carried the most nurturing instinct and warmth about her. At that time I was unaware that she knew I was anorexic. I thought that unless I flat-out told someone, they couldn't tell.

Peggy had offered to check in on me that weekend. When she

called and said she could come down, I accepted. When she and her yellow Labrador retriever, Martsi, arrived Friday night, my sunken, bloodshot eyes and unkempt appearance were enough to tell her how I was. Peggy suggested we go for a drive to calm my nerves. Instead of feeling sorry for me, she engaged me in conversation about school, rock climbing, and yoga. I had been meaning to try yoga. We talked about my date. She asked if I wanted to go to a café, but I wasn't ready to face a public space. I mentioned how much I missed exercising. I was an invalid and it wasn't because of a broken leg, which would eventually heal. I just wanted to pick up where I'd left off, get strength, and be active again. Maybe more moderated. Peggy told me I wasn't ready for exercise just yet but I would be soon.

Back at home, Peggy drew me a bath, like a young child needing supervision so she wouldn't drown in the shallow water. With the calming illumination of candles and soft music on the stereo, I let myself relax for the first time in months.

But a glimpse of my own body caught me off guard. I really hadn't looked at it, I mean *really* observed myself, in a long time. In the shower, and in a mirror, you can disconnect from what you see. But in the bath, that really is you. I looked like an arthritic old woman with these little sticks on either side. For the first time, I knew that I had become much too thin.

To this day I swear by Peggy's bath, because that night I slept. It didn't make up for three months of insomnia, but it was seven hours of pure slumber. Peggy made me breakfast, asked me how I felt, and for once my answer was a genuine "good."

What meant the most to me about having Peggy as a stand-in for Mom was the company to and from appointments. I had made appointments to get my hair and makeup done. At my makeover, the Clinique gals gawked over my long and curly eyelashes. They were annoyingly perky. The rest of me still ached with apprehension, but my face glowed with beauty and life.

After two hours in a chair, getting my hair pulled into ringlets, curls, buns, bobby pins, and a slight shimmer spray, I emerged in elegance. With every step of preparation I gained confidence that I would be making it to, and through, my prom.

All the girls were meeting at Gaelin's house for last-minute touchups, or rather freak-outs, of makeup, perfume, and nitpicky perfectionist rituals. Gaelin had become my safety net at school, especially since we had physics together. Other friends pulled away, but Gaelin would always check on me and keep me in the group. She'd say, "Come on, we're going to get coffee." Or "This is what we're doing today." Gaelin was very nurturing at a young age.

Peggy handed me over to Gaelin's parents, who also had become very supportive during my struggles. Her mother kept telling me I looked stunning, just like a princess.

Up in Gaelin's room, I sat on her bed, watching my girlfriends fight for the mirror, eyeliner in hand. I felt as ready as I was going to be. Except that my dress felt tighter than when I bought it. Had I gained weight? I was bloated, and I hadn't had a bowel movement in at least a week. In my right mind I knew it was constipation, but my right mind wasn't in charge.

Gaelin asked how I felt and I said, "My dress feels tight." She sighed and looked at me with reassurance, telling me, "It's okay." There had been many times Gaelin didn't know what to say, especially when I believed I had gotten bigger. Telling me I was crazy wouldn't work. "It's okay" was the best thing to say.

The guys had been scheduled to arrive fashionably late. I was nervous to see Mike. I thought he was cute and liked what I knew of him, but it did feel like I was going to prom with a stranger. I remembered to bring him a boutonniere, and he had a big corsage for me. It looked enormous on my bony wrist. Then there were group pictures and mothers checking the tailoring on rented tuxedoes, fixing collars, and pleading, "Honey, smile!" Only I didn't have a nagging mother or an out-of-it-yet-proud father. Where the hell are *my* parents? On the other side of the country, celebrating Mom's James Beard award. Why at this moment? All the other girls' parents were here.

We were lucky to have our prom on the Santa Cruz waterfront, at the Coconut Grove ballroom. But it meant a long limo ride. More time to be anxious, nervous, and searching for topics of conversation with Mike. Luckily we were in a big group.

That evening on the coast, the sky was depressingly gray and the winds harsh. Although it was a quick walk from the limo to the entrance of Coconut Grove, my body chilled right away.

We were herded into a crowded foyer and then up a steep staircase packed with glamorous, boisterous teens. I tried my best not to crumble into a heap of panic. I focused on my breathing, slow and steady. My coats of makeup acted as a shield. At least I looked pretty and put-together! Mike was nervous, too. Instead of trying to think up interesting topics and then having those awkward pauses, we listened to the crowd and blended in. I counted girls wearing the same dress.

I was hungry, as usual, but at the prom so was every girl around me. Girls rarely ate at all on prom day, for fear of last-minute bloating. Most girls' conversations focused on their hunger. You could hear, "I haven't eaten all day" all over the room. For once my hunger did not set me apart from the group.

At one point, Mike asked if I liked the food or if I'd had enough to eat. I said yes, which wasn't completely false. I had enough to my liking and felt satisfied enough to focus on other matters.

My close friends gawked over my entire presentation, and people I didn't know all that well complimented my look. On one of my anxiety trips to the bathroom, one of my favorite teachers, Mrs. Peters, stopped me and said, "Wow, Lisa, you look beautiful, just beautiful; like a princess."

sheila: While Lisa was accepting princess compliments, I was meeting friends for dinner and a concert at Carnegie Hall, still believing I would have a premonition of disaster. Our niece, a student at Barnard College, got Ned's treasured ticket to the Beard gala.

Before Ned boarded the subway to JFK, we made our traditional run to Essa Bagel on Third Avenue. Luckily it was a Saturday, when trains aren't so crowded, or he would have made lots of enemies with a large duffel bag of bagels in addition to a suitcase. We had fine-tuned this routine since our first trip together to New York in 1978 (a trip so fun that we decided to get married), so that bagels and corn rye bread retained their freshness through six hours in the air and at least four in ground transit:

1. Call ahead, so bagels are ready (and just baked) when you get there. Also, to ensure there's enough of each variety you want, especially pumpernickel.

2. Keep bagels in paper sacks, even if they're still hot and make the bag sweat, until you get back to the apartment or hotel and can spread them out on a table or bed.

3. When bagels are cool, pack in freezer bags. The bagel place provides bags and twist ties.

4. The minute you get home, store bagels in the freezer.

The family was in crisis, but we were carrying out the bagel ritual as always. We wouldn't have to eat bland Bay Area bagels for a long while. And Ned would be there whenever Lisa needed to come home from the prom.

lisa: We ended up staying at the prom almost until the last minute. Mike and I danced, my nerves calmed, my fears went away. I stayed awake through the ride home, but for once I was awake because I wanted to be. I wanted to soak up the minutes and internally celebrate my success. Back at Gaelin's house, her parents had prepared a spread of cookies, pizza, sodas, and fruit. At the first smell of food, everyone swarmed the kitchen.

I asked Gaelin's dad to drive me home. I'd had a really good time. I had the chance to end it on a good note. I wasn't ready for the after-dance party scene.

And Dad was coming home from New York sometime that night. If I left now he could still see me in my dress.

He was sleeping when I got there. I woke him up. I didn't want him missing the firsthand image of me still dressed in pure formal elegance.

sheila: Ned was sleeping, but not soundly. He heard the door open and there was a brand-new Lisa, glowing and beautiful. She told him all the highlights, from the moment Peggy got there, and how she had worried, and going to Gaelin's house, more worries. But it had all worked out. "For that night, anyway, it was as if she was better," Ned recalls. "I could just be the proud father. I remember not even thinking about what tomorrow would bring."

A year later, Ned and I went to a workshop for parents and caregivers of ED patients, and finally began to understand why anorexia and bulimia aren't a matter of willpower, that they distort rational thought. But at this point Ned kept saying things like, "You can do it if you try." He felt Lisa just needed to concentrate and focus on finishing high school. He got angry more easily than in the early stages of her illness. He still took her on walks around the block and listened to what was wrong with each antidepressant, why she couldn't go to school, how she couldn't sleep, and the scariest, when she talked about the voices in her head. But he felt betrayed. Lisa used to be on his team, a fun-loving Himmel. Now that she had defected to depression, he gladly let me take charge, and she rarely called him at work. The question "What should we do now?" stayed in my court. We argued, but held each other up. That we weren't alone was something to be thankful for. We couldn't imagine how single parents, or parents who dislike each other, dealt with serious diseases.

How do people learn to be parents when things come up that knock you to the ground and then the bottom falls away? When you don't sleep, but don't want to get out of bed because the day will only bring something worse than what had already happened?

But after the prom, Ned and I could breathe again. Lisa seemed to have enjoyed herself. I kept a constant alert system in my head— what the bad possibilities were in each situation and what we'd do. It hadn't come close to being needed.

Although none of us thought of this at the time, maybe we all did our best on prom night. Jake showed up. He didn't know what to say or do, he didn't want to make the situation worse, but he wanted to show support by just being there. The anguished parents got ourselves out of the picture, and brought in a loving person who wasn't drowning in the family drama. I can't imagine Lisa would have accepted the idea of a bath and candles from Ned or me. And maybe it was better that Ned and I weren't there to jump into action for Lisa, or fall apart with her. She accepted help but also drew on her own strength. Now she could look back on a wonderful evening and even look forward, to the possibility of others.

But soon, Lisa was hearing voices again.

College

Lisa would get better in college, Ned and I were telling ourselves. She needed to leave the nest, have a roommate, find classes that rekindled her mind. Getting out in the world would be so much better than staying home, torturing herself—she'd see that right away.

We didn't know how bad she'd gotten. We didn't want to look.

lisa: An entry from my journal, dated May 4, 2004:

I'm trying to sleep but a swarm of confusion comes in my mind.
I lie in the dark, scared of what will come the next day. Every
day is a battle with myself to see if I can make it. Every day I
fail. The hands that hold me are so strong, and the more I try
to break free the tighter their grip becomes. Just let go of me!
I'm so young yet I can already feel great desperation, questioning if my life is even worth it. It can be hard to wake up to the
mess that surrounds me. I hate feeling like I am not worth it,

like I am not allowed to enjoy my last bite, or my drink on a Friday night. I always have to somehow ruin it by self-mutilation—no cutting, just severe and repetitive bingeing and purging. I have never cut myself but I have thought about it, when all I want to do is feel pain, and know that I can still feel, that I am not completely numb.

My jaw is so sore from all the puking. I have pimples around my mouth, my hands and feet are swollen, my tummy pooches out from lack of electrolytes. But nothing stops me. I still find some sickening pleasure in releasing the food from my stomach, a grotesque rush.

sheila: One gorgeous spring evening I picked Lisa up at the dorm to review a recently rejuvenated Italian restaurant with a great view ("Dine with the sea lions") on the Santa Cruz Beach Boardwalk. Her roommate had moved out. Lisa's stuff now easily filled the closets, beds, and all the floor space. The garbage can was no match for its contents. This time, though, a greasy-haired guy in his mid- or late twenties was there, bent over Lisa's computer. They had met online. Of course they had. What could be more natural? I tried to act glad to meet him, and asked if he wanted to join us for dinner. As if, oh yes, my daughter always invites strangers to live with her and we're fine with it. I didn't want to act shocked and annoy Lisa before we even left the dorm. So I asked and he declined. Later I figured out that he wanted to keep a low profile in the dorm, since he wasn't supposed to be there, and Lisa was bringing food to him.

Hidden on a hill, the UC Santa Cruz campus scatters a dozen separate colleges over two thousand acres of redwood grove and native grasses. A sweeping cow pasture and some old barn buildings are all you can see as you approach the campus. To me it felt mysterious and a little scary, like Brigadoon, the mythical Scottish highland village with a dark secret. Brigadoon's inhabitants lived in the past and disappeared in the mist. When driving to meet Lisa on campus, I couldn't shake the fear that she might have disappeared in the fog. There was so little of her at this time.

Even when sitting next to me in the car, she really wasn't there. On the way to Carniglia's, I kept myself on a short leash of non-confrontational questions that bored us both. But we got there without a fight. On the boardwalk, we passed two women and their children, eating fried shrimp in paper cartoons while the women relived fond memories of coming there in high school. The boardwalk, being a hundred years old, is like that for a lot of people. It still has a wooden roller coaster, and now a website featuring "Millions of Memories" about the saltwater taffy and Fun House days.

The boardwalk wasn't remotely interesting to Lisa that day or any other. Nor were her classes. Bulimia took up so much of her time, and she wasn't alone. The National Women's Health Center estimates that on college campuses, up to eighty percent of women students have binged and purged. The physical and psychological effects are horrendous. Following is a list from www.bulimiasideffects.com, a site sponsored by a bulimia treatment center in California. The sponsor has a commercial interest in the subject, but the list is consistent with those of nonprofit agencies. The fact of a website with this address speaks to the ongoing scourge of bulimia.

PHYSICAL	PSYCHOLOGICAL
Esophageal problems	Out of control feelings
Vocal chord damage	Mood changes
Stomach ulcers	Avoidance of others
Osteoporosis	Constantly thinking about food

PHYSICAL	PSYCHOLOGICAL
Hair loss	Depression
Digestive problems	Anxiety
Decreased body temperature	Unable to eat with others
Irregular heartbeat	Poor body image
Elimination problems	
Dental damage	
Organ damage	
Vitamin and mineral deficiencies	
Enlarged salivary glands	
Dry skin	
Decreased bone density	
Menstrual dysfunction	
Hormone irregularities	
Insomnia	
Low red blood cell levels	
Weak muscles	
Immune system damage	

Other bulimia side effects include difficulty conceiving a child, a larger risk of miscarriage, and premature birth.

lisa: I read lists of the physical effects of bulimia over and over again. I don't really know why I did it. Maybe to scare myself, and it did scare me. I wasn't scanning the list casually, thinking, "esophagus tearing, dehydration, la-de-da, muscle cramps, yadda yadda, bloating, hmm . . . that's interesting." No, it wasn't like that at all.

I guess it's the same with alcoholics who are fully aware that their liver has gone to hell. There is an underlying issue that cannot be resolved by having the shit scared out of you with statistics. Bulimia is an addiction. I could not make it through a day without my drug. It wasn't that I binged and purged every day, but I was always thinking about it.

I was just not ready to leave home and go to college. I clung to the guidance of my parents, but they weren't there supplying me with fresh groceries, nor did I have someone to accommodate my specific dietary requests. I found it very difficult to go to classes, study, exercise for two hours a day, and remain on a restrictive, meager diet. There was a lot of homework, more exhausting reading than I had ever experienced. Introductory sociology could not compete with hunger pangs. I was always hungry, and being a hungry freshman in college, a foreigner on new ground, blew out my tightly controlled system. I binged, at first not frequently, maybe once or twice a week and always on Fridays.

I started throwing up to alleviate the pain of being full. But I had absolutely no privacy in the dorms so purging proved tricky. However, with practice I got good at it. After a month I was *really* good at it. Still, it took forever. I'd be in the bathroom for forty-five minutes trying to get everything out until I saw the semblance of something—a "marker" food—that I'd eaten to begin the binge.

Initially, my roommate and I had been close companions, what any college freshman would hope for, but by winter quarter she couldn't take me anymore.

I had come back to our room from one of my two-hour gym sessions when she told me that after I showered she wanted to talk to me. I knew it was going to be something about my horrible organizational skills or that I had done something to annoy her. Anyway, I showered quickly as the communal showers never offered much of a relaxing comfort, and came back to our room, quickly dressed, and sat down to hear what she had to say. Every time she had something to tell me, she tensed up and interlaced her fingers together, fidgeting.

"I don't know . . . but lately, like, I've been getting uncomfortable with how messy your side of the room is all the time and one time I stepped on a piece of gum and, like, and that just really got to me. I dunno, it's just that our lifestyles are so different. I mean it's not your fault or anything, but you go to bed way earlier than I do and when I come back I have to remember to be quiet. Then you get up earlier than me, which usually wakes me up. So, I'm thinking it would be best if I moved out. I mean I really like you as a person . . . but we just can't live together. Do you understand?"

I understood, but I wished she'd said how she was really feeling, like, "Well, it's just that you're a crazy bingeing-purging bulimic freak and I don't know how to live with you." She knew I was bulimic. I had told her flat-out, and how could anyone not know, watching me wolf down thousands of calories in five or ten minutes?

My bingeing and purging got worse. Often I was purging up to ten times a day. I was almost hospitalized during what had become a monthly visit to the student health center. The doctor ordered an EKG and warned me that if my results came back abnormal she had no hesitation about sending me to the hospital. I barely passed, but it was enough to keep me living where I was and how I was. What I don't understand is why I gained so much weight. Statistics say most bulimics are slightly underweight or of a normal weight. Sometimes, I did eat normal meals of dining hall food, and my body was holding on to every calorie it got.

Bulimia wasn't working, but anorexia was definitely harder. It took so much willpower to convince myself that I wasn't hungry, that food was the enemy, that I was strong for resisting. I made up excuses for why I couldn't go out with my friends to eat, because if I went with them I would spend the whole time being paranoid about what to eat and how many calories I was consuming. It was much easier just to decline, go to the gym, and come home to my safety foods. Looking back, I can't believe I survived on such bird food. I would make these terrible creations and convince myself that they were good. I trained my mind to disconnect from what I was eating and respond with "Mmm, yes, this is filling me up, this tastes good. Yes, a quarter cup of black beans over lettuce with carrots, tomatoes, and balsamic vinegar is delicious." Oh, and if I felt risky, I treated myself to a scoop of Soy Dream.

With bulimia I didn't have to avoid food *and* I could go out with my friends. I could order anything I wanted on the menu because it sounded good, tasted good, and was a comfort. If I wanted to have a slumber party and munch on candy and other "bad foods" I could do it. I could be as fucking bad as I wanted as long as I got rid of it. That's the catch—indulge and then purge. Indulge and I *must* purge. I didn't have to worry so much about not being able to go out, or making excuses to get to the gym, because really I could "burn off" the calories with purging. And it became this drug that is so addictive and almost thrilling. Eating is a rush. Actually no, eating is painful, I hated it and still do. But I also hated being hungry. I hated those pangs that mock me, that swirling of liquids in my stomach, the emptiness that just begs to be filled. So of course I felt forced to do something about it. Sure, I had a meager list of foods I didn't have to purge: a bowl of cereal, fruit, some bread, but even those can become objects to be thrown up in the porcelain goddess. I hated being full. I hated losing control. I hated the feeling of entering the dining hall alone, finding no one to sit with, and being left with that stupid enemy food. Just me and my mocking thoughts that I failed as an anorexic and now I am just a gruesome bulimic! The voice would go off in my head, growing louder and louder and demanding: *Purge it, Lisa, stick your fingers in farther, just GO, fuckin' GO, GO, GO, you little weakling, go!* And there it was; it came out, dinner, lunch, breakfast, everything, puked up in the toilet. It was gone, and I was safe. "I'm okay," I'd say to myself, then . . . take a deep breath, wash my face, head back to my room, collapse on my bed, and cry.

I've wondered what it would be like to die. How would people react? Who would be affected and why? Once that year I truly wanted to kill myself. I believe it was a Saturday in October, the month of my birthday, when I decided I needed to die or escape, somehow. I was reading statistics on the web about bulimia and anorexia when I came across Karen Carpenter and ipecac syrup. Ah, there was my solution, ipecac. I would go to the drugstore to buy ipecac and swallow it and let the poison work its way through my body until I started vomiting and I wasn't going to stop vomiting until I passed out. Looking back now, I'm not sure if I wanted it to kill me or just land me in the hospital. All I really cared about was escaping from my pain.

I put on the blue striped polo shirt I only wore after a binge, and my stretchy stone-washed American Eagle jeans, and sat alone in my fat clothes on the bus, staring out the window and seeing only the reflection of my tear-stained eyes. At the drugstore I went up and down each aisle that had anything to do with health products. I must have spent ten minutes just looking at laxatives. But I couldn't find ipecac, and I was far too embarrassed to ask. What would I say if the clerk asked why I needed it? Poison control? I left with a bottle of liquid Ex-Lax instead. I later found out ipecac syrup had been discontinued. I don't know if I was disappointed, but I wasn't relieved.

At first I liked the idea of not having a roommate. It was difficult sharing space with another person. Now I had two of everything:

closets, dressers, desks, and beds. All filled up quickly. My parents made a special trip over the hill to buy me a little TV set and pillows for the extra bed, so it could be a couch/guest bed. And I did seem to have quite a few guests. I even had a full band (Halifax) stay with me, which should have been a dream come true but they all had girlfriends. They did not know I was a bulimic, nor would I give them any reason to suspect. After the show we went to Taco Bell, where I sat and engaged in conversation but ate nothing. We came back to my dorm room, smoked a bowl, I took a sleeping pill, and we all dozed off.

I kept a steady supply of pot, which I got from this guy who lived in the lower quad. My friends came over quite often to smoke out, but they never stayed long. It should have been the perfect setup, having my own room. But the emptiness produced loneliness, and made even more space for my habits. I started bingeing more frequently, most often alone in my room. After about a month I stopped inviting people over and they stopped initiating meeting up.

My mini-fridge and microwave nestled in the far-left corner of my room. And so, during binges, I'd huddle in that corner, and stuff myself full of whatever I had. I tried not to buy unhealthy food, but that didn't even matter when it came time to binge. I usually started with cereal, and I'd keep pouring a little more in, never letting the bowl empty. When I started getting down to the last few bites, I'd pour in more milk, but if there was too much milk I'd have to pour in more cereal. This would continue until I got horribly bored and moved on to another food, something sweet and completely sinful such as cookies dipped in peanut butter.

I could almost precisely measure that my cereal binges could account for a serving of seven to ten bowls. One serving could also be seven to ten bowls of Trader Joe's Cinnamon Cat Cookies or Teddy Grahams, the kinds of cookies you can scoop and eat by the handful. It's like my hands were on their own—they just wouldn't stop grabbing cookies and plopping them in my cup of milk. During a binge I seemed to shut down completely. Eating was my way of filling up on emptiness. So there I was on many nights, eating cat cookies in milk with a spoon, completely shut off from my surroundings and myself. Eventually something would click—either something in my head or my body—and I was brought back to reality. Now came my moments of panic and guilt, confusion, disgust, and hatred for my body, for my actions, for losing control.

The only way out was to purge. If it was a weekend, throwing up in the bathroom was easy because if anyone walked in they would think I was throwing up from being drunk. If I wanted more privacy I left the building and hurried to the individual bathrooms by the dining hall. I'd turn on the faucet to drown out the sound of puking, as well as have a steady stream of liquid when I needed assistance with getting the food out.

I eventually purged mostly in my room for complete privacy. I'd take plastic or paper bags, sit in my chair holding the bag open with one hand, and using the other to purge. Then I'd casually take my trash to the Dumpsters outside, as if it was normal garbage.

For a few minutes I was acceptable to myself because I had gotten rid of my binge. But depression quickly rolled back in, burying me in a dark pit of solitude with no one to pull me out. I just cried and wanted to die. I was crying so hard my entire body hurt, and my lungs ached from vomiting and coughing and constant crying. I had no set suicidal plan, no knife, no gun, no jumping off a bridge. But I was alone and it would be easy to take a bottle of sleeping pills with alcohol. No one would find me for a while. I'd probably get some phone calls from my friends and parents but the only people that would get suspicious would be my parents. They'd probably get worried and keep calling and eventually come up to see if I was okay, and I still wouldn't answer their calls. Maybe they would find my resident assistant to let them in the room, explain the situation; that they had been calling for a few days and I hadn't called back and now they're worried and they knocked on the door but I didn't answer, and I still didn't answer their phone calls. I would be dead in my room, either on my bed because at least it was a comfortable place for misery, or on the floor in a pool of vomit. The R.A. would let them in my room and they would find me. Their lives would be shattered. Even my R.A would have been shocked. He liked me and enjoyed my company from time to time. News would spread quickly and everyone who knew me would be lost for words because they had no idea I was that depressed. And maybe they would start questioning themselves for not seeing the signs or asking questions when my cheeks were always puffy and I became less and less social. Perhaps that's what would have happened if I had killed myself, but I never could do it. Something kept me going, and I still don't really know what it is. Maybe my parents or a distant glimmer of hope.

sheila: Every few days we called Lisa, praying she would pick up, and when she didn't, counting the hours until she called back, or we'd call again and again. We were happy to hear her voice even if she snapped at us or complained about something we said or did, or didn't say or do. We could deal with her contempt better than her despair. Maybe it was time to take Lisa out of school and bring her home, but to what? We needed a plan. I called psychiatrists who had been recommended as experts in eating disorders. Some called back, but their practices were full. Some didn't even call back. Then I heard about the UCLA Eating Disorders Program, which had helped a young woman who sounded a lot like Lisa. The friend of a friend had a severely anorexic daughter who left college and went into treatment at UCLA, starting with several months in the locked neuropsychiatric facility. Her mother generously shared their ordeal and hopes. Their daughter was doing well in school again, and though she would always be aware of her eating disorder, she had her life back.

I called UCLA and got an appointment to meet with the director in two months. Lisa and Ned would fly to Los Angeles in July 2004. Ned had an idea that they could go out to lunch, even have fun.

lisa: An entry from my journal, dated May 2004:

I think I'm going into a treatment program for my eating disorder. The bulimia has gotten so bad, twice a day at least. It hurts so much to swallow. Basically the doctor said I couldn't continue this pattern before something fatal happens. I am desperate for more help, I don't feel safe in any place and I need a stronger form of security. I can't let this continue. I think I might leave school early, if I feel I can't pass for the next three weeks.

It's really time I put my health first, I don't know what to do anymore. I really need intense daily treatment. I want someone to be there as I eat, as I go about my day, guiding me and being there when I get scared or anxious or feel like I can't control myself. But I'm scared to go into a program because then I'd be around a bunch of people who are starving themselves. And I know they will see me as fat and I will feel ridiculously fat, and I'm scared I'll try starving myself and I'll end up getting worse and come home really thin, or still throwing up. But then it could also be the best thing that's happened to me. I guess I'll just have to see. But the most important thing in the world for me is that one day I can have babies. If this is preventing that in any way, then send me to treatment now. I need babies. Most of all I need my life back, I know that I am beautiful outside and inside so I need to stop ruining that and loving myself and every inch of my body.

Damn this crazy cycle. Well, if I go, I hope people will come visit me.

• • •

July 7, 2004

Tomorrow we'll see if this "camp" will help me get past my eating disorder and start anew. I don't know, maybe. It's all complicated, but I'm still here for some goddamn reason and I won't give up . . . there's something out there for me and I'm going to find it . . . yeah . . . I will.

Tomorrow [July 8, Dad's birthday] I'm meeting the director of the UCLA program for eating disorders. I'm supposed to (according my parents) have a laundry list of questions, but this is my only question: Will I get better and can I stop? I know no program is going to fix me, there is no magical solution. I didn't become bulimic overnight and it won't just go away because I'm in a hospital. I have to completely change my mind and convince myself that I am better than this and better off without it. I have moved on from being 104 pounds—yes, I was once 104 pounds, I was even as low as 95 pounds. Look at me now and you wouldn't believe it. But even 104 meant unhealthy, it meant no kids, it was too little.

sheila: When Lisa and Ned went to check out the eating disorders program at UCLA, they did not have a fun day revisiting Ned's favorite restaurants. It was Ned's birthday, July 2004, and they flew to Los Angeles in stony silence, then met the staff. Lisa found the director and the place very forbidding. Maybe she had been expecting summer camp, but by the time the UCLA facility had an opening at the end of August, going there would have required Lisa to miss a good portion of school. She refused to go, and then miraculously got better, even bringing love into her life.

We didn't know how much Lisa was aware of the long-term

consequences of eating disorders. We were just learning ourselves. I was starting to notice well-dressed women in their forties and fifties with very thin, brittle hair and missing teeth. In restaurants I'd watch them order a salad with vinegar as the dressing, and nibble on lettuce and a couple of raspberries. Sometimes I'd find out who they were, and a pattern emerged: accomplished professional, prominent in her field; very thin; insomniac; no children, often no spouse or lover.

lisa: Deep in my depression I doubted any man's ability to love me, but I was glad to be wrong. In the fall of my sophomore year I took a stimulating course on the history of jazz, and there I noticed a charming yet reserved gentleman who always sat by himself. I surprised myself with my assertiveness, and he was even more surprised, but we hit it off immediately.

From that class on, we sat together, discussed our lives, family, friends, goals, and ambitions. Scott began to drive me home from school, which led to our first date, at a popular Thai restaurant. My heart told me to be honest. As we lay together on his vinyl sofa, covered in dog hair, I confessed that I had struggles with eating disorders and although I worked every day to pull myself through, I did not consider myself recovered.

Scott's piercing cobalt eyes caught mine and for several moments we just embraced. He said he wanted me to be happy and healthy, and that his attraction to me went beyond physical attributes. He saw a genuine, good-hearted person. He met and was attracted to the real me. He trusted in me to gather my strength. Even though it was going to take time, he would be supportive while I regained a sense of independence. Most important, we discovered balance in each other, establishing a stable relationship based on love, some grief, anger, and sustaining companionship.

Yet even with my incredible relationship I still felt such extreme self-hatred, and most of it stemmed from my eating disorders. I wrote in my journal:

> I don't know how Scott finds me at all attractive. Every time he picks me up I want to enjoy the moment but I can't stop thinking I'm too heavy for him. I hear him breathing like he's lifting too many weights and as much as I wouldn't actually want to hear his truthful answer I ask, "Am I too heavy?" He always says no. I'm convinced he's lying. My stomach is supposed to be flat—not poochy. I'm too short to have thick thighs and wide hips. If Scott seems distant I think I've done something wrong. Maybe he's just stressed, but I assume it's me. He says no and I get frustrated because I think he's holding back.
>
> I hate myself for not resisting temptation and losing control. I hate myself for being out of shape and not pushing myself harder to lose weight. I hate that I can't work out for as long as I used to be able to, that I my chest hurts and when I sneeze I cough up mucus. At the moment I hate my body . . . No, actually I hate my body most of time. I feel repulsive and fat. I hate the way my thong stretches across my big thighs and behind. I hate my love handles. I hate how my saddlebags fold over my thong. I hate myself for eating cookies sometimes and craving sweets and liking cheese so much. I hate myself for caring so much.

Now, I realize, the love handles and saddlebags were only imagined, but at the time they felt real.

sheila: The first time we met Scott, he was down at the Santa Cruz Harbor, working for a fish wholesaler. Lisa was calling him her boyfriend, but we didn't know what that meant. Confronted with parents, this blond kid in rubber boots and a bloody apron was properly shy but not stand-offish, warming up when we expressed interest in seafood. When he offered us some soft-shell crabs, Ned and I thought, "How sweet. This guy could be a keeper."

Lisa and Scott fit immediately. He moved her stuff twice and then they moved into a studio apartment together, a feat that had to prove they were in love. He brought us lots more fresh fish, news of the seafood industry, and a heroic level of caring. How Lisa was just suddenly ready for a relationship, three months after nearly going into treatment for bulimia, we didn't get. But they were so in tune. She made soup for him when he was sick, introduced him to more exotic fare, and waited up for him when he had a long film project for his major. They moved to a one-bedroom apartment, acquired furniture and kitchenware, and sweet memories. Until it all fell apart again.

lisa: During my senior year, I began to feel the familiar intense loneliness return. I couldn't really put a reason behind the loneliness, and this time I wasn't actually alone. I had Scott, I had friends, I had a job. I baked and gave the cookies away. Trying to ignore the scent of fresh-baked morsels quickly encouraged the rebellious bulimic voice: "Eat a cookie, *do it*! You know you want it!" I refrained for what felt like forever but was most likely five minutes—until it was almost as if a sumo wrestler shoved me from behind, forcing a cookie down my throat. One bite and all sense of control disappeared. I felt so good to be so bad. Cookies broke so many of my anorexic rules: They're full of fat, white flour, butter, sugar, and chocolate. But that was okay, even if I ate five because that "fear" disappeared with a trip to the bathroom.

I was purging again and with the purging came depression. I was crying daily and suddenly. There was this intense loneliness inside and no matter what I tried to do to escape it just grew worse and I would start to cry. Then I'd tell myself to stop crying, that I am okay, and I'd get it together, but that just made me cry more. I felt sure that no one else was going through what I was, that I couldn't quit or recover from purging. There was a part of me inside that was always crying and reminding me of the horrible times I have suffered.

I became afraid of reliving my last semester of high school, when hunger kept me from sleeping and even if I did eat a satisfactory amount I was still too exhausted even to watch television. There were always noises in my stomach. Wherever I was, I was waiting to get through it. To do what? I had no idea. Thinking about it now, I understand why people commit suicide. I understand that intense sorrow and excruciating pain inside that no matter how hard you try to escape it, you can't. It won't go away, no one else can make it better. I once thought everyone would be better off with me dead, but I think I couldn't face suicide just as much as I couldn't face life. So I decided to stay stuck in the middle.

I was suffering every day from my bulimia, depression, loneliness, and intense pain inside, but I didn't give up.

twelve

Relapse Spring
Warning Signs Prompt Action

On Mother's Day 2007, Lisa was working at a store in Santa Cruz. Ned, Jake, my mother, and I went to see a play in Berkeley that afternoon, and Lisa met us for dinner. Though tired from standing all day and dealing with customers, and the long drive, she was cheerful and brought me a gift. We enjoyed seafood at a cool new restaurant. The second time Lisa went to the restroom, my mom asked, "Is she all right?"

I laughed. "Oh yes, she just has a small bladder! She always has to go a lot."

Two months later, Lisa had a breakdown.

There were signs, as there had been four years before, but none of them struck Ned or me as emergencies in themselves. That it was her senior year in college, and the previous disaster happened during her senior year in high school, had occurred to us. But she had come so far since then. She emerged on the other side of anorexia.

She got a job, was doing well in school, and lived with Scott, her wonderful boyfriend. Nobody wanted to go back to that horror, so how could it happen? Please, let the plague pass over our house this time. Maybe what we were seeing was just bits of backsliding that wouldn't stick. They would remind her of the worst time in her life, then she would bat them away.

At this point we were pretty familiar with the warning signs. Just about every book and website on eating disorders has a list of warning signs, but none of them was defintive. As with the possible side effects of medications, your experience may vary.

We've been reading and writing lists since we became parents, to help organize our thoughts and actions, and to draw comfort. Sometimes the lists and flowcharts telling you what's an emergency can lead you astray. A friend will never live down having whisked her baby to Urgent Care because of the white spots in his mouth, an alarming sign of thrush, a fungal infection. The spots were drops of breast milk. On the other hand, your child spikes a fever but doesn't have a stiff neck. Check the list. Okay, phew! Probably not meningitis. We print out lists, like Signs of Choking, and post them by the phone.

The warning signs of eating disorders can be trickier. There are so many possible symptoms, and they often describe feelings that aren't out of the range of normal, or they are open to wide inter-pretation. At the very well-respected site www.somethingfishy.org, there are thirty-two signs and symptoms of anorexia/bulimia, and eighteen for compulsive overeating/binge eating. Some are helpful, others not. Who doesn't, for example, occasionally "make self-defeating statements after food consumption"?

Parents might turn to page 21 in the book *Help Your Teenager Beat an Eating Disorder* by James Lock, MD, PhD, and Daniel Le Grange, PhD. There are two very specific lists. First are the heads-up signs, then the signs that mean it's time to call in an expert.

Warning Signs of the Development of an Eating Disorder

- Diet books

- Evidence of visiting pro-anorexia or eating disorder websites

- Sudden decision to become a vegetarian

- Increased picky eating, especially eating only "healthy foods"

- Always going to the bathroom immediately after eating

- Multiple showers in a day

- Unusual number of stomach flu episodes

- Skipping meals

- Large amounts of food missing

Act-Now Signs and Symptoms

- Fasting and skipping meals regularly

- Refusing to eat with the family

- Two skipped periods (in girls) in conjunction with weight loss

- Any binge eating episodes

- Any purging episodes

- Discovery of diet pills or laxatives

- Excessive exercise (more than an hour a day) and weight loss

- Persistent and unremitting refusal to eat nondiet foods

- Refusing to allow others to prepare foods

- Extreme calorie counting or portion control (weighing and measuring food amounts)

- Refusing to eat with friends

Our observations were limited to visits and phone calls, but in the spring of 2007, just before Lisa was to graduate from college, some of the most common warning signs were adding up.

1. Criticism of Other People's Eating Habits

Lisa started mentioning what she didn't like about what other people ate. She had done the same thing in high school, in great detail, when she'd gone overboard into the sea of nutritional facts and figures. But since then she had pretty much stayed on the positive, nurturing side of food. She introduced Scott to fresh produce and stir-fries, and they now had a kitchen stocked with quality utensils and cookware. She replaced Ned's ancient set of barbecue tools and gave me *The Essentials of Healthful Cooking*, to encourage me to cook a little more, now that I worked from home. She scouted out restaurants, selected places for her birthday dinners, and enthusiastically joined us when we went out for restaurant reviews. She called to talk about the great teriyaki chicken dinner she had made, and the one that flopped.

We always criticized food. Constructively, I like to think. It is my job and my nature, as well as Ned's, to tease out the details of good and bad meals. We encourage people to try new foods, although as a writer I keep in mind that what you eat is like how you pray: your own business. Not to be forced on others. Worship at Burger King or Chez Panisse, depending on your tastes, wallet, and personal needs. It may be that you need a mediocre Thai restaurant to stay open, because you like the owners and there's nowhere else to eat in your neighborhood. Just don't make me go there.

Around Christmas of Lisa's senior year, her tolerance of other people's tastes and needs started slipping. It was especially evident around food.

"Can you believe *this*?" she called to tell us. "They like casseroles made with cream of mushroom soup!" And after a holiday party she ranted, "There were five giant desserts for six people!

Everyone ate way too much and the leftovers were gross!" No kidding! Had she ever been to a holiday party? Except for that horrible anorexic time in high school, Lisa used to laugh at food quirks, like we did with my father's fondness for I Can't Believe It's Not Butter.

2. Overbuying Clothes

Lisa worked at O'Neill, where the employee discount allowed her to buy lots of clothes. There were mirrors everywhere, feeding a young woman's insecurity and self-consciousness. As she started losing weight that winter, she went to a consignment shop with clothes that had become too big for her. The rest she brought home, bags of them, for us to take to Goodwill. Sometimes we said, "No, you have to take them yourself," and "Isn't this the blouse you got last month?" But mostly, we cringed. I wondered, "Have we ever seen this jacket before, or these shoes? Does Lisa ever wear the same outfit twice?" And when I recognized a sweater, "Phew, she doesn't have clothing bulimia, if there is such a thing, which I don't want to know." Later I learned that overbuying clothes can be a way to fill up the emptiness inside.

3. Frequent Restroom Visits

During the three years since Lisa had started recovering, we were on alert, oversensitive, and ready to panic, as I assumed my mom had been on Mother's Day in the seafood restaurant. Just because Lisa went to the restroom a few times didn't mean she was bulimic. Young women check their appearance constantly. When she did this, we would worry about it until the next time we saw her or talked on the phone, when we could feel out her mood. Most often, through the spring, she'd have a funny story about a customer at O'Neill, or a progress report on her anthropology class, which meant, to us, that she was engaged in the world. Good, if true.

4. Disinterest in Old Friends

That spring, when Lisa came home, she made no effort to get in touch with old friends. She claimed they weren't interested.

She did go the YMCA. Rodney Aley, the Y trainer who had noticed Lisa overexercising in high school, had kept in touch with her. He noticed all the anorexics and exercise bulimics at the Y, and intervened when he could. He was especially sensitive because he had worked as an orderly at Stanford Hospital's ED unit, and he'd been close with a young woman who died. Lisa had a photo of Rodney on her wall. One day in May, Rodney was going to be in Santa Cruz visiting with his daughter. Lisa had told him to call. Now she didn't answer the phone, or even call him back. When Rodney asked me if Lisa was okay, I made excuses: "She must've been at work."

But when she was home one weekend and went to the Y, Rodney tried to talk to her. Later, he told me he could see the change in her eyes. She listened politely but he could tell she was thinking, "Get this jerk out of my face." She flashed the same look at me the day we went to the gym together and I said one round on the elliptical trainer was enough.

5. Overexercise

Earlier that year, Lisa had stopped going to the gym on campus. She said it was crowded and she had to wait too long, so she joined 24-Hour Fitness.

We argued: "The gym on campus is free. You have to pay for 24-Hour Fitness."

"I'm working thirty hours a week, I can afford it."

"We don't want you to work thirty hours a week. It's too much when you're in school full-time."

So far she was doing well enough in school. She said she didn't like to have free time, and this was a healthy way to fill it. Scott was working in San Francisco and was away a lot, and except for a handful of work friends, Lisa's social circle was tiny. Maybe joining a gym wasn't a sign of exercise mania.

6. Menstruation Stopped

Lisa's menstrual cycle had been erratic since her anorexia in high school. After getting her period back, she went on birth control pills for a while. When she started menstruating again regularly, she got severe cramps and heavy flows, and never resumed a dependable cycle. Then as she started losing weight again, her periods became lighter and less frequent. Alarmed, I encouraged her to eat better and go to the doctor. The latter she did. That spring, she went back on the pill.

7. Trouble Sleeping

Lisa's phone calls increased. Often she said, "I can't sleep." She called at two in the morning. We would put down the phone and she'd call again.

We sympathized, Ned more than I, since he knows what it's like not to sleep. We tried to think of concrete solutions, like a hot bath and cutting out coffee. We tried to be calm and supportive, understanding that it's natural to be anxious at this time of life, leaving college and going out into the world. Most everyone goes through something like this, we said. "It must be nerves. Let's just focus on finishing spring quarter." We helped with schoolwork where we could, coaching her through assignments, devising a schedule for studying.

8. Easily Upset, Mood Swings, Depression

A million little things happened, as they always do, until one put Lisa over the edge.

The previous summer, in July 2006, Lisa glowed as the flower girl at her cousin's wedding. Being older than the usual flower girl made it even more fun, getting a beautiful dress and having her hair done with the bridal party. It was a wonderful weekend in the wine country. Scott came, met the whole family, got the seal of approval. They were so sweet together.

Six months later, Lisa was calling with anxious worries that devolved into convoluted rants. Ned and I fell into the routine from when Lisa's eating disorders had surfaced in high school. One of us answered the phone, one stood by, gauging from the comments and facial expressions whether it would be constructive or confusing to join in. Spelling each other like this helped, saving strength for the next loop of complaints: "I have no friends." "My stomach hurts." "I tried (whatever we had suggested); it didn't help." She lost patience with a customer and was sent home from work.

Occasionally something good happened. She and Scott went out to dinner, she liked her classes, a customer at O'Neill appreciated her. We pounced: "See, it's not so bad! Look at all these good things in your life." Lisa couldn't summon the energy to sound convinced.

She had a plan: Go to summer school, keep working, finish up her degree in the fall. But she wanted to know what would come after that. She'd have a degree in American Studies, not computer science.

Who knew? Who ever knows? American Studies was a great major for a teacher or a counselor, and for other careers beyond our knowledge. Lisa had been promoted to shift manager at O'Neill and she could work there full-time for a while after graduation. Or get another job while figuring out what she really wanted to do. This is what Scott had done, and six months after graduation he got a job he loved, in the very competitive field he'd studied: film. They had worried that he might have to go to Los Angeles to break into the film industry. But this TV show needed a gofer and was based in San Francisco, and there would be some opportunities to help with camera work.

Scott drove back and forth most days, a three-hour commute. They planned to stay in their current apartment until Lisa finished school in June, and then find a place closer to San Francisco. They thought they had worked it out with their landlady that they could stay after the lease was up, and rent month to month until June. But in April, the landlady said they had to be out in two weeks.

Scott took it as an inconvenience, but Lisa took it as a stab in the back by their landlady, a personal affront. She flipped out.

One weekend in May, Ned helped Scott and his dad move into the new apartment. When Lisa came home from work, she was very tired. She hadn't been sleeping. As Ned drove away he watched Scott and Lisa walk back arm in arm, holding each other up.

Lisa struggled that spring with anxiety, hormonal swings, insomnia, undereating, overexercising, various and changing medications, and self-medication with marijuana. We don't know exactly what happened, but she unraveled. There were still unpacked boxes when we moved her stuff out of the apartment four months later, when Lisa's hospitalization made clear that she wasn't coming back.

Within a month of noticing Lisa's rising anxiety, we took action. Several actions. They were just the wrong actions. We encouraged Lisa to go back to the ED therapist she had made a little progress with during her sophomore year. At least they wouldn't be starting from scratch. We also insisted Lisa go to the student health center on campus, to see about medication. From one provider she got estrogen to restart her period, and from another doctor, drugs for anxiety and insomnia. While you're there, we said, ask about Prozac. This was the antidepressant that had helped Lisa untangle her destructive circular thinking.

It was a clean sweep of bad moves. She took Ambien too often, too late at night, so that even when she did sleep she was exhausted the following day. She was jittery and couldn't concentrate, which she thought was because of the Prozac. Her period did come back with the estrogen, but so did cramps and mood swings. But the worst was the ED therapist (see Chapter 15) who gave us a long scary speech on bipolar disorder and suicide. Lisa's many diagnoses had never included bipolar disorder. When we left, I had to think the bar to hang your therapist shingle on must be way too low in California. Lisa and I got to the car and agreed—she wasn't going back.

We were back in All Lisa All the Time mode: canceling, rescheduling, ears constantly to the phone. Ned and his best friend, David, get together once a year. It was to be the first weekend in June, in Portland, where David had a business meeting. I had a colonoscopy appointment that Friday. At first, the plan was that since Lisa didn't have Friday classes, she would drive me to the clinic and be home while I slept off the anesthesia. As the weekend drew near, and Lisa was still in school but very anxious, I asked a friend to drive. But what if something happened in the afternoon when I was out of it and Ned was in Portland? Ned canceled the trip. It was easier to reschedule than a colonoscopy.

Lisa was frantic about getting a final paper done. She had a solid idea, lots of notes and sources, but nothing in any kind of order. The paper counted for eighty percent of her grade. She liked this class and the teacher. One Saturday, Scott was working, so we drove to Santa Cruz to help her. We brought newspapers and books, stopped at a Chinese restaurant for takeout, and settled onto the porch while Lisa worked just inside. We couldn't get her to eat much, but like coaches, we helped her assemble supplies and map a plan. Go, Lisa! She started typing. And stopped. We checked, voiced encouragement, and listened for more typing. There was a little, then nothing, really nothing. She couldn't do it. She wasn't sleeping or eating, and she couldn't concentrate. She needed a doctor.

"Please, hon, you seem so sad," Ned said. "It seems like your brain isn't functioning. Maybe we should go to the hospital."

Lisa agreed. All of us felt a little hopeful at the nearby hospital, as medical professionals took over. Lisa even ate a sandwich there. After a couple of hours, she was deemed stable and discharged with a new prescription. Maybe a time-release sleeping pill would work better. To make sure, we brought her back to our house for a week.

She seemed a little better and had been back at the apartment for a few days when I called and she didn't answer the phone. My mind went immediately to the bottle of sleeping pills. I started driving to Santa Cruz, calling every few minutes, talking myself down, batting away horror. This can't be happening. This can't be happening. It takes almost an hour to drive to Santa Cruz. At last I got to the apartment complex, saw Lisa's car, ran up the concrete stairs, and rang the bell. No answer. No sound inside. Banged on the door. Called from my cell phone. Banged again. It was probably only a few minutes, and I was about to call 911 when she shuffled to the door. She'd been sleeping, deeply, that was all. Never mind, we were going to the doctor.

At the student health center, Lisa walked out a little clearer. Later she met several times with a very kind, experienced psychotherapist, and, again, seemed to make progress.

Ned and I had to make a decision. Again, it seemed we could choose our pleasure or Lisa's welfare, but this time my mom was involved. A year after my father died, my mother wanted to go on a cruise with my family and my sister's family. We couldn't find a time that worked for everyone, and Jake and Lisa had to be in school, so in mid-June Ned and I were going with her on a National Geographic cruise from Istanbul around the Black Sea. Then we would spend four days with friends in Paris. We would be gone almost three weeks.

As opposed to the James Beard awards in New York, this trip had no professional value. It was something my mom wanted, though, after many very tough years taking care of my dad. We'd been looking forward to it, too; it was our first trip in a very long time. Lisa isn't going to ruin this for everybody, Ned and I agreed. The world can't always stop for her. We were back to the question: What is manipulation and what is real need? And what good was it doing Lisa for us to be running to Santa Cruz?

Lisa agreed to let me meet with her and the student health center therapist. I was very impressed with her knowledge, attitude, and her rapport with Lisa. When she suggested residential treatment, though, it was a shock. She gave us a brochure for a facility that the school had had good results with, and the name of a local psychiatrist who specialized in eating disorders, for when Lisa returned to Santa Cruz. The glossy brochure showed healthy, earnest young women, writing in journals and conversing amid handsome Southwestern furnishings.

This place was in Arizona. At first, we thought no way. But Lisa would be safe there. This program had helped other students. Wasn't it worth a try? The average stay was six weeks. We could go to Europe and be back in time for the facility's Family Week.

Back in high school and early in college, Lisa had wanted to go to a hospital or residential treatment program. "I think that's the only thing that will help me," she had said, frustrated with the slow pace of weekly therapy and nutrition appointments. I suspect her vision of residential treatment had been one part summer camp, two parts health spa. Now that it was on offer, though, and we were in favor, she didn't want to go. But the facility's intake supervisor delivered a convincing spiel, including, "Making the decision to come here is a great sign that you want to get better." If only.

The packing list made clear this was no spa. Bring: alarm clock with no radio; one small cosmetics bag with no mirrors, toiletries in original containers with no glass (alcohol not one of the first three ingredients); conservative clothing including a one-piece swimsuit.

Do not bring: music, books, cell phone, sports equipment, iPod.

But Lisa did bring her iPod, we learned later. And a severely negative attitude.

thirteen

Fetishes and Talismans
Desperate Parents

When your child gets sick, it is such a reversal of the natural order that at first it seems cruel and wrong when the rest of the world goes on as before. How dare they? Desperate parents go into a defensive crouch, intent on beating back the threat to someone they would die for, mobilizing the rest of the family into the emergency. Between the illness, its treatment, and recovery, nothing else matters. We had to figure out how to accommodate the unwelcome new reality. Each step was like recovering from a stroke, laboriously figuring out a way to do something we used to do without thinking. Other steps, we found during Lisa's struggles, involved inventing little games, like fetishes, and collecting little objects, like talismans. It's surprising what can help when your mind goes into triage mode.

First, the practical. You have to get out of bed and go to work like everybody else, even if, like me, you work at home. Sounds obvious, but it's not so easy if you've spent the night imagining all the possible bad outcomes of your child's illness, and replaying missed opportunities that might have changed all this, except that you didn't know at the time, and you know it's not all your fault, you do your best as a parent, but it feels awful anyway, and there must've been something . . . and so on. Then, perhaps, a little sleep. This is when I wake up, sweating, momentarily wishing I just had a terrible nightmare.

Then you put in calls to doctors, hassle with insurance, visit the hospital if that's where your child is, eat and, too quickly, try to sleep again. You may need to practice some mental gymnastics. Push away thoughts of how long this horror could last or where it could lead, the worst that could happen or even the best. (Worse is okay, just not worst.) You must focus. Cut through your regular to-do lists, and all the well-meant advice and referrals. As with suggestions when you're job-hunting in a bad economy, tips about the treatment that worked for somebody's cousin can pan out, or they may be your friend's shot-in-the-dark attempt to stay connected. Which is a good thing, but there's only so much input a person can absorb.

It's game time, you're out on the field, and you may not win. You really may not win. But as kids learn in little pants and long socks on the soccer field: "So the referee made a bad call, your throat is sore, and it's starting to rain? Honey, this is what you signed up for. Play on."

We signed up to raise children. Oh, right, that means not just when they're darling infants or even surly teenagers, soiling the nest because they're about to leave. If they need us later in life we have to be there. We can argue about how young adults these days are so much less mature than we were, that we were self-sufficient at their age and they should be, too. But the world has changed. Adult children often spend some time living with their parents, and pediatricians sometimes see patients over the age of twenty-one.

There were times when Ned and I crumpled and wailed at home.

We snapped at each other, most often about household mainte-
nance, which got very slipshod.

Conversations went like this—attack and extended defense:

"You forgot to pay the utility bill."

"Me? Why is it always my job? I couldn't find it! Where did you
even put it? Who can find anything in this house!"

And the constant haranguing of whichever one of us talked to
the doctor and neglected to ask the critical follow-up questions,
such as: "How long until this medication works, if it's going to?
What the heck is PRN? Should we look into brain imaging?"

Occasionally we ran down the endless possibilities starting with
"if only" and "if not for" just to the edge of outright blaming each
other for this calamity. If only we had seen this coming. If not for
Ned's freaking out that Lisa would be like his sister. If not for my
family's heredity of depression. If only we were smarter, more tal-
ented, totally different people . . .

Lisa was hospitalized, was barely able to walk or feed herself. She
and Scott had planned to get an apartment closer to his job in San
Francisco once she finished school, but now that was hazy and the
Santa Cruz apartment was an extra expense. A friend at Scott's job
had a room in a house he could rent month to month for now.
When we explained the plan to Lisa, in all its rationality and tem-
porariness, she cut through the details and asked, very quietly, like
she'd lost the right to know, "But where will *I* live?"

No one could say. How awful is that. Our little airplane was
sputtering, with nowhere to land. But to Lisa we came up with
concrete possibilities: a halfway house for a while, home, Santa
Cruz, anyplace other than Santa Cruz. We'd figure it out. Don't
worry. We all love you. Please believe us, wrinkled and weary as we
are, as if we know. Lisa's question rebounded off every plan in our
minds: "But where will *I* live?"

Once Scott was able to negotiate with the landlord and find a new tenant, we drove down to get Lisa's clothes. Scott was stoic, packing and labeling boxes, as usual getting the job done, making it easier for us. He would get a storage unit for the furniture and cookware.

On the drive back, instead of "if only" we lapsed into a litany of how things could be worse. Not the unspeakably worst, but that she could have had an incurable disease. Or we could have been destitute, had no health insurance, hated each other, and been screaming about every little decision. At this point, we still had hope that one of the medications would kick in and Lisa would return to normal, a fantasy that struck us as funny because we are not optimists. Quite the opposite, and yet here we were again, the critic and the grump, playing the Glad Game. The name of the game comes from an early twentieth-century series of books, but we knew only the Disney version. In the 1960 movie *Pollyanna*, blond Hayley Mills is the poor but sunny orphan child who makes the best of all bad situations. The Glad Game was invented by her sainted father. When he wrote to a charity and asked if they could please send his daughter a doll at Christmas, there was a mix-up and instead of a doll they sent a set of child's crutches. She could be glad about getting the crutches, he said, *because she didn't need them*!

The Glad Game became the all-purpose fetish for me, especially. Ned was less into it. But when we hit bottom, I could say: "We're so lucky. Lisa's in the hospital and nobody can figure out what to do, but it's a world-class hospital and only three miles from our house!" And when we just needed a laugh: "We're glad that the hospital has such a nice cafeteria!"

Turn the Glad Game inside out and you have Catastrophic Expectations, our other go-to fetish. We found that you can dim their power just by writing them down.

Years ago, one of mine was: "The neighborhood teenagers drive too fast and will run over my children." Time passed and I re-checked the list. My children were teenagers themselves. Now there was real reason for worry. They were the drivers. They could run over somebody else's children.

More recently: "Lisa can't find work. She will be jobless, then homeless, then have needle-pocked arms and eat out of garbage cans." Am I really worried about a death spiral like this? Yes, but I try to put it on the shelf with global depression, war, climate change, and massive earthquake, all of which are happening or going to happen to some degree. What can I do to influence events or pre-pare for disaster? I support Lisa's treatment. I drive her, I listen, I build up a nest egg for her, I sign off every phone call with "I love you." The likelihood of the Catastrophic Expecation (hers and ours) that she ends up living on the street? Come on. Lisa is three courses away from graduating college. She is not refusing help nor using crystal meth. She's afraid of needles, for heavens' sake!

Many of us have always lived in fear of doing the wrong thing and causing irreparable harm. But when you become pregnant, the pos-sibility is real. The rational path is to prepare, study, learn, adapt.

I have never let go of Catastrophic Expectations. They don't cover what actually happens, we hope, but when your child is seri-ously ill, the sun may as well not come up in the morning. Angry mythical gods are laughing at you, bellowing: "You thought you could raise children and keep them safe? We've let you come this far, but now you're going to know the truth!" Having children forces you to concede that you're just one of the deeply flawed mortals, and now you have another life to protect. Whatever thought or action that may help is worth trying, including fetishes and talismans, to make her well again.

Ned and I also dove into our own little obsessions. He loves to study other cultures and plan trips. He planned a lot of fantasy trips during those years. For me, tennis became a bit of a fetish. I joined a league and welcomed the spring season of tournaments on TV, a mix of drama and hypnosis that can go on longer than a football game. Playing tennis, I might wear the lucky shorts, socks, sweat band. I might repeat a mantra in my head, like, "We are winners! Winners don't quit!" Most usefully, though, playing a sport reminds you that when a strategy or technique isn't working, don't keep using it. This is a useful rule in medicine.

We made deals, of course. Please make Lisa better, and we'll be much better people. We said "Lisa Himmel" for many years at the moment in the Sabbath service when congregants softly speak the names of those in need of healing. We talked with Lisa about places we'd go when she got better. Ned made up a game in the hospital called Improve with Improv, trying to remind Lisa of the fun they used to have with improvisational games, and watching the TV show *Whose Line Is It Anyway?* He'd pick up an object and invent its function, a game called Props. Then it would be Lisa's turn to make up a use for the spoon or stuffed animal. She could never do it.

We seriously considered nonconventional therapies. A neighbor recommended a faith healer, and we took the phone number but never called. We investigated a brain-imaging company in San Francisco that claimed success with eating disorders. More recent research has lent credence to this technique, because bulimics often show less activity among the neural pathways that help control impulsivity. But at the time, brain scanning for eating disorders wasn't widely known and we dropped the idea.

Instead, we went to Chimayo to collect "healing dirt."

Chimayo, New Mexico, is the little town between Santa Fe and Albuquerque some call the Lourdes of America. I was more than skeptical, but Ned loves to discover offbeat sites, even if they aren't about food. Lisa was starting her sophomore year of college, very lonely, bulimic, and depressed. We had escaped to Santa Fe for a couple of days, so why not check out the healing dirt.

Chimayo does not make a powerful first impression. You can

drive into town, but there is nowhere to park unless you are disabled or a souvenir vendor. The rest of us park in a field and walk a quarter-mile dirt path, along a chain-link fence full of fading flowers and photographs, like the makeshift memorials often posted on highways and railroad crossings where people have died. When we got closer to the fence, we could see that there were also lots of crosses made from twigs. They were little shrines for beloved family, from wrinkled patriarchs to heartbreakingly happy-looking children.

As the modest adobe church came into view, I had to look at Ned and ask, "We drove two hours for *this?*" Except for people sitting on the ground selling religious items, Chimayo looked like a very small Southwestern theme park in its off-season.

With a handful of elderly people, we entered El Santuario. Daylight poked through one unceremonial window, so that at first it was hard to see what was there, but there wasn't much. Wooden benches, candles, a simple altar, a total lack of grandeur. To the side was a room with crutches, no longer needed. The small back room held the healing dirt, in a round pit in the ground. Everyone seemed to understand that we were allowed to scoop out a little, but there was no sign, no guard, and no explanation of the dirt's holiness.

We took our turn, filling a small plastic medicine bottle, and stood there for a few minutes to make sure we weren't missing anything about the Lourdes of America.

At home, we gave some dirt to Lisa, and saved some for ourselves. Lisa carried hers around in her purse for a while, and I have to say, that time coincided with her getting a lot better. Within months she got the job at O'Neill, got more interested in school, met Scott, and moved into a much better living situation. That is why we keep our holy dirt in the medicine cabinet, just in case. We also bought silver earrings from a Native American vendor on the sidewalk around the square in Santa Fe. She told us the symbols meant healing for Lisa and peace for me.

That was the start of the collection of oddments. Anything that mentioned healing, we latched onto. A friend of Ned's gave Lisa a clear, smooth stone with an angel in it. On a trip to Israel, we bought a keychain in the shape of a hand, the Kabbalah version of warding off the evil eye.

A friend studying Japanese calligraphy made a beautiful painting using pictograms saying: "Out of pain, joy is born." We had to have it.

fourteen

Treatment Centers and Their Aftermath

If a friend or family member wants to visit a patient at Stanford Hospital's eating disorders ward for adolescents, first they have to know it isn't at Stanford. These patients, up to fifteen at a time, are housed at El Camino Hospital, ten miles away. You can't just walk in. It is a locked facility, with evening visiting hours. When researching this book, during the time Lisa was in college and doing well, I asked if there was a standard tour for parents that I could join. There isn't. Individual tours are by appointment only.

Here there are girls, mostly in their teens but some as young as eight, in wheelchairs with intravenous tubes, bent over and drawn, as in a nursing home. At a distance, they could be grandmothers. Most of the patients have anorexia, which is harder to conceal than bulimia. They are little skeletons, with flat hair and bad skin, some with downy body hair. It seems to me that anorexia attacks the body somewhat like progeria, the rare disease that also strikes in childhood or young adulthood, causing premature aging. Initially, the Stanford adolescent patients are "on beds," which means bed rest, until their medical stability is established. One patient sits on her bed with a heart monitor and a portable commode.

The schedule features a pet visiting service twice a month and theater groups twice a month. Otherwise, from 7:30 a.m. to 11:00 p.m. the schedule, at least on paper, has a narcoleptic sameness. Vital signs are taken eight times a day. Patients are weighed, without their being able to see, each morning. Nurses wear pagers connected to patients with bad heart rhythms.

Patients stay from two weeks to two months. A teacher from the Mountain View School District works with them on weekdays from 10:15 a.m. to 11:45 a.m.

Parents of younger patients may request that they not mix with the older patients, justifiably fearful that they'll get new ideas about starving themselves. Some of the patients' identities are confidential. As at celebrity hospitals, if people call for them and the caller isn't on the approved list, nobody will let on that they're here.

When I visited in March 2007, the ED patients ranged from eleven to nineteen years old, but staff had been seeing an increase in eight- and nine-year-olds. About one in ten was a boy. A sizeable minority comes through twice, and there's handful of what in hospital lingo are called "frequent fliers."

Three months later, all of this research went from my notebook to my gut, when Lisa's eating disorders landed her in another locked ward, and she became one of the young women who looked very old.

But first, we made a detour, with the forbidden iPod, to Arizona.

Lisa and I took the one-hour flight to Phoenix, she in sullen resignation, me trying to lighten the mood with talk of what we'd do when we all got back together. I brought food. Before we got off the plane, I had Lisa give me her iPod, which wasn't allowed at the center. At the baggage claim, the center's driver met us and scooped Lisa and her duffel bag into an industrial-size van in the adjoining parking structure. It took maybe five minutes from hello. Suddenly the van was driving away, with Lisa the only passenger, and her head barely visible. I had kissed her and told her I loved her, so many people loved her, reassured her that her life would get better, but now I wanted her back. Maybe it would help if she heard all of that one more time. I stood in the garage and studied the parking space where they'd just been. I tried to tell myself what I'd just told Lisa, that things would get better. This place would help her.

Back inside the airport, I had a book and two hours till my flight home. Ah, I could have music, I remembered, since I had Lisa's iPod. But I didn't. It wasn't in my purse or pockets or the bag of food I'd brought. I raced back to the baggage claim, then to the helpdesk, security, and the Southwest Airlines counter, to see if anyone had turned in the iPod. They hadn't. I left our phone number at each place. Later we found out that Lisa had snuck it back into her purse. Deceitfulness is also one of the warning signs of eating disorders.

lisa: As soon as we arrived, I knew someone had made a grave mistake. The brochure had deceived me and all other patients. The small converted bed-and-breakfast ranch secluded in the desert was less a comforting home away from home than a small prison where all my necessities would be taken away or monitored. That meant shampoo, toothpaste, razors, anything with alcohol in the first three ingredients, my iPod, and my backpack. The therapist also took away the book I'd brought, because it was about a young woman and too closely related to eating disorders. I wasn't *that* bad off. Anyone who saw me wouldn't have guessed I had an eating disorder, right? I weighed 104 pounds, not big, but not starving by any means. Granted my body was shaking as they tried to take my blood pressure and heart rate, and a blond Kirsten Dunst look-alike demanded, "Hold still!" After my vitals and EKG were completed, the insurance coordinator came in and greeted me with a cheerful yet seemingly insincere smile. "Hi, Lisa, welcome to the center. I'm Susan." She extended her hand. "I hope you got here okay? Now it's time for lunch!" I tried to answer: "Oh, I already ate . . ." She grabbed my arm and led me to the office, which was really a large portable building.

For some reason this irritated me, that the office wasn't even a *real* office. It seemed unprofessional. Again, I wanted out. I had eaten breakfast on the plane with Mom. So, okay, breakfast had consisted of a banana, a bag of Total cereal, and a cup of coffee. Still, I doubted any of the other girls had had breakfast or anything else to eat before their arrival. Susan presented me with a paper plate containing my lunch. I stared at two croissant-like fluffs of dough sandwiching ham and cheese. I immediately scowled and said, "I don't *eat* ham." Susan stared at me in disappointment. She asked, "Now, is that an eating disordered behavior or is it religious?" I paused. I had not eaten ham since I was fourteen and saw the movie *Babe*. I felt sorry for that poor innocent pig and declared that my relationship with any pig product was over. "It's for religious reasons," I said. "I'm Jewish, I keep kosher." My first hour at a treatment center and already I was lying to avoid food.

"Oh well, okay. I am so sorry, we did not have that written on your file. I'll get you something else." Susan spoke through her walkie-talkie, explaining to somebody: "Ms. Himmel keeps kosher and would like something else for lunch." A few minutes later a different young lady walked in holding a turkey sandwich on wheat. She told me to start eating and that the side cup of ranch dressing was for the carrots and I was to keep my hands placed on the table at all times. I bit into the semi-soggy wheat bread trying to locate the turkey. I got through maybe half the sandwich, the entire unripe plum, and a few carrots but couldn't face the ranch dressing. I'd worked at a pizza parlor for two years and noticed the chemical ingredients of ranch dressing, and swore off it for life. I ate what I perceived to be a good portion, and then stopped. It turned out that the clean-plate club was not something strictly for picky child eaters, but for ED patients, too. I had already broken the rules by leaving food on my plate. As punishment I was forced to drink a glass of Ensure to equal the number of calories' worth of food left on my plate. What kind of sick place was this? They were supplementing me on my first day. Ensure appeared at almost every meal on someone's plate in place of any bit of food they had failed to consume. It seemed that eating until your stomach says "STOP!" meant we were reverting to anorexic behavior.

That first day I believe I ate more often than I had ever in my life without engaging in some kind of ED behavior. Not more than an hour after lunch, while I was getting my first round of preliminary survey questions, the nurse announced snack time. I thought to myself, "Are you fucking kidding me? Snack? I just ate!" As she asked me basic questions such as age, when my anorexia started, my goal weight, and so on, I reluctantly munched on bland crackers. I had to finish those, too. Meanwhile she asked if I thought I was fat. Of course I thought I was fat. I was at a treatment center for an eating disorder. Every girl here thought she was fat! At dinner, other patients tried making conversation with me about home, school, work, and my boyfriend. I just felt petrified and angry and disgusted by how much food I had to eat.

After dinner I got introduced to Meal Processing. One girl handed out a sheet of paper with a list of numbers from one to ten rating our hunger and fullness levels going into the meal and leaving it. I immediately circled a ten (meaning Thanksgiving dinner full and about to burst). I had not felt hunger going into the meal and left with more discomfort than from my last big binge. However, dinner did not conclude a day of meals at the center. Oh no. From their nutritional standpoint, the refeeding process required patients to eat three meals and three snacks each day. That night our snack consisted of two blueberry muffins and a glass of two percent milk.

I knew by the creamy taste it wasn't low-fat or nonfat. I felt poisoned. No sane person eats muffins right before going to bed.

My nutritionist told me we were eating no more than seventeen hundred calories a day, but one girl had heard we were eating around four thousand, and I more readily believed this. Anorexics and bulimics memorize, calculate, and recalculate the calories of every food on the planet. I may have struggled in astrophysics but I sure knew fruit from vegetable and the caloric contents of breakfast, lunch, and dinner entrées. Seventeen hundred calories? Yeah, maybe at breakfast, where biscuits, gravy, and sausage patties were piled in front of us. Coming from California, I wasn't familiar with this kind of southern food. While my mind shouted, "Purge, purge, *purge!*" my body had to take it in, all of it. Each bite felt like a glob of fat and cholesterol, with no relief in texture or taste.

Some rich meals have safety valves; an omelet may be cheesy but at least you have the option of substituting fruit for potatoes and leaving out buttery toast. Fried chicken can be served sliced over a fresh salad with lots of veggies to dilute the grease-covered poultry. Even desserts like cake can be made less filling when served without frosting and instead with a little fruit compote. But there were no substitutes at the center. It's not that all the food was necessarily bad or grossly rich, it's more that because we were required to finish every crumb I felt disgusted and positively stuffed to my breaking point. As a longtime bulimic I had many occasions following a meal where I could feel my food creeping up into my throat, wanting so desperately for me to grab my toothbrush and stick it down to gag myself and release my meal. One night after eating spicy enchilada pie, I couldn't help but bend over the toilet hours after dinner, in my room, and release the globs of food creeping up my throat. I did it only once and kept it a secret.

Some days it was the quantity more than the quality that got us. The portions so severely surpassed normal that I felt as if we had walked into the Cheesecake Factory, especially on "dessert challenge" days. After a meal of large pulled-pork sandwiches, with potato salad on the side, the "challenge" was Key lime cheesecake. Every girl there stared at the bathroom after that meal, wanting so desperately to make a mad dash and puke. At Meal Processing everyone came out of the meal at ten and felt incredibly disgusted.

The nurses always watched me, as I tried to find ways to revert back to ED behavior. We had turkey wraps for lunch one day and, as had been customary for me, I started to peel apart the tortilla to eat mainly turkey and lettuce. The nurse who sat with us that day scolded me, "You can't do that, Lisa. You have to eat it whole." I wanted to fling back, "Fuck you! I'll eat this damn wrap how I want to." Instead I slowly chewed and swallowed, wondering how this could possibly help. There was one nurse, however, that I was incredibly fond of and I think she felt the same about me. I feel like she saw the real me—not simply an eating disorder—and she always encouraged and cheered me on at the table, telling me to eat slowly and that it was okay, that I was okay. When she sat at my table I didn't mind eating so much; she had such a kind face that made it much easier to tolerate whatever it was we were eating. One other nurse also helped me feel a little more comfortable, by asking about school and my boyfriend. She must have seen how desperate I was, always near tears. Some of the patients also helped distract me from the meal with conversation.

We were allowed to omit three foods from our menus but those three foods had to be very specific and could not be from the same food group. For example, I did not eat beef or pork, yet I could only omit one of these and it could not be all beef or pork preparations; I could chose hamburger or steak. But my nutritionist actually made an exception for me since I was very adamant about my dislike of beef. I also was not allowed to eliminate a fat addition such as oil or butter. I remember feeling so overwhelmed when trying to make this list of only three. I chose beef and nuts, but I don't remember the third food. All I remember is that I regretted it and wished I had said pasta or bread. I was however able to have soymilk instead of regular, so I was saved from a glass of creamy cow's milk at our nighttime snacks. And since I suffer from acid reflux, my nutritionist allowed me to omit spicy foods as well.

I felt as if I had no time ever to process my feelings because all we ever really did was eat. Every two hours at most we were eating, and not just small snacks here and there to stabilize blood sugar but real hard-core meals. We were also timed during snacks and meals and if we didn't eat within the allotted time, or we left too much on our plates, out came the cup of Ensure. One time I opted for non-compliance instead of drinking the Ensure. I felt too full and angry to bother following whatever dumb rules they had laid out. I don't remember how many noncompliances I received but I didn't care. All that it really meant was that I couldn't go on the morning walk, which was fifteen minutes of monitored walking at a moderate pace. The only other thing close to exercise was equine therapy. The brochure shows two women riding horses off into the sunset, but in my experience equine therapy was playing games, like trying to lure a horse into a rectangle shaped by ropes, not riding. On days we had equine therapy we were forced to guzzle down an entire bottle of Gatorade with breakfast. Do you know how much sugar is in a bottle of Gatorade? I found it dull and ultimately discouraging when the horse refused to follow my commands. As if standing in the blazing desert for more than five minutes wasn't torture enough, attempting to rear a horse into a small, roped-off area over and over again proved my theory that I really was in hell.

When I was asked if I had any pain and I would say yes, in my stomach, the nurses would say, "You just need to eat more," and I would say, "No, it's because I am eating too much!" Every meeting I had with my therapist seemed to fall during snack time. She'd ask how I felt and I'd say I was overly full, I felt fat and gross and depressed, and then in would come my snack and she'd look at me like a naive child and say, "Crackers will help." It is mean to say this, but

I hated the fact that she was severely overweight and always talked about food. She claimed to have been a recovered bulimic, which said to me that in order to be recovered I had to be overweight. In fact, it seemed every member of the treatment facility was overweight, and I felt like that just did not fit the scene. How could a group of overweight women tell me how I should go about recovering? Is being overweight healthier than starving or purging? This whole setup focused too much on food rather than on feelings, and I wanted out as fast as possible. I wanted to work one-on-one with a nutritionist as I had four years earlier and work out my own food plan rather than being force-fed and lied to.

Many girls cried at meals, but I just felt numb and doped up on food. As much as I wanted to cry, the only emotion I ever really exhibited was anger and that got me in trouble, which made me angrier. How could they get mad at me for my feelings? I said I felt like I couldn't deal with the amount of food and I did not see myself as thin. My therapist got angry with me. They fed us a ton of fiber and bran cereal to try to regulate our bowels. Yet that combined with the blazing dry heat failed miserably. Most girls went days or weeks without going to the bathroom. I went once the entire time I was there and it was nothing to write home about.

Some of our meals were actually quite delicious. Chicken salad served with sliced tomatoes, avocado, and sesame crackers made a perfect summer meal. We also had Asian-inspired marinated chicken and rice. However, the pleasure of fresh grilled chicken was obliterated by a greasy, rich dessert of fried wonton skins and caramel ice cream. We ate peanut butter by the quarter cup, drank milk by the glass, and ate cereal by the cup.

I needed to gain back some control and I knew that was not going to happen in that place. I felt horribly misled and trapped. I wanted to get treatment, just not in this intense of an environment. I needed to slow down, to work it out with someone who would let me go slow and ease back into the swing of eating normally and trying new items. When control is completely taken away from me, I freak out. I felt like no one listened to me, that that place was not the right fit for me. My parents, my boyfriend, they didn't listen; the nurses, the other patients, even the sweet maid did not listen. I needed to escape back to my safety foods and the gym. I needed to be back in Santa Cruz and surround myself with organic produce and vegetarian options and my large salads with fat-free dressing. I wanted my large light-roast coffee, not one cup of bland decaf. I wanted mustard instead of mayonnaise and to pull apart my turkey wraps, to continue eliminating pork from my diet, eating only three times a day, and deciding my own portions. I did not want to be forced to eat dessert when my stomach shouted *stop*. I did not want nighttime snacks of muffins or bran cereal and a glass of soymilk. I wanted to wake up in the morning and go to the gym again and come home to my own prepared meals. I never wanted to eat biscuits and gravy again or pork sandwiches or BLTs. I wanted to choose how to prepare my own pizza without having to eat pepperoni. I wanted some sort of control back and I was not going to get it, and I knew I had to leave and find some other way of healing because that place and that treatment plan were not working for me or making me better.

sheila: Maybe this center's twelve-step treatment plan was never going to work for Lisa or maybe she just didn't give it a chance. I spoke with her therapist, the intake supervisor, the psychiatrist, and others, but from a distance I couldn't tell whether this could be the right place, and Lisa's resistance was normal. Lisa called several times a day to complain. Of course, it wasn't meant to be fun. Could it really be as bad as she described? Then she said she'd walk away. We could have held the line and told her to stick with it or don't come home, but we didn't. After a week and a half, the day before we were to leave for Europe, she flew home, promising to contact the day program in our area. Scott and Jake would stay with her at our house. Our sisters would fly in if necessary. We had other family in the area, ready to pitch in. We had no idea we'd need them all.

Ned and I flew away, guilty yet grateful for a long, cramped trip through eight or nine time zones, sealed away from any news.

It came soon enough. Lisa called the ED day program near our house, but she sounded so bad that the intake person told her to have someone take her to the emergency room or they would send an ambulance. Lisa was admitted to the psychiatric ward at Stanford Hospital. It was a place that we had joked about, in a previous lifetime. Years earlier, when we knew the place only vaguely, we'd called it SMI, Stanford Mental Institute, as if you had to be very smart to go there. Big joke. Now my daughter was attending SMI.

My sister flew down from Seattle to stay at our house, and then Ned's sister came from San Diego. Also there were Scott, Jake, our nephew and his wife, and my cousin Peggy, who had helped Lisa through the prom. We met my mom in Istanbul, where the cruise would start. She offered to fly home. If anybody flew home it should have been us. We felt like assholes, but we got on the ship.

We checked our email and called home. Elaine was making dinner for a full house, then they'd go to the hospital and visit Lisa. She told us Lisa seemed about the same. Doctors said it could take a while to find the right medication.

We had warned our friends that our stopover in Paris was doubtful, but when we changed our flight, the soonest we could get home was the following day. Part of us desperately needed to be with Lisa, our child. Part of us was incredibly relieved to have one glorious day in Paris with wonderful friends.

lisa: When I got home from Arizona, I immediately resumed my old habits. I tried to restrict my food and to exercise as much as possible, and I lost five pounds fairly quickly. With my parents gone on their trip around Europe and Scott at work, I was alone all day with my disease. To fill my loneliness I binged and purged. I'd been home a week when Scott found me in the garage covered in cake crumbs. He took me to the emergency room, and I was admitted to the psych ward. It was our second trip to the ER. Two days earlier I had been on the phone with the intake coordinator at El Camino Hospital's day program for eating disorders, the place I had turned down when I chose residential treatment. This woman feared for my safety and urged me to admit myself overnight. We went to the ER but the thought of being in a hospital with patients who were severely mentally unstable was too much. I promised to take better care of myself. But every time Scott went to work and I was alone, I would binge and purge until I coughed up blood. I went into the garage freezer to chow down a chocolate cake, and as I was leaving to purge, Scott came home. He looked at me, and I looked at him and said, "I just want to die." His only response was "Okay, get your stuff. Let's go." And I knew we were going back to the ER and this time I had to stay. In the car I told him I didn't know how I was going to do it but I planned on ending my life, that I had nothing to live for, and that I promised to leave a note. He snapped, "Well, that's great, that's fucking great!" I did not blame him for his anger.

We returned to the Stanford ER and they had to place me in the lookout room, a place for suicidal patients that had a security guard at the door. I was allowed to have one visitor at a time. The guard sat and read as I lay on the bed staring at the blank walls. He told me I looked too young and innocent to be this sad, and he prayed that I would get better. We talked for a little while about activities I used to like and my boyfriend, and then he brought me a magazine. I told him I was only twenty-two and wanted to die. He said there are too many people in the world who would be distraught if I died. I wanted to believe him.

After hours of waiting I was brought upstairs in a wheelchair. A nurse asked me routine questions and made sure I would not hurt myself. She took my vitals including weight (ninety-eight pounds), and we put together a standard schedule and treatment plan. My aunt had flown in to take care of me and to her surprise ended up sitting with me in a hospital room. From my room in the psychiatric wing, located right by the entrance to the ER, we heard sirens and saw panic. My room was also located next to the nurses' station, making it nearly impossible to sleep at night. They gave me earplugs. I covered my eyes with my blanket, but every hour or so a nurse came in to check on me and shined a flashlight in my face. Most of the night, I followed the slow tick of my clock. Early in the morning a lab attendant came in to draw blood, finding it difficult to locate my veins as I squirmed. An hour later a nurse came in to take my blood pressure, heart rate, and weight. We started a weight curve with where I was and where I needed to be. My doctor explained they hoped to see a steady incline. I always went down. Unlike inpatient treatment centers for eating disorders, the hospital let me know my weight each day. I wanted it to go down.

Meals were at 8:00 a.m., noon, and 6:00 p.m. I had extreme difficulty choosing items on the menu, but my dietitian, Johanna, patiently sat with me as we tried to figure it out. I just wanted fruit and nonfat yogurt. The hospital did not have nonfat yogurt and she said I couldn't have it anyway because I needed to gain weight. She required me to have soymilk with each meal to get more calcium, in addition to calcium supplements. Many meals I ate mainly vegetables or just the chicken off my salad. Unlike at the treatment center, no one watched me eat. I circled how much I ate on my menus so Johanna could monitor my weight and caloric intake. She said they hoped I was getting at least eighteen hundred calories a day, but I wasn't—not even close. One of the interns, Jennifer, often sat with me at breakfast and asked me why I wasn't eating. I told her it all looked like binge food to me and she asked me why it was a binge food, and I said, "It just is." I wouldn't let myself have french toast, scrambled eggs, or potatoes. Most days I had oatmeal, a banana, and cholesterol-free eggs. They kept opening Ensure shakes. Johanna explained that I was not getting nearly enough calories and needed the Ensure shakes. But I saw them as a one-way ticket to fat land.

In the hospital I felt no relief and no healing. I felt like a helpless mental patient when in reality I was incredibly sick, lonely, exhausted, confused, scared, and longing for someone to talk to. The doctors barely had any time to listen to my thoughts and feelings nor did it seem they even cared when they did lend an ear for two seconds here and there.

sheila: Our nephew had set up a hospital meeting for Ned and me the day we got home from Europe. Seeing Lisa in a hospital gown, disheveled, hardly speaking, we could only say to ourselves, "She'll get better." We agreed to the suggestion of a new medication, and thus began the torture familiar to patients with mental illness and their families. The medication may not work, or may have terrible side effects, but in any case it'll be at least a few weeks before you know. Meanwhile, Lisa was having delusions and decided she wanted to leave the hospital. She was put on a seventy-two-hour-hold.

In California, a person who is demonstrably a danger to herself or others, or gravely ill, can be held involuntarily for three days if authorized by a physician or police officer. The patient has the right to contest the hold. One afternoon I got a call from the patients' rights advocate, who reported that Lisa had filed a petition to overturn her involuntary hospitalization. The advocate said the mediator who considered these petitions would decide based on Lisa's ability to feed, clothe, and care for herself. Then she asked me, "Does she have a place to go?"

I stumbled. "What if I say no?"

"Then it's highly unlikely the mediator will approve her petition."

I said no.

My own daughter could not come home. I woke up at night and each morning, sure I'd dreamed all of this. No? It's real? The walls of our bedroom were still pale yellow, the trim white, and Lisa was still in the hospital. I knew I wasn't going back to sleep, but if I didn't get out of bed, maybe nothing bad would happen. Or it would happen without my participation. I could stay in bed and not answer the phone until I became like the Jennifer Connelly character in the movie *House of Sand and Fog*. She stops paying the bills, stops taking care of everything, and holes up in the house that is no longer hers. Like Lisa, she has no other place to go.

When did these cotton sheets turned to lead? I couldn't move. Sweating, I waited for a sign, something to tell me it really would be better if I got out of bed, but on that day, like day before, there was no sign.

The only shopping we did was for food, and Ned did most of that. If we went to a movie and ran into someone we knew, we'd stonewall. Well-meaning questions struck me as judgmental. I didn't want to hear about other people's children, or that a friend of a friend's child had trouble with eating disorders and they could get the name of the place she went for treatment. My left ear ached from being plastered to the phone. Sometimes I would remind myself to use my right ear, but if I had to write something down, that didn't work. I stopped answering the phone or returning calls for several weeks.

Ned and I scrabbled around for words that would sound like improvement. "Yes, she is a little better today." "She has a lot more energy today." Or, "Not as good as yesterday, but you know, two steps forward, one step back." We said "better" so many times, it became an anvil chorus in my head. "Better better better better better better," like the end of "Hey Jude."

The psych ward is on the second floor, near where the maternity ward was when I had Lisa. The last time we were in this hospital, Lisa was eighteen months old, having tubes put into her ears so she wouldn't get so many infections. The other child in the room had leukemia. We felt very lucky.

Stairs are quickest, but the stairwell often smells of urine. The elevator is for wheelchairs. The escalator is the best way. It feels like a department store. You can forget for thirty seconds that you're not on the way to the lingerie section.

One week after Lisa was admitted, I arrived for the midday visiting hours to find that visiting hours were now only 6:30 p.m. to 8:30 p.m., and that surely we had been informed. Maybe we had.

Lisa was so thin, she often used a wheelchair, and she was threatened with tube-feeding if she didn't gain a few ounces. Roommates and other patients came and went. One of them, a graduate student, came back to visit and told Lisa she looked better. "When people tell me that, it makes me feel worse," Lisa told her.

It also seemed to make Lisa feel worse when other patients commented on what a nice family she had, coming to see her every day, how lucky she was to have parents who obviously loved her.

At the time, Lisa took this to mean that, with support like us, being sick must be her own fault. She interpreted any encouraging comments as, "This isn't cancer, Lisa. Stop feeling sorry for yourself!"

Doctors said they wanted her to stay until she was well enough not to come back. Her diagnosis, in addition to anorexia and bulimia, was major depression with psychotic features. Not that the TV was talking to her. Psychotic features were defined as "excessive worries that don't respond to assurances, or fixed false beliefs." One recurrent theme was that she was committing insurance fraud, being in the hospital when she shouldn't be there, and that the police would be coming to arrest her. Later, her therapist explained the logic of this, because in Lisa's mind she wasn't sick enough to be hospitalized. Another psychotic feature was: "Holds self to impossible standard." She was convinced she was the worst patient ever. "I'm not following my treatment program" and "I messed up," she repeated without end.

After six weeks, we were suddenly informed that Lisa was being discharged in a few days. What? She could hardly walk and was still hauntingly thin. We only knew that if at all possible, she had to get out of the hospital. The department's helpful social worker lined up an interview with the director of La Casa, a residential treatment facility in the community since 1979. Only eight to twelve people live there at any one time. It reminded me of a great old house in Berkeley I used to live in, cozy living room with over-stuffed couches, a big dining table, young adults milling around. La Casa had therapists, medical supervision, house meetings, and chores, including cooking dinner, and an offsite day program to work on reentry skills. Ned and I were thrilled to learn such a pro-gram existed, and that Lisa could leave the hospital and be safe there. Previously, our knowledge of halfway houses was as charities or mentions in a crime report: Someone from a halfway house was beaten up while walking downtown.

Lisa stayed two nights at La Casa, but her medications made her tremble uncontrollably, and then she got so scared that she called 911 and told the dispatcher, "I think I just killed myself." She was having what doctors called a dissociative episode, a sort of out-of-body panic attack. Sirens blaring, the police came and took her, handcuffed, back to the emergency room.

When I was allowed in, there was a security guard posted at her room but the handcuffs had been removed. Because of the sui-cide threat, a security guard would be there the whole time. Lisa was more cogent, though, and even smiled when I arrived. A real smile, appropriately sorrowful. She talked about "goofing up" this time—not her whole life, not "I'm the worst person in the world." Could something have clicked? For a few hours Lisa shared a room with a severely anorexic young woman, immersed in her laptop and being extremely snotty to her mother. She knew the staff, and she displayed deep knowledge about eating disorders, electrolyte imbalance, and irregular pulse. She repeatedly mentioned her potassium levels. Lisa and I were able to watch this display at a remove, which gave me hope, even though Lisa was back in the hospital. Scott came to the ER, but only one of us could visit at a time. Their relationship was unraveling. Embarrassed, Lisa wanted him to go home. Ned and Jake were away for the weekend, using the Portland tickets and hotel that Ned had canceled for Lisa's emergency in June, but I wasn't left alone. My cousin Peggy came to the hospital with her sweet Labrador retriever.

On a Saturday night, the ER was so crowded that patients were sleeping in the hall. The psychiatric ward, too, was fully booked. One of the half-dozen young doctors we saw that day told me Lisa was going to be transferred to another hospital. Where? Oh, don't worry, it'll be somewhere in the Bay Area. That could be two hours away. Could this day get any worse?

At 11:00 p.m. Lisa's bed was wheeled to the trauma room, which in contrast to the rest of the ER was empty and quiet. Lisa and her security detail spent the night there. When I arrived in the morning, the guard told me that the trauma room had been quiet, and Lisa had slept well. And Lisa had good news—she wouldn't have to travel after all. There was a bed at Stanford. The place none of us had ever wanted to see again now looked good, even the heavy automatically locking double-door entrance.

Lisa got out in two days, stayed at La Casa for four months, and made at least one lasting friendship. But for another year, Lisa couldn't get any traction in her life. Again, everything we did had a bad outcome, except for finding a psychologist, at last, who clicked with Lisa and had experience with ED patients. Lisa started to get some perspective, making two steps forward, one back, or the other way around, but she was *moving*.

lisa: I felt like I had lost everything: my job, apartment, school, friends, the man who loved me and I loved. Didn't somebody have to pay for this? Maybe that is why, after leaving La Casa and moving back with my parents, I still threw up and hurt myself. I couldn't quite express my true feelings to others.

That can also be why I took money from my parents without asking and drove off to San Diego or Santa Cruz without telling anyone. Maybe I felt like I didn't owe them an explanation and I still felt like shouting, "Fuck you for going to Europe when you knew I was sick!"

Instead, I popped a blood vessel again. Third time in one week. My hazel eyes were camouflaged by a piercing red dot. It was unattractive; as I stared in the mirror, it stared back. The visible repercussion of me being bad. People asked what happened, and I lied and said that I had allergies or got poked in the eye. I couldn't tell them the truth, and I didn't think anyone really cared to hear it. But maybe somebody knew. Perhaps Mom or Dad heard the faint murmur of me gasping for air as I gagged and choked and thought, "She's doing it again." Or they found evidence in the bathroom or had first noticed a certain food missing, such as buttery croissants intended for Sunday brunch or the Mitchell's creamy vanilla ice cream that they all too easily controlled each night, dished out in tiny bowls that could never be enough for me. I had been so bad in my behavior that I had to punish myself severely.

I know how to make myself suffer and I know how to make myself just want to raise my arms in the air and shout, "I give up! Let me go!" So many times I have tried to leave behind my badness for a life more ordinary and less complicated. I might make it a few days, weeks, or months and feel proud that I might taste normalcy again. But the desire to fuck up always crept up on me and even when I wanted to push it away like a child pushing away vegetables at dinner, I caved. I needed the guilty pleasure of stuffing myself full of forbidden foods in a numbing trance, knowing that I was going to rid myself of that awful binge soon. I needed that rush of adrenaline from purging my food. I needed the pleasure in knowing I wouldn't gain weight because I faked eating.

I got used to the bruised and cut fingers, swollen cheeks, protruding stomach, and red, watery eyes. In the hospital all I thought about was sneaking past a nurse into my bathroom after each meal and vomiting until I saw stomach bile like I used to. But no, I followed the rules, all the while knowing I was an incredibly bad person and the worst patient of all time. I tried to convince others and they didn't buy it; they wanted me to gain ten pounds in the hospital. Instead, by carefully counting calories, I got admitted at ninety-eight pounds and discharged at ninety-three.

Then, all I wanted to do was eat. Not that I ever felt hungry or full. I never felt anything in my stomach, more like I had a head and legs and arms but no middle. I became a shell of a being who seemed to respond to some vocal advancements and could semi-carry a conversation and seemed to be getting better, when really I just felt numb. Soon, I was back in the bathroom.

sheila: After a breakdown in the spring, a hospital stay in the summer, and a halfway house in the fall and some of winter, Lisa was holed up at home and began edging back into the world again. She started seeing friends from high school. At last, she felt comfortable driving, a relief to me because she could do errands and get to appointments. And then she took the car and disappeared.

Occasionally she answered our pleading emails, and once she picked up her phone when I called. Twice she came home and then disappeared again. Should I have taken the car keys? Of course. What about putting a clamp on her ankle? Or kicking her out of the house?

But she wasn't just being defiant. We knew she'd stopped taking her antidepressant and that she wasn't sleeping. One friend had seen her, had initially let her stay, and then told Lisa she really needed to go home. Lisa cut her off, too.

We called the police and seriously considered reporting the car stolen. Until we realized it could involve guns. Officers in Palo Alto and Santa Cruz called Lisa's cell phone, and she answered and sounded reasonable. One set up a meeting, which she blew off. The Santa Cruz police had a BOL (Be on Lookout) for her and the car. But even as we panicked, we realized that in a college town with a colorfully radical reputation, another runaway student was not a law-enforcement priority. Especially because she was an adult. As anyone knows who ventures into any major American city's downtown, a person can't be taken away for having disorderly thoughts.

That's why we seriously thought about abducting our daughter. Lisa was hitting the Santa Cruz bar scene, and we knew some of the bars. If only we could find her, though, she would see the love on our faces, come home, get a good night's sleep, and go see her therapist in the morning. We would all cuddle again as our *Good Night Moon* family. I even mentioned this plan to a police officer. He talked to me as if I were sane, reminding me that kidnapping was a felony and probably would only push her to run farther away next time. Still, we had to do something. It was as if she'd been kidnapped and we were bargaining with criminals: Please, let her be alive, let her come home, we'll do anything just to hear her voice.

I thought to call John Hubner, a colleague from the *Mercury News* who has deep experience with juvenile justice, courts, and cops. John's first job was as a probation officer in Chicago, in one of the busiest corrections systems in the country. He and Jill Wolfson wrote a well-regarded book, *Somebody Else's Children: The Courts, the Kids, and the Struggle to Save America's Troubled Families*. John lives in Santa Cruz, though I didn't know where or if he was even still around. We hadn't spoken in six months.

I called at 5:00 p.m. and gave him an hour's worth of the Lisa saga. He talked me out of arrest and kidnap, and got to the core question: Is this behavior or biochemistry? Since it wasn't just bad behavior, but real sickness, the options were complicated.

John knew every bar I mentioned. These were upscale places, on a circuit traveled by young couples and singles from UC Santa Cruz. These are "drinking and talking" places, he reassured me. The police reporter in him had to notice that in running away Lisa had chosen Santa Cruz, not San Francisco or Los Angeles or any other big city where she could more easily hide. Her memories of Santa Cruz, especially in the last months, had been awful. To us, that was puzzling, worrisome self-punishment. John saw something else.

I described Lisa, and John had an idea of what she looked like. A couple of years earlier he had gone to O'Neill, where she worked, and introduced himself as my friend. That day, Lisa remembered him from newspaper events. Lisa's memory for people has always been astonishing. Supplied with her car's license number and details, and the address of a recent parking ticket, John found the car within thirty minutes. It still had a "Mercury News Employee" sticker in the front window.

Now what? Leaving a note might scare her off. John reported that the car was parked properly, within the lines, a detail that somehow mattered. There was a popular café near the parking lot. He went in and saw a young woman that could be Lisa, with a guy, but John was doubtful. Does Lisa drink coffee? Yeah, but who doesn't. Then he went to one of the bars and saw another suspect, slouching. Does Lisa slouch? Again, not a distinguishing clue. In the third place, John recognized Lisa sitting at the bar with a nice-looking guy. He sat down next to her, ordered a beer, and struck up a conversation:

"Want to make a bet?"

"Uh, okay."

"I bet your name's Lisa."

John has a soft, nonthreatening voice, employed over many years as a reporter in getting reluctant people to tell him their deepest feelings. He doesn't look crazy and he wasn't hitting on her, though she later told us she wondered why some old guy had sat down next to her. Once he started talking, Lisa's people memory ignited. She recalled that John lived in Santa Cruz and had come into O'Neill, and that he and I had worked together for years. All very cordial. Then she turned away, back to her companion.

John handed her his cell phone and said, "Call your parents. They just need to know you're safe."

And she did. Lisa sounded good, said she would call, said she would go to her therapy appointment the next day.

In some ways, it didn't matter. All we needed was to hear her voice, to know she was alive, and to get John's description of their conversation. He made her keep talking to him.

As he told us, "I'm looking hard at her, into her eyes. She looks really healthy, relaxed, and happy."

Of course, it was early in the evening. The drinking was young.

John got to her story, though. As she told us, loud and often, she hated being back home in shallow Palo Alto. But unlike us, John sympathized and talked up Santa Cruz as a more stimulating place for a young person.

"Sounds like this is a walk on the wild side for you, but in a safe place?"

"Yeah," she told him. "I could've gone to Compton!"

Before leaving, John threw Lisa a safety net. "If you ever need a place to crash, please, knock on my door. Here, take down my address."

She got up and went behind the hostess stand for crayons and a napkin. She'd been to this bar before.

A month later, even Lisa was laughing about her incident with the Sam Spade of Santa Cruz. A little time, distance, and humor don't make eating disorders go away, but they offer reasons to believe.

One morning I picked up the phone to hear: "This is a non-emergency call from the Palo Alto Police Department." Still, this was a live person calling, not a recording, so it wasn't about flushing the sewers or the May Fête Parade. My mind basically stopped until the officer continued.

Ned had taken the train to work, ran late, and apparently hadn't paid attention to where he parked his car. It was blocking someone's driveway. If I could come get it now, they wouldn't tow it away.

No problem!

fifteen

The Trouble with Experts

Sometimes you have to remind yourself—and it's not your first thought when your child is in pain—that professional health providers also have mouths to feed. They may be kind, understanding, generous, highly skilled, even brilliant. People who choose to work with eating disorders, which are notoriously difficult to treat and have high fatality rates, often have the noblest intentions. But like most of us, they work for a living. They are professionals.

As a child, I thought if a person was a "professional" that meant he or she was tops in the field, like a professional golfer, wrestler, or chef. Men, mostly, went to work, whatever that was, and came back with money. They were professionals. This worldview began to unravel when I started working in the family jewelry store. Filing invoices and receipts was a snap, but I was miserable at wrapping packages, especially during the Christmas rush when harried shoppers stood there, waiting. So what if I got the job through my father. I was getting paid. Did that make me a professional package wrapper? Certainly not. But this was a small store, not Macy's. There were no professional package wrappers. Then I began to notice that many adults weren't very good at their jobs, either, and that sometimes all that distinguishes professional from hobbyist is that the former is lucky enough to find someone to pay them. Like authors and bloggers, for example; some make money, but many don't.

In the growing field of eating disorders, usually the patients or the families pay the bills. Insurance companies have been slow to recognize medical issues categorized as mental or behavioral health, including eating disorders, on a par with other chronic, deadly diseases. This should change with the federal Mental Health Parity Act, which as of this writing is scheduled to go into effect January 2010. Even with good health insurance, your coverage is likely a lot more comprehensive for cancer than anorexia, which is still widely regarded as self-inflicted. Trying to get coverage for eating disorders, I felt like I was shopping in an impossibly disorganized store with a "You break it, you buy it!" policy. Patient or parent, you're on your own to sift the useful wheat from overwhelming chaff in treatment options, most of which will cost you just to open the box. On the chaff side are amateurs and hucksters sniffing desperation, unproven therapies, and expensive treatment centers staffed with little-trained former patients. As with drug and alcohol rehabilitation treatments, there are many bona fide professionals and institutions out there. But which is right for your child?

To figure that out, we naturally ran to the Internet. I've scoured the websites, finding good information about current research and conferences. I've been glued to features like "Famous People who Have DIED from Eating Disorders" and "Famous Celebrities who Have Spoken Publicly About Their Suffering with Eating Disorders (*This List Is Constantly Being Updated*)." Also constantly being updated, unfortunately, are websites *promoting* eating disorders. A web-security company found the number of pro-anorexia and pro-bulimia websites increased 470 percent between the end of 2006 and the end of 2008. The company reportedly tracked a random sampling of three million websites from around the world and found a "rapidly increasing amount of dangerous and illicit content on the Internet." But no surprise, fright is good for business. This company sells content filters and other security measures, the better to help businesses and families cope with Internet predators.

Similarly, when patients and families Google "eating disorders," we find a gusher of information and likely don't drill down to the source. Desperate for help, we may not notice the fine-print disclaimer that says something like, "Referral information is supplied solely by the providers themselves and is not checked or warranted by this website. We do not endorse or recommend practitioners."

Profit or nonprofit, many websites function like a club. Providers pay a membership fee that entitles them to list themselves on the site, in the language of their choice. The sites offer tips to professionals on how to snag more clients by, for example, advertising on the website. The treatment center that's "peacefully situated on thirty-six wooded acres next to its own private five-acre lake" may be a marketer's hallucination. Phrasing like "dedicated to delivering the best possible service available and a broad spectrum of treatment modalities" is open to interpretation. The site may list famous, well-respected centers such as the Menninger Clinic in Houston as well as the bottom-feeders.

All compete for our ED dollars, whether we pay directly or are blessed with health insurance covering behavioral health, the industry term for mental health. They are professionals if somebody pays them. They may genuinely care for patients, but they depend on insurance, donations, and endowments—or tens of thousands of dollars from the family.

Hospitals and clinics have budgetary concerns when recommending one treatment over another. They may have invested in new equipment and need to justify the expense by using it a lot. But if the experienced physician recommends a procedure, puts his hand to his chest like a politician promising truthfulness—a gesture we saw often—and says if this were his daughter, he'd go for it, it's hard to stay rational. We did get second opinions, but in our experience, they were expensive time sinks. Doctors backed each other up.

To rule out a brain tumor, physicians suggested Lisa undergo an MRI, which requires the patient to lie still in a long tubular scanner. At the time Lisa was taking medications that made her body shake uncontrollably. Did an MRI make any sense? We weren't sure, but a doctor had said "brain tumor" so we went for it. Lisa couldn't stay still long enough and the result was inconclusive, except that at a time when Lisa felt that she couldn't do anything right, that in fact she was the worst person in the world, she got to feel bad about failing another test.

My deeper concern with health professionals treating eating disorders is whether they are open-minded. Behavioral health is atomized into specialties that may prescribe antipsychotic medications or dialectical behavioral therapy (DBT), a twelve-step program based on Alcoholics Anonymous, or a $1,300-a-day residential treatment facility on the beach. For eating disorders, alternative treatments, such as acupuncture, equine therapy, herbs, and probiotics, are becoming more widely available. In addition, discoveries in brain chemistry are very promising, using electroencephalogram (EEG) data to help guide treatment decisions. We looked into that for Lisa.

If you're lucky, you can find a multidisciplinary treatment team of experts who are used to working together. They might include a psychiatrist, psychologist, dietitian, and social worker. Too often, though, the specialists speak different languages. They don't even hold visas to each others' countries. Health professionals, like lawyers, naturally compete with and often openly disdain each other, in a way that makes their effectiveness very hard to assess.

Are they good or just self-confident? With all the controversy around the causes and treatments of eating disorders, and the wide range of people affected, patients and parents may simply have to try something new or untested or unproven. A treatment may be evidence based or just based on an individual practitioner's experience, and still the best hope for your child's recovery is that it may take years.

lisa: In high school my parents found me a tremendous therapist. She didn't specialize in eating disorders, but was still able to listen to my food and body anxieties and professionally analyze my situation. She had a maternal approach to therapy and when my health severely diminished, I sought safety and solace in her office. We met only once a week and each session I came with an overload of thoughts, feelings, and worries. Unfortunately, we had to end our therapist/patient relationship when I moved to Santa Cruz for college. She let me go with care but worry and I, too, left in complete apprehension.

Once I was in college, Dad researched therapists in the area who specialized in eating disorders. He found one in downtown Santa Cruz, and I took the bus to see her, a plain-dressing, gaunt woman who appeared to be in her mid-fifties. We never connected. I questioned her own eating behaviors, and she disapproved of my impulsive tendencies. In her office I felt criticized, not safe, so that I began to keep to myself. She sat in her chair, staring at me with this look as if urging me to talk more. But she never asked me leading questions nor could she carry a topic for very long. I began blowing her off and ignoring her phone calls, then I'd go back, and then skip appointments again. My parents made me stay with her, even after I tried telling them how she was in no way helping me get better.

Finally, I wrote her a letter saying I wasn't coming back, that we weren't a good fit.

I took a break from therapists for a while. My parents, especially Dad, constantly urged me to find someone else, thinking it would help with my bulimia and just to have someone to talk to in general. But I resisted. I didn't see the point of spending money for therapy because I knew I wasn't really ready to change. I became so incredibly reliant on my bulimia that I felt somewhat threatened by professional help. What would happen if they took my disease away? In truth, I had stopped seeing it as a disease and more of a lifestyle. If I didn't binge and purge every day, I felt anxious and unsettled.

But after I had to move to a new house for the third time in a year I gave in to Dad's suggestion and contacted a local therapist said to specialize in the treatment of eating disorders. I went to see her and immediately I felt her practice style to be a little overly holistic for my taste. She favored herbal remedies, DBT, and questions like, "Find where your feelings come from in your body. Is it your heart? Your stomach? Your head?" I honestly had no discernable feelings location, so I made stuff up.

I did learn a few things from this therapist, but in her office it was as if she was leading a slow-paced, spiritual yoga class while I was blasting cardio pumps in the corner. No connection.

I didn't see her again for several years, until my relapse in the spring of my senior year of college. By that time it was probably too late for any medical professional to pull me out. I was hardly sleeping, eating very little, and exercising way too much. Dad suggested I contact the most recent therapist, and I was scared enough to try, but by our second appointment I had already fallen too ill to comprehend her holistic approaches. My weight got down too low and my insomnia made it nearly impossible to connect. After Mom came along to a session, she withdrew me from her care.

At the ED treatment center in Arizona, every girl had an assigned therapist, out of a whopping two. I hated mine. She approached therapy as if disciplining an animal. I didn't feel that she saw me as a human being with my own feelings and needs. Rather, I had to adhere to her rules and guidelines and recovery approaches. I understood that she had herself recovered from bulimia nervosa after suffering a heart attack, but it didn't make her more approachable.

Then in the hospital, the medication coupled with my eating disorder led me to believe I would never be normal again or feel at all like my old happy-go-lucky self. I had forgotten how to take care of myself, although looking back I blame this on the medication. I shook when I walked, became unsure of how to feed or dress myself, and feared I had sealed my fate as an invalid for the rest of my life. I couldn't trust the doctors and nurses or my family, who had okayed the prescriptions. No one wanted to take care of me or let me come home. I had been left completely alone, I realized, and I truly thought I would die in the hospital. But I found hope. My parents managed to make a very smart decision on the advice of their friend, a psychoanalyst. They found me a new and highly recommended psychologist for when I got out of the hospital.

sheila: When you're the desperate parent, you might expect and even welcome the sure-footed professional—until the treatment clearly isn't working and all that's prescribed is more of the same. Sometimes it looked to us like the experts were juggling medications and treatments and just hoping something would catch.

Eating disorders often involve more than one diagnosis, for the patient and possibly for the family. The "comorbid" condition in our family being depression, Lisa was diagnosed with depression and anorexia. I picked up a hint of pride when Lisa spoke of having a dual diagnosis, as if that was more impressive than just being, say, bipolar. Whatever the combination, ED patients and parents deal with mind-bending complexity at a time when everyone most wants one bulletproof answer. In less than a year, Lisa's possible diagnoses spanned the *Diagnostic and Statistical Manual of Mental Disorders*, the standard used by U.S. mental health professionals. Experts mentioned obsessive-compulsive disorder (OCD), bipolar disorder, major depressive disorder, and generalized anxiety disorder in addition to plain-old anorexia, bulimia, and anorexia nervosa, binge-purge type. And then, psychiatrists mentioned schizophrenia, with Lisa present, as a possibility that couldn't be ruled out for several years.

In our experience with Lisa's illness, if the professionals had doubts, they weren't divulging them to us. Once they had a theory, made a diagnosis, or read a colleague's report, that was that. New information was only going to cement their opinion.

Asking about taking other tacks, we were told:

"No. We don't do that here."

"No. We haven't given this treatment plan a chance."

"No. Studies show that this works."

As a journalist, I know that studies can show anything, even when dressed up in evidence-based data. Results of medical trials, particularly, can be skewed by a high dropout rate. Even if the study being cited is totally credible—with a large enough and representative sample, a control group, accurate reporting, and no strings attached to the funding—do the results apply to your child? An overworked clinician may not necessarily know. And yet, to calm you down or appear in control, he trots out his Ivy League training and doesn't turn back. We were only too eager to buy it. When confronted with this attitude during Lisa's stay at Stanford Hospital, we thought, stupidly, "Well, yeah, this is *Stanford*, for heaven's sake. They must know what they're doing!"

There are gifted experts in the field of eating disorders, without question. Still a patient's progress is glacially slow because of the nature of the disease. Patients don't want to change their eating habits, gain weight, or lose attention and emotional support. Even if the patient agrees to try medications, the initial dose is usually low and takes a while to work, if it's going to work. Meanwhile the drugs have debilitating side effects. You must wait for your child to reach the therapeutic dose. And that's only if medication is even a possibility. With severe anorexia, the patient first needs to gain weight. With severe bulimia, pills may not stay in the body long enough to do anything. Ned and I were told to hold on and be patient when it made sense but also when it should have been time to fold our cards, shuffle, and deal again. Too often, we clung to every turn of medical phraseology, as if we could squeeze the right answer from analyzing each word and comma. When Ned and I talked about what the doctor said, we had to wonder whether he or she was telling us something just to make us feel better. Later I learned a helpful way to think about listening to oral reports. Anthropologists doing fieldwork have a different way of listening to their subjects' words, and it applies equally well when listening to experts: "It is true that he said that. But what he said may not be true."

It is also true that no patient or parent wants a wishy-washy doctor. With any disease, we would want them to be clear, hopeful, and open to new information.

Until being forced down the rabbit hole of eating disorders, I had the usual strongly held opinions. These diseases were somehow the parents' fault, and anyone who wanted to could just decide to get better. Why in the world would anyone get started on an eating disorder like anorexia? It made no sense to me. When I'm hungry, I eat. Food is health, love, community, and fun. Back then I didn't see the irony in my opinion. I used to be the One Who Didn't Eat, and then became a no-fun vegetarian, and now I can't see why anyone would go that route? Ahem.

Four experts helped me reframe the question as: Why do some people get eating disorders and not others? In a thin-worshipping, food-obsessed culture, where we like to think that with willpower we can control most aspects of our lives, it's a wonder everyone doesn't have an eating disorder. I was lucky enough to encounter these four experts—a psychologist, a college adviser, a dietician, and a high school English teacher—while navigating the thicket of ever-changing information. A former Olympic athlete also pitched in. Each of them cleared up an issue or two for me, Ned, and Lisa. They helped us recognize the surprising expert who finally got through to Lisa.

The Psychologist

sheila: Louise Stirpe-Gill was one of the most clear-sighted people we met on this journey, perhaps because she'd been immersed in the field of eating disorders and had taken a step away. Lisa and I met her when we gave a talk about eating disorders at our synagogue. Stirpe-Gill had specialized in ED for many years. She still sees some binge eaters, bulimics, and anorexics, but she found it more therapeutic to widen her practice—for herself as well as her patients. It's very hard on a physician to treat so many people that close to death. At first, she saw mostly female college students. Then they were high schoolers. In the mid-nineties, Stirpe-Gill started getting male patients with eating disorders. That hasn't let up, although men are still more vulnerable to feeling shame about mental illness and therapy, and more likely to stay away until a physical ailment requires action.

A short, trim, and feisty grandmother, Stirpe-Gill traces the obsession with size to the Twiggy era, the late sixties. After that, it never really went away.

In a reversal of what women believed in the Marilyn Monroe era—that sexuality involved flesh—skinny models like Twiggy promoted the notion that women could be thin *and* sexual. Now, the ideal has changed again. As Stirpe-Gill puts it: "Be as skinny as you can be, but have big boobs." She has seen anorexics getting breast implants. How confusing to have a physically impossible body image in mind, along with the rest of a typical young girl's worries about becoming a teenager: "I'm going to be so fat! The boys aren't going to like me! I won't have any friends!"

I remember those feelings. The waiting, waiting, waiting, and then, in my case, not a whole lot happened. One day in the college dorm, a girl I thought was a friend said after we'd changed into our swimsuits: "Where were you when they passed out the waists?" I will never forgive her, whatever her name was.

As Stirpe-Gill says, a lot of children hear the anxiety from their parents: "I was so *bad* today. I had dessert!"

Young people get the message from parents and other adults, that it's what's on the outside that is important. Their inner hungers get shoved aside in desperation to look a certain way and they develop an insatiable desire to match an imagined standard. But what is the hunger really about? Attention from parents and teachers, yes, but at the core, what's important is to have a life that means something to you.

As kids can see, most of the adults are hungry, too. We may look like we have it all together, but most of us just figure out how to make do with our limited talents. That's the big secret kids have to learn, and adults have to remind ourselves.

Stirpe-Gill also helped us by talking calmly to Lisa on the phone, during a time when we were all falling apart.

lisa: I know that we did have what Mom remembers to be a lengthy conversation on the phone before any treatment plans had been decided for me. But I was in such a state of extreme anxiety and doubt that I felt capable of having a real conversation with anyone. Louise asked about my eating disorder and my mental state, including what became a frequent inquiry: "Are you depressed?" I can't recall many of my answers. I'm sure I told her that I did in fact feel depressed, but I wasn't sure if I was actually clinically depressed. I had become so against antidepressants that I didn't want to think about needing them again. I told her that I felt I wasn't doing anything in my life right and had let everyone down. She said, "Gosh, Lisa, you are so critical of yourself. Why is that?"

The Student Health Director

sheila: I heard about Alejandro Martinez from a friend at Stanford University. As director of the student health center, he was the guy to help me understand why college is such an incubator for eating disorders. It was for Lisa at UC Santa Cruz. At super-elite colleges like Stanford, especially, students have achieved the dream of American children and parents everywhere. Their tickets in life would appear to be punched, with a superior education and connections. What could they possibly be hungry for?

Martinez started by admitting that student health professionals pretty much missed eating disorders until the mid-1980s. There were isolated cases of anorexia, which is easier to catch. A resident assistant in the dorm may notice a student's severe weight loss or isolation. But bulimics are often social and look normal. Before eating disorders became widely known on campus, the other way college officials were alerted was when students needed medical clearance to participate in a sport or activity.

Most students are extremely reluctant to get help. They've gotten to college through tremendous drive, and they've been praised for being outstanding, but in college everyone is exceptional. Control and perfectionism may have helped get them there. Who better than a perfectionist to take the societal ideal of thinness and achieve it better than anyone else?

What I hadn't thought of is that college is such a breeding ground for eating disorders because it's a very large community of people the same age. As Martinez explained, "There are lots of places to make comparisons. And they have pressure in almost every dimension of their lives. In high school, someone's watching over them. In college, they're in a group that's watching them and they're watching each other."

Or it could be a casual, overheard comment, like, "I need to lose five pounds." You look at the speaker and think, as Martinez says, "Hmm, maybe I ought to be losing a few pounds myself."

And then, "I just wanted to lose a few pounds and it became a waterfall that I couldn't stop."

The Dietitian

sheila: When Lisa slipped badly down that waterfall, her senior year in high school, she found dietitian Karen Astrachan to be helpful. I had gone to Lisa's initial appointment and been impressed with Astrachan's straightforward approach.

In researching this book, I returned to Astrachan's office to see what was new in the street-level treatment of eating disorders.

Astrachan played intercollegiate tennis and became interested in how food fuels the body. She was introduced to eating disorders by observing other female tennis players. "I developed a comfort level because I saw it in the bathrooms," she says.

Why are sports so often the trigger? I wanted to know. It seemed to me that athletes needed all the energy they could get. Later, I met an Olympic downhill skier who said she and her teammates all used eating disorders to keep off body fat, the better to fly down the mountain, despite being extremely cold. Coaches encouraged this. In sports like gymnastics and ice-skating, the same aerodynamics apply. Astrachan had a patient who wanted to be an ice-dancer, but was too heavy for the lifts and flips, and eventually picked another sport. Ski jumping is a high-risk sport for anorexia, for both men and women. The extra problem for boys and men is that they don't have a key physical clue—the lack of menstruation—telling them something is very wrong. Again, it's usually up to the parents to notice.

Like Stirpe-Gill, Astrachan was seeing younger patients. A ten-year-old exercise bulimic wanted to spend time with her father, a busy Stanford doctor, so she went to the gym with him. This made me think about all the young children I've been seeing at the Y. Not only on school holidays, but on regular weekdays. What are they doing inside with a bunch of adults, strapped to heavy equipment, monitoring their calories? I wondered why they weren't outside playing baseball or soccer. Then again, a person with eating disorders can turn any activity against herself.

lisa: I did ballet and gymnastics in my younger years but preferred the intensity of kicking a ball across a soccer field. In soccer, the focus is more on strength and endurance. With twelve years of soccer, muscle sculpted my legs, and even when I had lost a great amount of weight, my legs were never thin. When I was seeing Karen, I mentioned my distaste for my "soccer legs." She explained how everyone has a set-point weight, where her body is most comfortable, and while I might desire a certain weight, it may not be where my body can function. We talked about how I could always find a reason to hate my body or feel bad about not having a thin frame and skinny legs. And then she asked, "If you didn't like your ears, what could you do about it?" I hadn't heard of anyone having plastic surgery on her ears, so she had a good point, and she had many others throughout our sessions.

The High School Teacher

sheila: I met Linder Dermon years ago, when our kids were on a swim team and our job was to stand over the pool for hours with stopwatches. Our children also went to the same elementary school. In addition to teaching English at the high school, Dermon was the elementary school's resource specialist, the friendly face in the Cottage, where kids went for help with learning difficulties like ADHD. My kids didn't have those difficulties, so I had to wait several years to get the benefit of her gentle wisdom.

Kids in Dermon's and my generation used to "go out and play." We would knock on the neighbors' door and say, "Can Jill come out and play?" Whatever the game, parents never lined up on the sidewalks to cheer. That was good, but in my town, being a good student was a mark of weirdness. I remember an older, blond, sophisticated neighborhood girl snarling, "You like to *read*?"

For kids these days, reading too often can be just another place to keep score. It's about standardized test scores, not learning and certainly not pleasure. All of this starts at birth, when the month is crucial. As Dermon has noticed, "If your kid has a June birthday, you keep them back, so they'll have an edge later." She explained the rules of the game to me, an average parent who wants her children to be above average. As a resource specialist, Dermon sometimes sees what the trade calls "the genius disabled." If children aren't doing well in class, they must have learning disabilities.

Right up there with grades, sports, and honors, how you look is a matter of competition. Being thin becomes another area to keep score.

Dermon personally gets the weight issue, and is realistic. As she told me over dinner in a Thai restaurant: "I've been on a million diets. I'm not sure we can prevent it as parents. It would be nice to catch it earlier, but a lot happens in secret."

What does one do with the feeling that he doesn't measure up? Some kids are promiscuous, others get into substance abuse, others diet.

Dermon remembers Lisa being a panelist at a community meeting about stress, in which she spoke up for being average. "If there's any good news, it's that girls have become much more forthcoming."

lisa: At my elementary school, everyone knew and adored Linder. She ran a reading and writing program out of a portable building called the Cottage. Even though students of the Cottage had learning disabilities, mainly dyslexia, I wished I could go there because of Linder. Later I did get to experience Linder's amazing warmth and fabulous teaching skills, when I took her Film Literature class in high school. It was when I was suffering from anorexia, though, and my focus was very shaky. When I confided in Linder, she reminded me of a time, just the previous year, when I showed amazing courage. I got invited to be on a public panel with a few other students, two teachers, and a guest speaker about stress in high school, especially for people who didn't get all the awards and attention. Talking with Linder helped me remember that, somewhere, I still had that strength and honesty.

The Psychoanalyst

sheila: Even less than dealing with the police did we ever expect to consult a psychoanalyst. If we hadn't played tennis with one, and through her meet other psychoanalysts, we would have sailed merrily along assuming the breed was pretty much extinct. Last seen, psychoanalysts were being lampooned in Woody Allen movies. My view swept in the couch, the self-indulgent rehashing of childhood traumas, and the expense. Whatever would Sigmund Freud know about eating disorders?

In the hospital, Lisa had seen several nutritionists and a psychologist specializing in eating disorders, but nobody was getting through. In desperation, I took my tennis friend's referral to an analyst who specializes in eating disorders.

lisa: The woman I'll call Dr. Cohen approached therapy as none of my former psychologists had. From our initial meeting I felt immediately comfortable. She didn't judge me, even though I could barely talk and Mom or Dad had to sit with me because I shook so much. After getting out of the hospital I was beyond timid. Everything seemed too bright and moved so quickly, I just wanted to hide. But with Dr. Cohen, I felt I could slowly come out of my shell and try to understand what happened to me in the hospital. On our first meeting she said hi to me in such a sweet, soft, and soothing voice. Her manner was never critical or too aggressive. She knew I was incredibly fragile and let me go as slowly as I needed. I lay on her couch, just staring blankly at her. As I recall our conversation began like this:

"Hi, Lisa. I'm Dr. Cohen."

"Hi." I spoke in the pitch of a painfully shy young child.

"How do you feel?"

"Bad."

"Yeah? Is there anything else?" Still, she remained soft and soothing.

"Sad . . ." My voice trailed off.

"Why do you feel sad, Lisa?"

"Because of the hospital," I said, looking up at the ceiling. I couldn't think of anything else to say, as if my mind allowed me only a few words at a time.

"What made you so sad in the hospital?"

I felt so small lying on her couch, like I had truly shrunk into a child again. It wasn't so much that I felt skinny but actually short and little.

Our first few sessions went exactly like this. I needed time to open up and be in the world a bit. She and my parents agreed that for a while I needed to see her every day and she was determined to pull me out of my dissociated state. She knew she could uncover the old Lisa by digging into my past, especially having me go back and try to detail my breakdown in May. Every day she was there for me, even when I freaked out after two days in the halfway house and ended up back in the locked ward. She came to visit me and promised to get me out of there. She told me I did not belong in a hospital and I needed to be out in the world with people who loved me.

For once, I had a medical professional telling me I was, in fact, *not* crazy and did not need a lockdown and did not need the medication, and she wanted to listen to me and she actually understood me. When I thought I hadn't made any sense, she told Dad we were making progress. When I became trapped in bingeing cycles, she tried to make sense of it, at first explaining my tiny body needed the calories and then, when I had been gaining weight, tried to devalue food. In her office I felt safe and comforted to have someone who "got me." I no longer felt misunderstood and forgotten.

Dr. Cohen promised to help me get back to my normal self, and after months of intense therapy I regained a great deal. I was able to tap into my emotions. I stopped feeling so numb and disconnected from my environment. Early on, I described to her how I felt like a cardboard cutout, with no insides. I didn't think I really existed, like I told the police when I called 911, that I wasn't a person. I truly believe she made me a person again.

I still talk to Dr. Cohen three nights a week, at least. I put my complete trust in her. She knows when I'm withholding feelings or information, even if we're having a phone session. Dr. Cohen told me never to pretend with her and that it was okay to be sad or have trouble and to bring all of my emotions to her. So I did and I still do, and I often find our sessions too short.

sixteen

Ten Things We Learned About Eating Disorders

I spend a lot of time at the Y. The more stress, the more rowing. One Saturday afternoon, a tired, gray-haired man settled a disabled teenager onto a treadmill, showing her what to hold on to and what buttons to push. He looked like he could've been her grandfather, but he was probably her father. The strain of caring for her may have put years on his face. While going through my strength-training routine, I spun out a colorful fable about his family, what they were living with, how it made our plight seem trivial. I felt sad for this family and yet, incredibly, a little envious. Their pain had an obvious cause, a severe physical disability. Of course this heroic man looked exhausted. Ned and I were slackers in comparison.

Parents with seriously ill children often follow an unwritten handbook of public decorum—of question and response. Mostly we act as if life is normal but we walk around with our guts clenched, fearing the next phone call, tuned to the "fight" setting of the fight-or-flight instinct. On the phone and in person, we feel out our contacts for their capacity to hear a complicated, worrisome story that may not change and has no visible end.

Sometimes, instead of "Fine" in response to "How are you?" I start talking. The news isn't easily packaged. Soon I get lost and stumble around for an appropriate way out, embarrassed that I haven't thought to ask anything about them. But sometimes I don't want to hear their news, good or bad.

We gauge how helpful people really can be right then, by how much work it will be for us to fill them in and deal with their reactions. "Fine" is often the best conversational tool. Many people want to be helpful, but we don't know what to have them do. Then the burden is on them, the would-be helpers, and we all feel bad. They are like workers at a soup kitchen that gets slammed by enthusiastic volunteers at Christmastime. The volunteers end up standing around with nothing to do or trying to socialize with needy people who may be embarrassed to be there.

We go to events about our child's illness. They can be like mental health trade shows, where you cruise the booths and pick up pens with organizations' names on them, maybe find another doctor or treatment to try. At the September 2007 kickoff event of the Eating Disorders Resource Center in San Jose, there was a wine and cheese reception followed by experts giving talks and panel discussions. Melissa and Don Nielsen, founders of the well-respected National Eating Disorders Association, spoke movingly about their daughter's fourteen-year battle with anorexia. "She took pride in being the Queen of Anorexia," Don said. Exactly! Ned and I thought. Lisa acted that way, too. This was between Lisa's two worst episodes. We didn't know she would soon take pride in regarding herself as the worst patient Stanford Hospital ever had. Don Nielsen continued, as if speaking directly to the Himmels, "Each hospital made her worse, and we tried dozens. Everything we did was wrong."

Bingo again. Maybe every parent in the auditorium felt this way. Eating disorder parents, like the patients themselves, can get to thinking that if the sun doesn't come up, it's their fault. The encouraging news was that Nielsens' daughter got her life back. She is now married, has two children, and works as a therapist. What they finally did that wasn't wrong, but that actually worked, was to give their daughter an ultimatum: Go in for long-term care or get no contact from us, and no support.

The first time Lisa seemed to have recovered, when she was a sophomore in college, people would often ask, "What helped?" We didn't know, except that around the time Lisa turned twenty, something clicked and she decided she wanted her life back. We latched onto the UCLA experience as a turning point. When she refused to go to that treatment program, we were paying her tuition and supporting her in every way, but we didn't say, like the Nielsens, "Go in for long-term care or we can't help you anymore." We didn't say, "Get better or go to UCLA." She just decided, "It's a locked facility. I don't like the director. I'd have to miss school. I'm not going." A few months later, she got a job, met her boyfriend, moved into a new house, and was engaged in her classes.

Our Lisa was back! Why mess with success? For a while we insisted that she continue in psychotherapy, but she hadn't made a good connection with either therapist in Santa Cruz, was blowing off appointments, and didn't want to try another one. Professionals call a phase like this a "flight to health," meaning the patient hasn't dealt with underlying issues or followed a treatment plan, but just wants to fly away and try to have a normal life. We were worn out, and naively hoped that acting healthy could become being healthy. It was a false start, but Lisa did have almost three manageable years before crashing again.

In the end, what helps? Here are ten things Ned and I learned we needed to deal effectively with Lisa's eating disorders:

1. **One professional who really relates your child.** For Lisa, a psychoanalyst who specializes in eating disorders turned out to be the one. We were as surprised as anyone, but right from the start, when Lisa was trembling from medications and barely spoke, Dr. Cohen conveyed understanding and hope. And soon we saw progress. It's been very bumpy, but Lisa has pretty much traded in the protective rigidity of anorexia and the oblivion of bulimia for a real life. That is a huge success.

   As we discussed in the previous chapter, experts on eating disorders run the gamut of credentials and degrees, including pediatricians, psychologists, psychiatrists, nurses, and nutritionists. In addition, their theories and practices range from dialectical behavior therapy, based on a concept that everything is composed of opposites, to structural family therapy, focusing on how family members communicate and solve problems. What matters is that the expert listens in a way that makes your child feel heard and talks in a way your child understands. You'll know it when you see it. Most important, this person should be someone both you and your child trust. The ED industry is only too willing to take your money. Progress is so slow and full of setbacks, parents have to wonder if even the most highly regarded experts know what they're doing.

   But first, you have to get your child to go. Teenagers tend to resist any kind of help, and with young adults you may have zero leverage legally. If your child is over eighteen and refuses treatment, you can withdraw support and force the issue, knowing that the risk is finding them on the street or dead. (A recommended book on the subject of when to force treatment is Xavier Amador's *I Am Not Sick and I Don't Need Help!* Vida Press, 2007.)

2. **Your village.** Our nephew and his wife camped at our house. When we were away and Lisa was hospitalized, our sisters flew in and organized the troops, which included my mother, my aunt, and our cousins in the Bay Area, Chicago, and Portland. Friends, neighbors, and colleagues circled the wagons.

There may be an overload of advice. Often it is best to say thank you and be on your way. It's great that your hairdresser's son had success with Abilify for bipolar disorder, but that may not be relevant to your situation. Remember that they are only trying to help. Other friends and family will make you dinner, force you to go to a movie, hold you together. They may also be the best source of referrals—we found Lisa's doctor through a friend—and backup—when Lisa ran away, a friend helped us find her.

A family support group may also help, but it needs to have a skilled leader, more like a teacher than a physician. Stressed parents and siblings easily go off topic, dominate the discussion, or hold back when they need help the most. A good facilitator makes sure group members get what they need, whether it's a resource, referral, or empathy.

3. **Books about other subjects.** Whatever gives you comfort, read it again and keep it close. During Lisa's runaway month, someone gave me Jumpha Lahiri's collection of short stories, *Unaccustomed Earth*. Lahiri writes about being the adult child of aging parents. The stories resonated for me, in a completely different situation with adult children. I read this book of stories twice.

I also returned to *The Runaway Bunny*, one of Lisa's favorite books as a child. It is the flip side of author Margaret Wise Brown and illustrator Clement Hurd's hypnotically calming *Good Night Moon*. When the little bunny comes up with ever-more fanciful plans to run away from home, his mother doesn't panic or get angry, but keeps saying, basically, Raise the ante all you want, I'll be there for you. "If you become a sailboat and sail away," said his mother, "I will become the wind and blow you where I want you to go." All of this, "Because you are my little bunny." These lines soothed me, helped me cling to a belief that whatever was tormenting Lisa, whatever her hungers, Lisa still carried this feeling.

Of course, we also read books about eating disorders.

4. **Exercise.** No thinking, just doing. It's hard to ruminate while rowing. Find an exercise that gets your heart going, or at least gets your mind off its disaster movie. Some people swear by Bikram yoga, an hour and a half of sweating that, like rowing, includes your whole body and pretty much excludes thought.

Since Lisa became anorexic in high school, my exercise regimen has ramped up, from the treadmill to the elliptical trainer, weight-training, and rowing. At the worst times, I felt if I could just lift the same weights as yesterday, or even add a little, I could handle whatever trial was coming next. I loved the feeling of warmth in my muscles and my Michelle Obama arms. As a collateral benefit, our nearby YMCA is the place where we find out all the neighborhood news.

5. **Laughter.** Science has shown that humor helps patients relieve stress and heal. The same is true for caregivers and families, but if you've just spent an hour weeping into a pillow, good luck getting up and finding something clever. I often felt our situation was too precarious for laughter. Movies and TV shows that once seemed funny did not do

the trick anymore, and often made me feel worse. As in, "I used to laugh at that dreck? How pathetic. Nothing else makes me laugh, either. I have completely lost my sense of humor."

It wasn't true, exactly. I found other dreck to make me laugh, including flings with *Desperate Housewives* and *What Not to Wear*. Also, I am married to someone who makes me laugh.

6. **Work—paid or volunteer.** The tendency to obsess about your child's illness is overwhelming; work is a great diversion. It was easy to lose myself in a story or momentarily forget my troubles as I discovered a new food or restaurant. I also appreciated the time I was able to participate in the outside world—a world beyond illness. During Lisa's first descent into anorexia, I kept reviewing restaurants and writing about food for the *Mercury News*. Four years later, when she crashed again, the media world had darkened. But I had taken early retirement from a newspaper I loved and was able to devote more time to Lisa. We were fortunate to have health insurance from Ned's work, so I was able to write this book and pick up freelance assignments.

I volunteer at a local elementary school twice a week, in a program for English-language learners. Not only does it give me something to do besides worry endlessly about Lisa, if not the economy, I get to help somebody in a concrete way. One year, my third-grade student started in September at a 2.3 reading level (equivalent to the third month of second grade) and in June scored at 4.6. He did the best out of the program's ninety students. At some point during that year, I could see the joy of reading clicked with him. Even when I felt like a failure in my relationship with my daughter, working with these kids gave me a sense of purpose and accomplishment.

7. **Early intervention.** I recently met a woman who did intervene early, and I admired and envied her. She happened to be talking on the phone to a friend one day as her fifteen-year-old daughter measured out portions of food. The daughter had become a vegetarian, and then started measuring portions to the nth degree, which the woman mentioned in an "isn't this funny" kind of way. Her friend said no, this could be serious, take her to the doctor right now. The pediatrician recommended a nutritionist that the girl saw, often unwillingly, for a year. She never developed an eating disorder.

Unfortunately, we had no such aha moment with Lisa. Ned and I didn't recognize the problem until it was full-blown. Even then I'm not sure we would have found the right help. Were we oblivious? In denial? Maybe, but it isn't easy to decipher the difference between actionable behavior and the normal hormonal hit-and-run of puberty and adolescence.

Your child was walking around the house singing yesterday, but slamming doors and moping around today? Does that mean she's bipolar? Are moodiness and monosyllabic answers signs of an underlying problem, or typical of teenagers? You can come barging in, and the effect is too much too soon, or you can hang back, keep a watchful eye, and do too little too late. As NEDA's Don Nielsen said, you often feel like everything you do is wrong. It is better to jump in, ask questions, and offer help—and risk overreacting and alienating your child—than to risk a downward spiral into severe depression or severe eating disorder. It would be great if parents could always spot the warning signs and save the child, sparing everyone a lot of agony in the moment and years later when we mull over our many mistakes. Ned and I do occasionally rewind that movie, but not so much anymore. It's useless. Don't do it. You love your child and you got help as soon as you were able.

8. **Getting out of bed.** I sometimes wake up and study the way the pillow forms a canyon landscape with the sheet and blanket, or how the quilted blue comforter looks like a calm ocean. I could lie there and study linen shapes all day, or doze a little longer, and maybe some problem will have gotten better without me. But I know I have to get up and do something, if only to stand around and worry until I get to sit down or go back to bed. Otherwise how will I ever know about the improvement?

9. **Vacations and trips.** Take them. Lisa still resents that Ned and I went to Europe when she was clearly very sick. We still second-guess that decision. But I don't know what we would have done to change the outcome had we been there. Would she not have ended up in the hospital, where at least she was safe? Impossible to know, but what I do know is that our canceling the trip would have made Lisa feel guilty and given her another incident to prove what a bad person she was. In this book, we focused on that trip, and the weekend that forced a choice between her high school prom and my James Beard award, because they highlight our most exquisite moments of torture. This may leave the impression that Ned and I were constantly jetting off to Europe and New York, leaving a desperately ill daughter to fend for herself. Well, no. Every time we went anywhere, we assembled a multifaceted contingency plan and spent hours with Lisa on the phone in transit and at

our destination. At home, we canceled events at the last minute if Lisa seemed fragile. Now I think we did that too much. Lisa needed to grow, and we needed to recharge. The unrelenting pressure a child's illness places on parents physically and emotionally is tremendous. Sometimes all you can do is take a recess, so that everyone gets some fresh air. You do have to take care of yourself in order to take of your child.

10. **Eating well.** Bodies are nourished and sustained by good, healthy food. We have to eat, and eating is fun in all kinds of ways, as I have learned in my life with Ned. Lisa and I disagree about how much my job and our food-centric family life contributed to her eating disorders. I suspect a bit of defensiveness and guilt on my part (and Ned's), and a bit of immaturity and the need to blame on Lisa's part. But we are gradually loosening up our fighting stances. We can even enjoy eating together again.

These are ten things that worked for Ned and me. You may find others to add to the list. Somewhere in the thicket of emotional needs and cultural pressures, we all hack our way through. Lisa has a list of her own.

lisa: I still have issues with food and my weight and I probably always will, although there are days when the idea of an eating disorder seems something foreign and horrible from my past. Other days, I have to meditate into a comfortable, nurturing quiet to avoid purging. I can't help calculating the caloric contents of nearly every food. I control my portions reasonably, but I don't use measuring cups. I examine food labels and nutrition facts, and the words "fat free" still send a shiver of excitement through my veins, but I also read the benefits of heart-healthy monounsaturated fats found in my consistent supply of olive oil, avocados, and peanut butter. I can better understand what my body needs and wants and the joy in learning how to balance and incorporate all the food groups in moderation. I've come to enjoy and appreciate the relieving effects of a glass of wine—good wine—with dinner, or to unwind at a bar after work with friends without obsessing about calories.

Many people, mothers mainly, ask me how they can help with their daughter's or son's fear of food. The questions make me sad and worried that I'm going to disappoint them. These diseases vary so much. Among my friends with anorexia and bulimia, we all played by our own schedules and rules. I'll do my best with what I do know:

1. **Watch those transition years, from middle school to high school, and especially from high school to college.** If your child is struggling, encourage her to take time off and get healthy. College won't make issues go away.

2. **If you're worried about a friend, sibling, or child, it's okay to say something.** Don't accuse, but do express concern. Often the ED individual takes silence as an insult. A reality check may be just what they need to realize they have an issue.

3. **Be careful with what you say about someone's appearance.** Say, "It's great to see you!" instead of "You look great!" which young girls often take the wrong way. I know I did. Hear it often enough and you think your outer shell is all that matters.

4. **Go out to eat, but avoid buffets.** One evening I was watching the TV show *Intervention* (which should be called *How to Be a Better Addict*) featuring a bulimic woman

named Selena. Her sweet husband, Neil, wanted to take her out for dinner after work, but he picked an all-you-can-eat pizza buffet. *Intervention* then filmed Selena, up close, heaping piles of pasta, pizza, salad with creamy ranch dressing, baked potatoes, soup, ice cream, and finally cinnamon rolls onto her little plate. She kept going back, while Neil sat there helplessly. They had driven separate cars to the restaurant, so that while he was paying the check Selena rushed home in plenty of time to purge. She didn't use the toilet, which he would have noticed. Her system was to throw up into zippered plastic bags she kept in her closet and take them out to the trash when he wasn't looking. A young bulimic could've gotten a few tips from watching *Intervention*, but it did demonstrate the hazards of buffets.

Many in recovery find it easier to just eat alone for a while, because we take any comment about our meal choice the wrong way.

Of course, eating alone can backfire. I've had my own Selena scenes, alone in Fresh Choice. I had a system, too. I took my plate and began with greens, healthy enough, and then started piling on the forbidden items like bacon bits, ranch dressing, and croutons. I got a real drink instead of a diet soda and my money's worth from the restaurant's soup, salad, pizza, baked potato and bread sections. I especially loaded up on cheesy bread, fried chicken wings, and spaghetti sauce (the juicy-smooth quality of the sauce made it easier to purge the rest). It was like a trance. While I didn't feel my stomach at all, I knew exactly what I was doing: bingeing and purging. In order to get a good purge, though, I had to hit up the ice cream machine, swirl out the vanilla and chocolate soft serve, and top with caramel sauce, chocolate sauce, and Oreo chunks. I ate this faster than a kid with birthday cake and then dashed to the bathroom. It didn't take long to see the evidence of my binge before my eyes, to see the baked potato and sourdough roll, the chicken and dumpling soup, and the entire salad bar. I spent $8.99 to continue my disease. Still, my meal wasn't complete until I went to the nearby donut shop where I bought two donuts, or an apple fritter and a glazed twist, then ate them and threw them up, too.

At the time, I was working at a reading program for mostly Spanish-speaking kids. I spent each lunch hour bingeing, ending with donuts in the car. Then, I'd go back to work, head straight to the bathroom, jam my fingers down my throat, wipe up vomit here and there, and keep jamming my fingers down until I got all the food out. Back in the classroom, I helped a child distinguish words with a soft *g* from those with a hard *g*. I was posing as a good person, as a tutor and mentor to kids. All they wanted was my help for an hour, but I still needed to satisfy my sickness.

5. **Don't talk about food during meals.** Very difficult, I know, but there is nothing more uncomfortable than discussions of last week's fried chicken bucket and mashed potatoes while a recovering or hopeful recovering anorexic and/or bulimic sits hesitantly picking at her chicken and potatoes with a side salad, trying so desperately not to engage in an ED behavior. Don't bring up body image, weight, the pretty girl you used to play tennis with, or anything to do with eating disorders. My parents often did this, and asked me over dinner if I'd thrown up that day. A hard

shot of embarrassment paralyzed everything. How do I answer that? If it's a yes, how will they feel? If no, will they believe me?

6. **Consider modifying the foods you keep in the house, at least temporarily.** Maybe ask the person with the disorder for a detailed list of binge trigger foods. I know it can be hard not to have ice cream around the house, but buy it and it may not even last a day. Don't fool yourself into thinking that writing your name on whatever you buy will make an impression on a bulimic. I ate one roommate's entire ice cream carton and bag of chips and didn't bother replacing them. I figured she was stupid for buying this kind of food, knowing I was bulimic, and for doing nothing about it. She could have called my parents, asked me about it, done something to show concern. As with drug addicts, with ED it doesn't matter who you trample on to get your fix because if you don't get it you will explode. I couldn't have ice cream in the house, because all too easily I would start eating it right out of the carton, and even when I tried scooping smaller amounts into a bowl for portion control, all of a sudden it would be gone and I'd be bending over the toilet, puking it all out.

Baked goods, chips, salty crackers, and frozen or fried foods couldn't be in the house. Dad would sometimes buy baked goods and try to hide them in the freezer, but during a binge I would scoured the shelves for treats and would always find them. I'd stick to cereals like Special K that aren't all that interesting to binge on. At my worst, though, I could pretty much binge on anything: a whole block of cheese or a loaf of bread with a stick of butter. Now that's pretty hard to purge. Bread turns to clumps in your stomach and almost hurts to get out, but I never quit until I was sure. I have, at times, baked cookies or cake not intending to binge and purge them but ending up having a little, and then a little more, and then more until I had no choice—in my mind—but to purge. Once, as a peace offering to my parents after we had gotten into a huge fight, I baked a cake from scratch and spelled out "I'm sorry" on the frosting with chocolate and butterscotch chips. My parents never saw it. I tried a little corner piece, just as a taste, but then the surge of adrenaline passed through my body and a little turned into more, which became me taking a fork and diving right in.

In September 2008, I became horribly exhausted from my extreme bingeing and purging. At the time of this writing, six months have passed. We'll see. Sometimes I start eating something like chips and have to tell myself to stop. I buy baked chips, for when I really need a salty snack, but, like many salty or sweet treats, there is no satisfying limit to them. I think about bingeing, but know it could ruin my relationship and living situation. I now live in a house with five other people, where there's very little privacy, and the toilet gets clogged easily. That for sure keeps me from purging.

7. **Know that often you can't say anything right.** If you mention that you think your daughter's skirt is too short, prepare for a reaction like, "Oh, so that means I'm *fat*?" People with ED are beyond self-conscious. When I was eighteen and anorexic, I purchased a denim miniskirt and giggled in the excitement of wearing a loose-fitting size 0. When I got home to show Mom, she disapprovingly commented, "Don't you think it's a little short?" No, I thought I looked cute! I didn't want her protective mom reaction. I wanted her to have the same giddy feeling I had

to this new skirt and instead of seeing her as my mother, I saw her as a harsh critic. When she said "a little short" about the skirt, I heard it as something was wrong with my body.

Mom was very careful about making *any* comments about my physique. Still, at times no matter what came out of her mouth, she set me off. Or it was the tone or the situation.

Maybe I'm overshooting this, but it seems mothers and daughters will always be in some sort of competition with each other. Either the mother struggled with weight her whole life and her daughter went the other direction as a thin, beautiful young lady; or you have a slender mom and a dieting daughter and the mom—maybe disapprovingly, maybe she thinks she is being helpful—makes comments about the daughter's weight, which makes the girl even more internally conflicted and uneasy in her own skin. Maybe they are competing for the same body, or they share clothes, or they act like best friends and get coffee together on weekends and exchange shoes for different events, but really, on the inside, one strives to be better than the other.

Mom has mostly, as far I have seen, had the pleasure of being on the slender side. People ask me how she stays so thin yet gets paid to eat, and I don't have the faintest idea. Good genes? Maybe. All I know is I've always been envious of her lean legs. Mine get buff. Every time I get bent on exercising, my legs return immediately to my soccer legs, not to those of lean, petite girls like Mom.

Often Mom makes a comment she means to be complimentary, but I take it in a negative light. If she tells me I look healthy, I take that to mean I look *fat*. If I'm healthy by her standards, I'm no longer thin and therefore must be fat. Once when I was no longer starving myself but secretly bingeing and purging, she told me I shouldn't eat so many carrots with my lunch, because they were starchy. I couldn't understand why she bothered giving me grief for eating a vegetable! Too much cheese I could understand, but carrots?

Parents, there's often not much you can do. Your child has an eating disorder and until that is resolved you may have to keep walking on those eggshells or just keep your mouth shut. Whatever the actual words or tone of voice, those of us with eating disorders often only hear:

You aren't good enough.

Everyone is constantly judging you.

No matter how hard you try you won't succeed.

The way you talk, sing, dance, act, paint, exercise, eat, pray all are wrong.

And of course, someone else always looks better, even your own mother.

8. **Question the experts.** Eating disorders and their medical consequences are vast and varied, and I have seen more than enough treatment methods. I know some patients have been helped by psychiatric medicines. My experience with them was terrible. Rather than genetics or a chemical imbalance, I think a lot of my problems were the result of poor nutrition and depletion of oxygen to the brain. My anxiety, depression, and panic attacks subsided with the progress of talk therapy, moderate exercise, and regular eating habits.

For so long I just kind of sat back and listened to doctors, nurses, psychiatrists, and various therapists. When I tried to challenge a diagnosis, I felt like I was met with more criticism and patronizing words. Soon enough I just went along with everything. In the end, I got my way and managed to (silently) prove everyone wrong. I don't need medication or, in more textbook medical professional terms: There is no conclusive evidence indicating my need for psychiatric medication.

And yet I am often sick. Bulimia does its damage. They were right about that. I have more difficulty breathing when exercising, and digesting food takes a horribly long time.

Being the patient, I don't know what my parents went through during those hospital visits. I'm sure the experience gave them nightmares and made them very sad. I never meant to hurt them and although my illness was not my fault, I can't help wishing I could take it all back and start fresh.

9. **Avoid fitness magazines.** If there's a difference between *Fitness* and *Shape*, I don't know what it is. I fixated on any piece of "expert" advice, reading in the April issue about how to get a bikini-body ready and in May, how to get the best summer body ever. Different titles, same content.

Since I read my first fitness magazine in high school, I have been trying to get the best bikini body ever and still haven't succeeded. Recently I scanned *Shape*, featuring "8 Minutes to Your Best Upper Body," "Bikini Body Countdown" (score! another way to get my bikini body!), "Best New Lower-Body," "Facts About Fat," "The Bikini Body Diet," "Carb Lover's Diet," "The Best Fast-Food Breakfasts," and much, much more. Three years ago I was almost certain I had found the best upper-body workout. I was also almost completely sure that I knew the facts about fat. Then I would pick up a magazine that told me I didn't know anything, and promised to teach me all there is to know. The problem is, the next month there would be something entirely new.

But of course, fifty experts give you fifty different plans, and then they change. It all becomes a mumbo-jumbo of information overload that is impossible to keep up with, but I tried. Pretty soon there was very little that I felt comfortable eating because at one point in one of my magazines I had read something "bad" about each food. One issue told me to get forty-five to sixty minutes of cardio a day; the next said no, lift weights.

I now realize that dieting and exercise are extremely individual, and what works for one person may not be beneficial for another. Making peace with my sweet tooth has been a good example for me. I have read over and over again that deprivation leads to bingeing and if we are truly craving something, the best thing to do is wait fifteen minutes and if that craving is still there to give in to one serving and enjoy every bite. Recently, however, I stumbled across this nutritionist's advice in a fitness magazine article on (surprise!) the bikini-body diet:

Many people have something sweet after they eat and I'm not in that habit—I think it's a habit you can get out of. One thing I do enjoy in summer is some ice cream. I go out for it so I don't have it tempting me at home. [When] I get the real thing—maybe four times over the summer—I have a small scoop and enjoy every bit of it.

Four times over the summer? A small scoop? Is that not still deprivation? The summer is three months long and so she basically has half a cup of ice cream once a month. What happens if she craves the ice cream in between? Does she wait four weeks?

For a long time I lived in fear of dessert. I thought that if I had just one bite I would immediately blow up. However, I do remember one time, when I was still deep in my anorexia, my friend's family threw a graduation party for me and a bunch of our friends. Mom had bought an ice cream cake. At first, I was determined not to have any. But as the time got closer to cut the cake, and I saw all the guests, especially my friends, enjoying their food, I somehow let myself go a bit and realized that maybe a piece of ice cream cake wasn't going to hurt me. And so, I had a piece and not just any slice but a corner slice with extra icing. And then, a surprising thing happened: I enjoyed it! I loved every slow bite. I didn't get fat. I probably could have had a piece of ice cream cake every week and I would have stayed the same size.

10. **Carry on with your life.** I remember when eating out was fun. I enjoyed scanning the menu for the most deliciously complex-sounding meal, trying new ethnic cuisines, and knowing just what I wanted in my burrito every time we went to La Bamba, the great *taqueria* near our house. As a kid, I got ridiculously excited when Dad caved in and bought Frosted Flakes instead of Cheerios. The year had a rhythm to it, when the Blenheim apricots came and Dad's favorite ambrosia melons, with the grand finale of potato latkes at Hanukkah and his holiday fudge. Before my senior year in high school, Thanksgiving was something to look forward to, not dread, as were Friday-night pizza dates with my friends. I remember giggling over pounds of sour candy and splitting fresh-baked cookies at the mall. I used to ask for french fries with my tuna melt. I loved family dinners, where we'd all practice our signature facial expressions—I did an adorable puppy, Dad touched his tongue to his nose—and talk about our days at school or

work, and I'd joyfully describe my newest career aspirations. I always had something exciting to talk about, something I saw in my future or an achievement I'd made in school.

I miss all of that, and hope to get it back.

seventeen

You Get to Sit Down

Years ago, when everything was splendid, Ned and I read a lot of John Cheever stories. Many of them delighted in the dark side of suburbia, where the residents lied, drank, slept around, and realized that no one really loved them and that they'd wasted their lives. We were so unlike these characters. We were blessed, along the lines of the Crutchmans of Shady Hill. As Cheever begins their story, "The Worm in the Apple":

> The Crutchmans were so very, very happy and so temperate in all their habits and so pleased with everything that came their way that one was bound to suspect a worm in their rosy apple and that the extraordinary rosiness of the fruit was only meant to conceal the gravity and the depth of the infection.

Exactly. When we were the Crutchmans of Palo Alto, I could think, "Life is sweet. We're very, very lucky, and temperate as well.

We don't squander the happiness that comes our way. We work hard, contribute to the community, maintain good values. And we're raising kind, ethical children (a girl and a boy, like the Crutchmans). People tell us they are jealous of our perfect family."

In Cheever's Shady Hill, jealousy of the perfect Crutchman family takes flight like this:

> Their house, for instance, on Hill Street with all those big windows. Who but someone suffering from a guilt complex would want so much light to pour into their rooms?

Uh-oh. Maybe *that* was the clue we missed. Our "midcentury modern" house has floor-to-ceiling glass. Also a flat roof—perhaps another architectural sign of moral decay. Rain puddles up there and pours off in sheets.

"The Worm in the Apple" continues in this vein, mining every possibility for the Crutchmans' comeuppance. Surely it will happen, if not when their son fails his junior year of high school and has to repeat, then because their daughter has such big feet. Resentment abhors a vacuum.

The Himmels' comeuppance was easier to find, though not by us. Suddenly, it seemed, we were expelled from the garden of happy families. Lisa's last year of high school, we thought, was the low point. Discovery of anorexia. Paradise lost. But her first year of college—bulimia and suicidal fear—was far worse. Then we had three pretty good years until Lisa's most devastating crash, involving people and places we never thought we'd see. The police, a halfway house, a psych ward, are you kidding? Now that our daughter's illness has been diagnosed and re-diagnosed, tamped down only to flare up in different ways, we cultivate Cheever-worthy jealousy of apparently healthy families. And now that we knew how much luck is involved, we can't help thinking, "Why them and not us?"

It gets uglier. It's not just wanting others to suffer. They have to suffer in the exact same way. I remember feeling this way as a child, certain that every other household lived the *Leave It to Beaver* life, not that mine was terrible, but I was sure my particular anguish was unique in the world and no one would ever understand. At least once, in elementary school, I wished physical harm to my friends. I had chipped a bone on the ball of my foot and was put on crutches. This was mortifying because it wasn't the normal sprained ankle or broken arm, and it sprang from no discernible event. My foot just started hurting and I made the mistake of mentioning it. Only time and lack of pressure would fix the foot. Having no plaster cast and no good accident story, I felt like an impostor of the disabled. Even the word *crutch* (like the name Crutchman) tortured me. Such an unbecoming word. A friend asked what she could do to help, and all I could think was, "If you are really my friend, go chip a bone in your foot so I won't be the only fool on these stupid crutches!" In the end, my foot stopped hurting as magically as it had started.

Another ugly Crutchman episode: I met Jim in the dorm freshman year. He was the first guy—ever—I felt like myself with, riding bikes at midnight, getting stoned, gossiping about our dorm mates. I would have liked to call him my boyfriend, but it never happened. After freshman year we had dinner a few times, occasionally saw each other around campus, then totally lost touch. Nearly thirty years later, Jim emailed me at work. I had taken Ned's last name, mainly because my family name, Highiet, was so hard to spell, but my paper trail made me "an easy Google," Jim said. We started updating each other, in an alumni notes sort of way. My headline was Lisa's illness, but otherwise life was good. I'd gone to graduate school but dropped out after one quarter. He remembered my parents, who were both alive at the time. His parents had died. However, he'd gotten a couple of graduate degrees, married a woman who was prominent in her field, retired to write screenplays, and loved to cook and go out to eat. Oh, and he had four outstanding kids, with closets full of scholarships and sports medals. Could my envy get any greener?

Still, he was going to be in the area, so we planned to meet for lunch. I learned that one of his children had been gravely ill, and that Jim had come out as gay. His wife, he said, "is patient with me." I didn't ask what that meant, but it sounded complicated. The little Cambodian restaurant near my office was especially noisy that day, and I didn't want to shout. I already had a headache. His screenplays weren't getting noticed, which was obviously bothering him. Maybe my agent could help? We made plans to meet again, but neither of us followed through.

I wished for worms in his apple and just got a big shameful stain on mine. What good did it do me to find that his life was not the polished work I had pictured? No good at all. I just felt remorse about my own bad character.

Still, I continued to look for suffering in apparently lucky families. What's the payoff? Maybe it's like watching *Jerry Springer* and thinking, "At least we don't have *that* problem," or "Thank God it's them and not me." It's ugly. But it is one reason—not an admirable reason, but one nonetheless—that people attend support groups. Of course, the good and healthy reasons are to find that others have been through similar trials and to share sympathy and resources. Whatever got me there, thank heaven I went.

At the first group I attended, parents had been dealing with their children's serious mental illnesses for ten and twenty years, while I had put in only two. How do they do it? A single mother didn't know for sure if her son was alive. He didn't answer his phone and when she went to his apartment, in a sketchy subsidized building for people on State Disability Insurance, nobody appeared to be there, and the neighbors hadn't seen him. A month later, she still didn't know. How do people live like that? Another couple returned to the group to report that they could sleep again, after many years, because their son agreed to return to treatment. Ah, that's how they do it. They stand around, as Annie Proulx put it, and eventually they get to sit down. Oddly, though, I remembered this phrase as being about an admirable character's stick-to-itiveness, and when I reread "The Bunchgrass Edge of the World," it turned out I was very wrong. Old Red, the grandfather who said it, was sick and nasty, and he outlasted everyone through sheer meanness. Does that mean you have to be an asshole to survive? I didn't have to find out right then. Lisa got stable and I stopped attending groups.

Three months later, Lisa ran away. I'm sorry I ever thought, "How do people live like this?"

Back at the family support group, the woman still hadn't seen her son, but she knew he was alive. He sometimes responded to her by email. A widow with two mentally ill children in their thirties told us about a momentous upcoming court date, about a conservatorship to care for her daughter, and while she was hoping for a good outcome, she rated the chance as fifty-fifty or less, and sighed. "Then I'll have to find another path," she said, without losing the sweet sparkle in her eyes. We learned that there is an actual personality disorder, listed in the *Diagnosis and Statistical Manual of Mental Disorders*, that causes patients to obsessively file suits and contentiously engage the legal system. I admire the way this woman has learned to shove anger away and save her strength for battle.

Also attending that night was a slightly bent man who must have been in his eighties. At first I thought he must have wandered into the wrong meeting, or he'd come on behalf of a grandchild. But no. He had a severely disabled son, fifty-five years old, who'd been diagnosed and re-diagnosed with mental illnesses including schizophrenia and Asperger's since kindergarten. The son lived with him, had never been able to work, and likely never will. The man's wife died three years ago. In her last decade she had Alzheimer's disease, so he was caring for both. Even among parents who've shouldered a lot of heartache, we wondered, "How does he go on?" Somebody asked him.

"You love them," he said. "You may be the only one who does."

That's it, exactly. The answer I've been seeking, even though our family situation is mild and blessed by comparison. Love is the hunger that matters, why we go on. All the parents there would give anything to heal their children. We have to be reminded that their impossibly complex illnesses aren't who they are, that they don't choose to suffer, that sometimes letting go is all we can do. But love survives. I wanted to cry, for this man's heroism and my flaws, and the great, lucky truth that I am not the only one who loves Lisa. We have a lot of hope. Lisa is young, she has mourned a wonderful relationship and found another, she recovered from a breakdown and wrote this book with me. We are talking and laughing and sometimes eating together again. Hungry? Not so much. But I can go home and hug her.

lisa: There is no happily ever after to my story. Like everyone with eating disorders, I look at food and feel conflicted. Sometimes I feel genuine hunger. I have, however, come to a point where I know I can do something else with my life, and I don't want to waste all of my energy retreating to the bathroom to punish myself for doing something as necessary and everyday as eating.

We all need food to live, to survive and thrive and grow. Our bodies are vehicles that require fuel to operate efficiently. Running on empty, everything shuts down.

I will always think about it, my relationship to food, and probably won't ever have the most normal eating habits, but I will be able to have a stable, consistent, and healthful life.

There are times when I just want to eat a whole mess of food and throw it all up. I feel a surge of anxiety. My whole body begins to feel the familiar craving and I need my fix. In the past I would have dived headfirst into an uncontrolled binge. Now I have learned to live with the urge and avoid it, although certain circumstances make this easier than others. For eight years my life revolved around the bingeing and purging and pizza and ice cream and late-night fast-food stops, candy, donuts, fried food, luxury dinner indulgences, dieting for weeks, exercising until my ankles bled, and taking diet pills and laxatives. I don't remember my college years and the two years thereafter as most of my peers do. Sure, I went to parties and celebrated my twenty-first birthday in a typical drunken escapade. I had roommates and moved many times and smoked pot in the dorms and then in the bathroom at work. I passed out in bars and dated many guys, then fell in love with one and gave him my heart. I had difficult schoolwork and lectures I fell asleep during, and lengthy papers to write that I usually saved until the last minute. I got A's and B's and C's but always tried hard. Teachers liked me and when I was motivated, and not sick or in the bathroom, I loved to participate.

And yet, I missed out on so much. All around me classmates grouped in cliques and tight circles that did everything together and called each other and made fabulous photo albums on Facebook. I longingly gawked, wanting so badly to have my own. I did not have super-close constant friends, but instead I floated from group to group never knowing who exactly to include in my posse. At dinner parties I retreated to the bathroom while everyone else talked and ate and laughed and drank wine. I'd come back and try to join in, start having fun, and then go purge again. I did have some great times, but mostly bad memories.

What I remember about college is trying to ignore the horrible stomach pains—from overconsumption of coffee or sugar-free candies or from hunger—as I sat in class. I woke up ridiculously early to work out before going to my job or school, beating myself up mentally and physically to go further and do better. I got pneumonia and bronchitis, and I saw too much of several hospitals. I remember wanting to die.

I know some days will be easier than others, and I will forget about my insecurity around food and my body. Other times I will probably have to work hard to keep myself from diving into a horrible binge. I'll need to figure out how to allow myself to eat something I might deem risky. I have learned to take hormones into consideration, that sometimes I want to eat all day and I can't get rid of the hunger—and it is genuine hunger.

I've heard it takes twice the length of time you suffer from an eating disorder to fully recover, so for me that would be about . . . sixteen years? Yikes. I think I've had enough of numbers, statistical analysis, and counting calories. I will just go by how I feel and hope for the best.

In a culture of black-and-white thinking, food has to be good or bad for us. With anorexia and bulimia, I took it further, and labeled my whole life as good or bad.

I'd like to call my new attitude toward food "mixed" but not "disordered." I have preferred methods of food preparation and still tend to gravitate toward fruits, vegetables, and lean protein, but does that have to be a problem? I told my therapist recently that sometimes I feel conflicted about food and find myself going back to analyzing everything I might choose to eat. Since I've been working out almost daily, I often question the foods that others might offer to me, wondering if having, say, a sloppy Joe for dinner will impede my fitness goals. When does awareness of what you put in your body become obsessive? This is the line I have to find. My therapist very wisely told me that it is okay to be conscious about my food choices, that just because I had an eating disorder doesn't mean that I always will, and that I don't have to show the world that I'm recovered by eating everything offered. I am not sick because I don't want the sloppy Joe.

I think I have at last found a fairly happy medium. There are no good or bad foods and I can instead allow myself anything in moderation. I eat nutritious and healthy foods for the bulk of my diet and allow myself a few treats, especially chocolate. I never say no to a strong craving. What I've learned is if I really truly want something I should have it in small portions. This way I will most likely avoid bingeing. Will I ever binge again? Purge? Starve myself and become too thin? I can't say. I'm just trying to focus on the here and now.

What has really changed is that I believe I can continue to improve and reach as much of a full recovery as possible. I no longer have the *desire* to starve or diet and binge and purge or just purge or restrict severely. I have not quite rediscovered a normal sense of hunger, but I know what I like and what I fear, and that I get into trouble when I put food into categories of good or bad. I will have hard times and I will have diet periods or days where I run or bike too much or refuse to eat something out of fear it will make me fat, but I'm not willing to make myself suffer anymore. There is no discharge from my treatment plan. All I know is that I see a new strength in me—a strength I had forgotten.

acknowledgments

Except for a few pseudonyms and identifying details to protect privacy, all the people and events in this book are real. Any errors are ours.

We are deeply indebted to our knowledgeable, clear-sighted trail guides in the publishing industry: editor Denise Silvestro and agent Jane Dystel. They helped us frame our mother-daughter drama in a way that we hope will be useful to other families.

At the birth of this project, *San Jose Mercury News* editors Rebecca Salner and Susan Goldberg were supportive midwives.

Joanne Martin and Fran Smith were astoundingly patient and generous writing coaches.

We got a lot of help from our smart friends Susan Cohen, Shela Fisk, John Hubner, Danelle Morton, Bob Okin, Mary Pratt, Olivia Rosaldo-Pratt, David Schrieberg, Ellen Sussman, Jill Wolfson, and Laraine Zappert.

Sheila's beloved study group—Connie Casey, JoAnn Gutin, and Paulette Kessler—read and heard about this book for years.

Jana Kahn is the physician who restored hope to our family.

The Squaw Valley Writers Community gave Sheila a week of bliss.

High school English teachers everywhere deserve applause. Sheila is sorry she never thanked Miss Rathert, Mr. Mayes, and Mr. Dessler for teaching teenagers the joys of writing.

Elaine Saville and Nancy Highiet Morse, our sisters/aunts, shared their stories and flew to the rescue.

Jake was there for us, more than he could know.

Ned/Dad read and lived *Hungry*, kept us well fed and, with heroic effort, laughing.

sheila: Above all, I appreciate the struggle that writing this book added to Lisa's life. Now that she has regained forward motion, the trademark sparkle in her eyes, and the total recall of *Waiting for Guffman*, there is no question it was worth the journey. I am incredibly grateful to have her back.

lisa: My mom put tremendous heart and dedication into this writing process. I know at times I've been difficult. But remember, above everything, I love you to pieces.

sources

Listed below are articles and sources referred to, or used as background, in the text. Web addresses are current as of April 2009.

Introduction

Marion Cunningham. "In Defense of Home Cooking." *Los Angeles Times* (September 16, 1998).

Eating Disorder Referral and Information Center, www.edreferral.com.

Sheila Himmel. "A Daughter's Inner Battle." *San Jose Mercury News* (December 7, 2003).

LiveJournal: Website Pro Anorexia, http://community.livejournal.com/proanorexia.

National Eating Disorders Association, www.nationaleatingdisorders.org.

National Institutes of Health, www.nih.gov.

Psychology Today, www.psychologytoday.com.

Lorraine Savage. *Eating Disorders: Perspectives on Diseases & Disorders* (Detroit: Greenhaven Press, 2008).

Alvin and Virginia Silverstein, and Laura Silverstein Nunn. *The Eating Disorders Update: Understanding Anorexia, Bulimia, and Binge Eating* (Berkeley Heights, N.J.: Enslow Publishers, 2009).

Something Fishy: Website on Eating Disorders, www.somethingfishy.org.
WebMD, www.webmd.com.

Chapter 3: Feed Me, I'm Yours

T. Berry Brazelton. *Infants and Mothers: Differences in Development* (New York: Dell, 1983).

Vicki Lansky. *Feed Me, I'm Yours* (Wayzata, Minn.: Meadowbrook Press, 1977).

Penelope Leach. *Your Baby and Child: From Birth to Age Five* (New York: Random House, 1978).

Chapter 4: Growing Gourmets

GoodPeople, "Hiring Managers Are Quick to Eliminate Candidates who Make These 10 Mistakes," www.hiregoodpeople.com/interviewtips_10mistakes2.html.

Harriet Lerner. *The Mother Dance: How Children Change Your Life* (New York: Harper, 1999).

James Marshall. *Yummers!* (Boston: Houghton Mifflin, 1973).

James Marshall. *Yummers Too: The Second Course* (Boston: Houghton Mifflin, 1986).

The Learning Center—Palo Alto Preschool, www.tlcpaloalto.org.

Marion Nestle. *What to Eat: An Aisle-by-Aisle Guide to Savvy Food Choices and Good Eating* (New York: North Point Press, 2006).

Michael Pollan. "Our National Eating Disorder." *New York Times Magazine* (October 17, 2004).

Chapter 5: Fat Girls, Husky Boys

Gary Grahl. *Skinny Boy: A Young Man's Battle and Triumph Over Anorexia* (Clearfield, Utah: American Legacy Media, 2007).

Judith Moore. *Fat Girl: A True Story* (New York: Hudson Street Press, 2005).

Mary Pipher. *Hunger Pains: The Modern Woman's Tragic Quest for Thinness* (New York: Ballantine Books, 1995).

Seventeen magazine (May 2009).

Shape magazine (July 2008).

Chapter 6: Middle School and the Great Job

Sheila Himmel. "Chore Leave. A Gift of Advice for Mom: If You Can't Stand the Kitchen, Get Out of the Heat." *San Jose Mercury News* (May 14, 1995).

Sheila Himmel. "Eatery Served Pork as Veal." *San Jose Mercury News* (February 23, 2000).

Sheila Himmel. "Chef Suspended as DA Investigates." *San Jose Mercury News* (February 24, 2000).

Peggy Orenstein. *School Girls: Young Women, Self-Esteem, and the Confidence Gap* (New York: Doubleday, 1994).

Mary Pipher. *Reviving Ophelia: Saving the Selves of Adolescent Girls* (New York: Ballantine Books, 1994).

Anthony Wolf. *Get Out of My Life, but First Could You Drive Me and Cheryl to the Mall: A Parent's Guide to the New Teenager* (New York: Noonday Press, 1991).

Chapter 7: You Are What You Don't Eat

Lessley Anderson. "By the Way, I'm Vegan: When Diners Drop the Dietary Bomb, Chefs Must Work Magic," *Chow* (May 11, 2007), http://c13-chd-www-lb.cnet.com/stories/10561.

Betty Crocker, Conversations: Holidays and Entertaining, "Favorite Meals and Treats of U.S. Presidents," www.bettycrocker.com/CommunityForums/forums.aspx/9/3535.

Susan Baker, MD, and Roberta Henry, RD. *Parents' Guide to Nutrition: Healthy Eating from Birth Through Adolescence* (White Plains, N.Y.: Addison Wesley, 1987).

Lori Ernsperger and Tania Stegen-Hanson. *Finicky Eaters: What to Do When Kids Won't Eat!* (Future Horizons, 2005).

Sheila Himmel. "The Muslim Market." *San Jose Mercury News* (November 2, 2005).

Sheila Himmel. "Whole Lotta Foods." *Mountain View Voice* (December 8, 2006).

Leon Kass. *The Hungry Soul: Eating and the Perfecting of Our Nature* (New York: The Free Press, 1994).

S. A. Klopp, C. J. Heiss, and H. S. Smith. "Self-Reported Vegetarianism May Be a Marker for College Women at Risk for Disordered Eating." *Journal of the American Dietetic Association* 103, no. 6 (June 2003): 745–47.

Ann Lien. "Vegetarian? Or Anorexic?" *Vegetarian Times* (September 1999).

The Phrase Finder, www.phrases.org.uk.

Robert M. Sapolsky, "Investigations: Open Season," *The New Yorker* (March 30, 1998), p. 57.

Brian Wansink. *Mindless Eating: Why We Eat More Than We Think* (New York: Bantam Books, 2006).

Women's Health Weekly. "Vegetarianism May Be Associated with Eating Disorder Risk in College Women" (July 31, 2003).

Chapter 8: Roots of Anorexia

American Psychological Association. Report of the APA Task Force on the Sexualization of Girls, www.apa.org/pi/wpo/sexualization.html.

Joan Jacobs Brumberg. *Fasting Girls: The History of Anorexia Nervosa* (New York: Vintage Books, 2000).

Carolyn Costin. *Your Dieting Daughter: Is She Dying for Attention?* (New York: Brunner/Mazel, 1997).

Jacqueline Detwiler. "America's Most Educated Small Towns," *Forbes* (January 5, 2009), www.forbes.com/lifestyle/2009/01/02/educated-small-towns-forbeslife-cx_jd_0105realestate.html.

Joan Didion. "In Bed," *The White Album* (New York: Simon & Schuster, 1979) p. 170.

Lovovico Ferretti. *Saint Catherine of Siena* (Siena, Italy: Edizioni Cantagalli. 1996).

Sheila Himmel. "Little Restaurant Serves Big Flavors." *San Jose Mercury News* (March 7, 2003).

Nobel Prize: The Official Website of the Nobel Foundation, www.nobelprize.org.

Michelle Stacey. *The Fasting Girl: A True Victorian Medical Mystery* (New York: Jeremy Tarcher, 2002).

Chapter 9: High School

Sheila Himmel. "There's Something Asian for Everyone." *San Jose Mercury News* (July 20, 2003).

Chapter 10: Our Big Nights

Sheila Himmel. "Serve You Right: Caring for Diners Is a Learnable Art." *San Jose Mercury News* (October 2, 2002).

Perri Klass and Sheila Solomon Klass. *Every Mother Is a Daughter: The Neverending Quest for Success, Inner Peace, and a Really Clean Kitchen* (New York: Ballantine Books, 2006).

Chapter 11: College

Bulimia Side Effects: Understanding Bulimia, www.bulimiasideeffects.com.

Chapter 12: Relapse Spring

James Lock and Daniel Le Grange. *Help Your Teenager Beat an Eating Disorder* (New York: Guilford Press, 2005).

Chapter 15: The Trouble with Experts

Optenet S.A. Press release: "The Number of Web Sites Promoting Anorexia and Bulimia Has Increased 470% Since 2006, According to Optenet Research" (September 23, 2008), www.optenet.com/en-us/new.asp?id=162.

Chapter 17: You Get to Sit Down

John Cheever. "The Worm in the Apple." *The Stories of John Cheever* (New York: Alfred A. Knopf, 1978).

Other Sources

Daniel Becker. *This Mean Disease: Growing Up in the Shadow of My Mother's Anorexia Nervosa* (New York: Gurze Books, 2005).

Pamela Carlton and Deborah Ashin. *Take Charge of Your Child's Eating Disorder* (New York: Marlowe & Co., 2007).

Laura Collins. *Eating with Your Anorexic: How My Child Recovered Through Family-Based Treatment and Yours Can Too* (New York: McGraw-Hill, 2005).

Sue Cooper and Peggy Norton. *Conquering Eating Disorders: How Family Communication Heals* (Berkeley, Calif.: Seal Press, 2008).

Carolyn Costin. *The Eating Disorder Sourcebook* (New York: McGraw-Hill, 2007).

Marya Hornbacher. *Wasted: A Memoir of Anorexia and Bulimia* (New York: HarperCollins, 1998).

Cynthia Kaplan. *Why I'm Like This* (New York: HarperCollins, 2002).

Gina Kolata. *Rethinking Thin: The New Science of Weight Loss—and the Myths and Realities of Dieting* (New York: Picador, 2007).

Steven Levenkron. *The Best Little Girl in the World* (New York: Warner Books, 1978).

Susan McQuillan. *Breaking the Bonds of Food Addiction*, Psychology Today edition (New York: Alpha Books, 2004).

Sidney Mintz. *Tasting Food, Tasting Freedom. Excursions into Eating, Culture, and the Past* (Boston: Beacon Press, 1996).

Michelle Stacey. *Consumed: Why Americans Love, Hate and Fear Food* (New York: Simon & Schuster, 1994).

Judith Warner. *Perfect Madness: Motherhood in the Age of Anxiety* (New York: Riverhead Books, 2006).

Joellen Werne and Irvin Yalom. *Treating Eating Disorders* (San Francisco: Jossey-Bass, 1996).